STUDIES IN MEDIAEVAL HISTORY

Edited by GEOFFREY BARRACLOUGH

Vol. VII

AN INTRODUCTION TO THE ADMINISTRATIVE HISTORY OF MEDIAEVAL ENGLAND

STUDIES IN MEDIAEVAL HISTORY

It is hoped that this Series, intended in the first place for students in the Universities, may help to bridge the gap between the text-books and the learned monographs in which England and continental scholars of the present day are re-writing the story of the middle ages. Its object is less to furnish an outline of facts. than to introduce the student to major problems of interpretation.

AN INTRODUCTION
TO THE
ADMINISTRATIVE
HISTORY OF
MEDIAEVAL ENGLAND

By S. B. CHRIMES

*Reader in Constitutional History in the
University of Glasgow*

THE MACMILLAN COMPANY
NEW YORK
1952

*First Published in the United States
in 1952 by The Macmillan Company*

PRINTED IN GREAT BRITAIN

PREFACE

Some years of experience in the academic teaching of English Constitutional History have suggested to me that undergraduate (not to mention more senior) students are confronted with considerable difficulty in grasping the significance and relevance for English history in general, and for the history of the Constitution in particular, of what is commonly called Administrative History. It is perhaps not too much to say that no general study of English Constitutional History at present exists which adequately incorporates and interprets the history of administration ; and no broad survey of Administrative History has hitherto been attempted.

The traditional emphasis upon the political, legal, and above all the parliamentary aspects of constitutional development has tended to obscure what after all has always been the most fundamental constitutional problem, namely, the limitation and control and definition of executive power. The nature of this problem in any given period cannot be understood without consideration of the nature of the executive itself, its organization and methods. The principle of the rule of law, and the growth of the common law, the development of the legislative, fiscal, and political functions and powers of parliamentary assemblies, vital themes though they are, were the expression rather than the essence of constitutional development in England. For the judiciary and the courts of common law and parliaments never have been, and are not, the government itself ; on the contrary, all of them were created by the action or acquiescence of governments. The general power of government which we call executive power resides elsewhere—in the Crown and Ministers of the Crown and their agents and servants, and has always resided there, except in times of revolution—indeed the usurpation of executive power by others is what ' revolution ' means. The essence of constitutional history in England has consequently always consisted in attempts of persons or groups other than the king's servants to influence, limit, restrict, or to control in some way the exercise of the executive powers legally vested in the king or the Crown.

Notwithstanding this obvious but basic fact, and notwithstanding the large emphasis which the English people at most periods of their history have placed upon government, the historical study of administrative as distinct from parliamentary development is comparatively new and is still comparatively neglected, especially in the more modern periods. Much has been done to illuminate the growth of judicial and parliamentary institutions ; much less has been done to explain the growth of those administrative organizations and methods without which the king's government could not have been carried on at all.

Bishop Stubbs apparently ceased to be much interested, after the time of Henry II, in the administrative side of the history he narrated, and this circumstance has inevitably been reflected in many subsequent expositions of constitutional history ; very little administrative history could indeed even begin to be understood or written until the vast records of administrative action which form the great bulk of the archives deposited in the Public Record Office came to be seriously explored and exploited by historians. The labours of the late Sir Henry Maxwell-Lyte and others of the Public Record Office made this task a practical possibility. Many scholars have shared in this task, but it was the immortal achievement of the late Professor T. F. Tout to have done more than any other scholar to use these archives on a scale large enough for the purpose of illuminating many of the central themes of administrative history. The publication of the six volumes of Tout's *Chapters in the Administrative History of Mediaeval England* in 1920 and subsequent years, and his numerous smaller contributions in the same field, laid the foundations of the modern study of administrative history. During the last thirty years the literature of the subject has grown considerably, in monographic studies and in articles in learned journals, in England and America and elsewhere.

The purpose of the present survey is to digest, put into perspective, and in some measure to interpret these extensive and much scattered contributions. The survey is not in any sense based upon a study of the original sources by me, but it

endeavours to gather together the results of other and more
expert scholars' researches and manifold labours, which are
indicated so far as practicable in the footnotes, together with
such interpretations and occasional criticisms and disagreements
as I have ventured to make. I have thought it best, in composing
the pages that follow, to pay more attention to perspective and
proportion than to matters of small detail; I have sought to
avoid those many matters of antiquarian interest which are apt
to beset the path, and sometimes perhaps to beguile the footsteps,
of administrative historians, and instead to concentrate as
exclusively as possible upon the essential theme. This theme
itself has been strictly confined to the history of the central
executive power; the vast field of local administration has been
omitted altogether, as well as the whole subject of judicial
administration. I have tried not to confuse the niceties of diplomatics with the substance of executive methods, and I have
concerned myself with how the government was carried on, not
with what it did, except when its action modified the form of the
administration itself. The point of view I have adopted has been
that of the centre of executive initiative and decision—of the
kings themselves and their administrative officials.

I have tried, as I have said, to maintain a due sense of proportion in covering this limited though still very large theme, but
inevitably the narrative is apt to expand or contract according
to the varying amounts of research work that happen to have
been done on the different periods and topics within the general
field. A generalized survey of this kind is bound to be in many
respects tentative, and indeed is always over-simplified, but it is
hoped that it may assist students to distinguish some of the wood
from the trees—at any rate where the trees exist, and that it may
promote the difficult but important task of ' thinking together '
the strands of administrative and constitutional history, so that
our understanding of English history may become more realistic
than it sometimes is.

I am grateful to Principal A. B. Steel for kindly lending me a
typescript copy of his forthcoming valuable work on *The Receipt
of the Exchequer*, 1377–1485, which brings together and carries
further his numerous and well-known studies in government

finance. Professor Geoffrey Barraclough, the General Editor of this Series, has made a number of helpful suggestions, from which this book has greatly profited. I am indebted also to my colleague Mr. A. L. Brown for a number of valuable suggestions and for help with proof-reading.

S. B. Chrimes.

CONTENTS

CHAPTER I

CHAPTER II

CHAPTER III

CHAPTER V

EPILOGUE

ABBREVIATIONS

A.H.R.	American Historical Review.
Bull. Inst. Hist. Res.	Bulletin of the Institute of Historical Research.
Bull. J. Ryland's Lib.	Bulletin of the John Ryland's Library.
Camb. Hist. J.	Cambridge Historical Journal.
C.H.	Constitutional History.
C.M.H.	Cambridge Mediaeval History.
E.H.R.	English Historical Review.
H.E.L.	History of English Law.
P.R.S.	Pipe Roll Society.
Rot. Parl.	*Rotuli Parliamentorum.*
Selden Soc.	Selden Society.
Stat. R.	Statutes of the Realm.
Trans. R.H.S.	Transactions of the Royal Historical Society.

CHAPTER I

ORIGINS: THE KING'S HOUSEHOLD BEFORE THE NORMAN CONQUEST

§1. | From the earliest days of organized communities during and after the Anglo-Saxon settlements in England, such executive power as existed at the centre of these communities, resided in the kings themselves.\ Whether or not it be true that ' war begat the king,' inevitably in the circumstances of the Anglo-Saxon migrations, conquests, and settlements, the primary need of the struggling communities was for military leadership, and we cannot doubt that the founders of the several royal dynasties among the communities established their sway by the successful wielding of military power. For such purposes, at least a rudimentary military organization must always have been a necessity, and the earliest Old English kings can scarcely have done without some form of administrative organization, which must have become less rudimentary as their kingdoms grew and the military problems became less simple. But the king himself was the leader in war, and he himself was the commander-in-chief, the wielder of military executive power.

The king, however, was not only the wielder of the sword. He was also the doer of justice. His function was not only to defend his people (and to attack other people on auspicious occasions), but also to exert himself and to use and improve his resources for the better enforcement of law and order as far as circumstances demanded and permitted. In the discharge of these duties lies the beginning of administrative history. For as the areas of government became larger, and the king himself more aloof from many of his subjects, the executive problem, the problem of executing his tasks, became far more difficult and complex. Such developments compelled some delegation of royal authority, and the use of administrative agents. In time the need for dealing in a competent way with available material resources evoked the rudiments of a financial organization, and in time

B

also administration came to be facilitated by the use of written records for certain purposes.

Until late in the Anglo-Saxon period, very little is known of these arrangements. No doubt 'the history of the royal household begins with the history of the kingship ',[1] but information about it remains vague or very scanty until the tenth century. We may well believe that from the earliest times the king had around him a band of chosen warriors, bound by solemn pledges to defend him and to fight for him, and that some form or other of the old *comitatus* publicized by Tacitus in his account of Germanic customs, written some three hundred and fifty years before the migration to Britain, survived, and was with differences reproduced in the Old English kingdoms. We know something, mostly from literary sources, of these *gesiths* who formed in the seventh century the warrior class around the king, and who supplied the military entourage for the king and his household. We have been told that the *gesiths* failed to become a permanent class, mainly because they did not acquire roots in the soil, so that as a legally recognized class they disappeared after the ninth century. But their functions could not disappear, and were carried on by a different category of men, who came to be known as the king's *thegns*. This designation is mentioned at least as early as the eighth century, and as early as the laws of Wihtred (c. 700), it is evident that the terms ' *gesith* ' and ' *thegn* ' are no longer, if indeed they ever were, equivalent. The *gesith* was a member of a class ; the *thegn* was a privileged individual. He was privileged because of his services to the king. Those services were doubtless primarily military, but some of the *thegns*, or perhaps all of them at times, were more than warriors ; they were the king's administrative agents, able and ready to carry out his bidding, to follow and serve him in his household or court, to convey his commands through his kingdom, and to execute them if need be. Their rewards were gifts from the king, above all gifts of land. Grants of land gave them a stake in the country, which, even if in the absence of assured hereditary rights, could not be permanent, was at any rate

[1] L. M. Larson, *The King's Household in England before the Norman Conquest* (1904), p. 76.

durable. Something like a landed official aristocracy arose in consequence of these developments, providing the king with persons of substance and standing to serve him at court, or with local dignitaries upon whom he could rely for service in the localities. But in the course of time, the connection between many of these *thegns* and the royal household became increasingly remote, until the time came when thegnhood implied superior social and legal status rather than special or continuous service to the king—a tendency sharply marked after the Danish invasions and conquests and the establishment of a Danish dynasty. Under Cnut the indispensable military and cognate service at court came to be performed by a royal bodyguard of *huscarls*. This innnovation by Cnut produced, at least at first, a body of hired servants rather than an official aristocracy, although moderate grants of land were by no means excluded from their rewards.

But of the organization, if any, of these servants and agents of the king, whether *gesiths*, *thegns*, or *huscarls*, we know next to nothing. Nor is it to them as such that we must look for the origins of permanent administrative institutions. For these we must approach closer still to the king himself, and examine the arrangements made for meeting his domestic needs, which being continuous and permanent, provided a firm basis for organization—organization which, although primarily and originally intended for merely domestic purposes, could readily be utilized for what we should call public service. From among the domestic offices of the royal household were to spring the first rudimentary administrative organizations of government.

It is a safe assumption that from the earliest days of the kingships, the kings, like any other men of substance and standing, built up around themselves the necessary elements for maintaining, in however primitive a fashion, a permanent household, primarily for meeting domestic needs, for themselves, their queens and families, and for such of their followers, great and small, as circumstances determined should be more or less continuously in attendance upon them. The king might not, and seldom did, reside in any one place for very long at a time, but wherever he went, he must needs take with him a considerable

entourage of attendants, and hence it was that the royal Household was in no sense a building or an establishment with any
fixed location, but *was* the king and his immediate entourage,
wherever they might be, and however at any given time they
might be composed. The important circumstance was that the
natural permanence of the king's domestic needs brought into
existence a permanent entourage, the nucleus of a court, the
members of which could, as occasion required, be put to tasks
which were more than merely domestic in character, and were
what we should call public and governmental. Permanence of
existence made organization feasible, and organization, coupled
with the growing demands of government, led in time to the
development of administrative methods, officers, and offices.
The beginnings of administrative organization are to be found
in the royal Households.

All the Old English kingships and Households were established and doubtless functioning in their primitive way before
the days of written records, or at least of surviving records, and
consequently next to nothing is known to us of the internal
arrangements of these early Households. When, in the seventh
century, we begin to get relevant written evidence, we are given
little information beyond the designations of various officers of
the royal Households, whose functions remain largely conjectural and vague, and concerning whom we should know nothing
if it were not for the circumstance that these officers figure from
time to time as witnesses to charters granted by one or other of
the kings. It has been suggested that the earliest evidence of this
kind dates from the reign of Ethelbert of Kent, and from before
the mission of St. Augustine in 597,[1] but it has recently been
shown that this evidence cannot be admitted[2]. No original
charter, admittedly genuine, survives from a date earlier than
679, and no copy of a genuine charter earlier than 670.[3] Very
little material evidence relevant to the royal Households

[1] *V.* Margaret Deanesly, ' The Court of King Aethelbert of Kent ', *Cambridge Historical Journal.* VII (1942), pp. 101–114.

[2] W. Levison, *England and the Continent in the Eighth Century* (1946), Appendix I, The Charters of King Ethelbert of Kent and the Descent of the Anglo-Saxon Charters, pp. 174–233. ' The Court officials of King Ethelbert dissolve into thin air '.

[3] *Ibid.*, p. 177.

exists for any period before the late ninth and early tenth centuries.

But the mere fact that very little evidence of court organization survives from before the tenth century must not blind us to the obvious fact that the kings of the several early kingdoms could hardly have sustained their rivalries, and have greatly extended the areas of their power and influence—especially in the case of Wessex—without using some reasonably effective organization at the centre. It is the evidence for this organization that is lacking, not the results of what must have been organization of a sort. Even when in the tenth century we begin to get a fair amount of relevant evidence, it still tells us little but the designations of certain officers of the royal Households, so that we continue to be obliged to infer their functions and place in the arrangements as best we may.

Such evidence as we have suggests that whilst the officers of the Old English court bore substantial resemblance to those of the Merovingian, and later, of the Carolingian courts, there were some considerable differences between them. The most important difference was perhaps that in the Old English Households there was never any officer comparable with the *major domus* ; in English history there were to be no mayors of the palace. 'At the court everything centred about the King's own person. In him all power resided, though at times he might share it with certain members of his immediate family.'[1] That is not to say, of course, that some of the officers of the Household did not attain to positions of dignity and influence. As early as the eighth century, a shadowy person, called the king's reeve (*praefectus regis*), figured among the witnesses to documents, but the nature of his position in the Household, if indeed he were a household officer at all, remains entirely conjectural. In the Anglo-Saxon period, no great officer emerged whose scope and authority exceeded the limits of a household official, even though the duties of some of them inevitably included tasks that touched upon the public as well as the private affairs of the king. It may well be that from the time of Alfred at least, the kings deliberately avoided the risks of developing any single officer of out-

[1] Larson, *op. cit.*, p. 117.

standing importance, by habitually appointing more than one person, often three persons, to the same office. So it was that, although by the tenth century we begin to hear of English equivalents of the four principal officers characteristic of Carolingian arrangements, the seneschal or steward, the butler, the chamberlain, and the marshal, none of these seems to have attained political importance or even much administrative importance outside of the Household. Their duties were essentially domestic in character, and consisted of supervising one or more of the activities needed to maintain the Household as a going concern. As there was often more than one holder of some of the offices at once, it is likely that they actually attended at court on some scheme of rotation, and this would be all the more probable as the office-bearers became more dignified and more substantial persons, and as the actual duties connected with their offices tended to become discharged by lesser and more menial servants, whose work and wages depended upon regular residence and attendance in or near the Household.

Broadly speaking, the *disc-thegns*, seneschals, or as they were later called, the stewards, were concerned with what we should call the victualling side of the Household—the maintenance of a good table and all that that involved. There is little evidence at this time of any special primacy of the seneschal among the household officials as a whole, and indeed there is no specific mention of him at all before the time of Athelstan. The *byrel*, cup-bearer, or butler is mentioned earlier, and his functions related to the provision of more liquid refreshment for the Household and its guests. The *burthegns*, *bedthegns*, *cubicularii*, *camerarii* or chamberlains, were the keepers of the king's bedchamber and wardrobe, and as such they were very close to the king's person—and to the king's treasures. With the chamberlains we come to domestic officers whose duties impinged on the more public aspect of the royal affairs, and we must examine them more fully in the next section of this chapter.[1] The *horsthegns*, or marshals, with their responsibilities for the royal stables, need not detain us in this period.

It seems that some departure from the Anglo-Saxon tradition

---

[1] *V. infra*, p. 8.

of avoiding a pre-eminent officer at court occurred after the accession of Cnut. From 1032[1] we begin to hear of an officer bearing the title, Norse in name and origin, of ' *staller* '. The *stallers* continued to figure in the records for most of the remaining years before the Norman Conquest; there were eight of them in office during Edward the Confessor's reign. Judging from the position which they occupied among the witnesses to charters and writs, we must assume that they were regarded as the highest dignitaries at court in this period, but their duties remain obscure. Perhaps the office was primarily military, and it is hardly a coincidence that we first hear of these officers from the year after that in which we begin to hear of Cnut's *huscarls*, and it may be that in effect they were the heads of this royal bodyguard. But the office had no future before it, for no more is heard of it after the Norman Conquest, and their military duties, if that is what they were, passed to the constables.

Among the witnesses to royal charters, especially in the later period, also appear, with growing frequency, persons designated under one form or another as the king's priests, and when we consider the nature of the functions of these, or of some of them, it is evident that we must postpone them for more detailed treatment in a later section. For just as among the chamberlains of the king's bedchamber we find the origins of the future financial organization of the court, so among the king's priests we find the beginnings of a *scriptorium* or writing office, and from these small beginnings two great departments of administration were eventually to spring.[2]

From an early date, therefore, the Anglo-Saxon kings acquired officers and servants in their Households, upon whose services they could rely for the discharge not only of domestic duties, but also of other duties that might arise from day to day. Inevitably the king looked to those in immediate attendance,

[1] The authenticity of the charter of that year, in which mention of the staller first appears, is doubtful. *V.* F. E. Harmer, 'Anglo-Saxon Charters and the Historian ', *Bull. J. Ryland's Library*, 22 (1938), pp. 339–67.

[2] In addition to the references given above, *v.* generally J. H. Round, *The King's Sergeants and Officers of State* (1911); ' The Officers of Edward the Confessor ', *E. H. R.*, XIX (1904), pp. 90–92 ; J. E. A. Jolliffe, *Constitutional History of Medieval England* (1937), pp. 129–34 ; Sir F. M. Stenton, *Anglo-Saxon England* (1947) ; G. O. Sayles, *Medieval Foundations of England* (1948).

to the *intimates*, the *familiares*, of his entourage, for assistance, advice, and suggestions in the performance of his royal functions, to share with him the task of reaching decisions and of taking steps to carry them out. His officers, priests, and *ministri*, with or without the spiritual and lay dignitaries not habitually members of the Household, figure time and time again as witnesses to his charters, and often they alone attest his writs. They, the officers, are always near to the king, but most of the greater men, the bishops, the *ealdormen*, the county *thegns*, and others who from time to time figure among the *witan* are with him only on infrequent occasions, perhaps at most two or three times a year. It is to the officers, therefore, not to the *witan* that we must look for the beginnings of a continuous king's council, always available to aid the king with advice and suggestion, and ready to attend the *witenagemot*.[1] and to give it something of what we should call ' the stiffening of an official element '. This kind of thing was to become more manifest and measurable in later periods, but the essence of the matter was already present before the Norman Conquest.

§2. In the nature of things, the early Anglo-Saxon kings, like any other persons, from the time when they acquired tangible wealth, money, jewels, costly clothing, and the like, in excess of immediate requirements, must needs have kept such things in the safest convenient place ready to hand and easy to keep under constant surveillance. The place within the Household that best fulfilled these conditions was the king's own bedchamber, the place which none but the king himself and a few intimate and trusted attendants need ever enter. The bedchamber, and its adjacent wardrobe, therefore, became the depository for the king's treasures, and in it are to be found the rudiments of what we should call a financial organization.

We begin to hear of household officers whose duties centred on the bedchamber (*camera*) from the tenth century at latest. The *burthegns*, *bedthegns*, or in Latin, the *cubicularii* or *camerarii*, or chamberlains as they eventually came to be called, were in charge

[1] *V.* Liebermann, *The National Assembly in the Anglo-Saxon Period* (1913), § 21, 36.

of the bedchamber and the arrangements connected therewith, whilst the *hraegelthegn* or *hraegelweard* acted as the keeper of the robes or wardrobe. The duties of these officers included the custody of whatever was stored in these apartments, and the things so stored might comprise almost anything of value for which safe custody near at hand was required, not only cash and jewels, clothes and equipment, but also, in time, records and documents. Inevitably deposits in and disbursements from such a store, in time, transformed this side of the chamberlains' duties into an administrative function, and as a result something like a financial office came into being. The office of chamberlain, from origins that were probably humble, increased in importance and came into the front rank of household officialdom. No single great office of this kind, however, emerged in the Anglo-Saxon court ; there were, it seems, always several chamberlains functioning at the same time, how many we do not know. But we know the names of three in the time of Edgar, of two in that of Edmund Ironside, and of three under Edward the Confessor.[1]

We know also that Edward the Confessor still kept a store of cash in a chest in his bedchamber, but before that time, the king's treasure had grown sufficiently to make resort to additional places of deposit needful. King Edred is said to have lodged records and money in Dunstan's abbey, and this report gives us our first allusion to what may be called a treasury located outside of the Household. From Cnut's time we have references to such a store at Winchester, and from Edward the Confessor's time the evidence points to a permanent treasury located there. In that reign, too, we first hear of the deposit (of a record) *in thesaurum regis*.

We do not, however, hear before the Norman Conquest of any one person as having charge of the whole financial side of the Household ; there was not as yet any ' chief hoarder ' or treasurer, and to the chamberlains, and such assistants as they may have had, fell the task of keeping, accounting for and disbursing the royal treasure. It is not likely that these duties were as yet more than part-time, and it would be unwise to over-stress

---

[1] Tout, *Chapters in Mediaeval Administrative History*, I, p. 71.

the degree of specialisation attained in this period. We know indeed very little of the methods employed at this time, but that a substantial financial organization existed seems scarcely open to doubt. The well-known account in Asser's *Life of Alfred* of how that king was able to divide his annual revenue into four parts implies that already the revenue could be viewed as a whole and dealt with on an annual basis. A considerable revenue was accruing to the king long before this time, and the evidence of Domesday Book after the Norman Conquest points to the existence of a matured financial system in full swing long before the Conquest, and this system seems to have received little modification for several decades after that event.

Already, long before the Conquest, the king's profits from lands were consolidated into farms or fixed renders from the shires, which the sheriffs had to pay over annually, but whether wholly in cash or partly in kind, is not very clear. *Wites* from the courts added to the receipts, and from 991 the large sums accruing from the occasional imposition of Danegeld, even if they did not represent much, if any, profit to the king himself, were assessed at the centre on an elaborate national system, collected, and disbursed. It is evident from the later Domesday Book, that something like an expert financial organization had come into existence, experienced and able to deal with these various transactions, competent to supervise the sheriffs' renders, making deductions therefrom on account of lands withdrawn from their charge, capable of keeping accounts, perhaps already partly by means of tallies,[1] and even able to maintain a proper standard of silver content in the coins received from the sheriffs, by testing them by weight, or by melting them and removing impurities. The assay of money, so prominent a feature of the later exchequer practice, was already in use well before the Conquest.

In short, by the end of the Anglo-Saxon period, a financial organization effective enough not only for contemporary needs, but also, as it seems, for the generation after the Conquest, had been built up. A firm beginning had been made with the foundation of an administrative organ of primary necessity to the king in what we should call both his private and his public capacities.

---

[1] *V. infra*, p. 54.

§3. From what date the Old English kings actually began to make use of written instruments in the conduct of their administration, it is hardly possible to say. Whatever the date was, obviously the transition from reliance solely upon verbal communications to written record was a momentous development, representing in the long run an enormous expansion of administrative potentiality, and of the range, scope, and effectiveness of the royal government.

But it has to be understood that the realization of this potentiality in practice was exceedingly slow, and in the absence of any literate class outside the ranks of the clergy, could not be otherwise than slow and for long of very limited utility. There can be no doubt that the principal, if not the only, motivation came from [Churchmen, who, with continental practice in mind, sought written record for the grants of land which were made to churches and religious foundations.] ' Perhaps ', as Hubert Hall wrote, ' we do not always sufficiently realise that practically the whole existing bulk of Old English charters has been both made and preserved through the agency of the Church '.[1]

It is not indeed until far into the seventh century that (so far as surviving documents are concerned) we begin to have evidence of any frequent issue of charters by the Old English kings. An exaggerated impression has often been given of the activity of the kings in issuing charters. Of the whole *corpus* of documents which are commonly called ' Anglo-Saxon Charters ', amounting perhaps to about 1500 items spread over some four and a half centuries,[2] several hundreds are of very doubtful authenticity ; a large number are miscellaneous documents

[1] *Studies in English Official Historical Documents* (1908), p. 176.
[2] A modern scientific edition of the Anglo-Saxon charters is still very much needed. From the existing collections, it is difficult to estimate accurately the proportion of genuinely royal charters. Miss A. J. Robertson's collection of *Anglo-Saxon Charters* (1939), in many ways the best edited of any, prints only charters in the vernacular, and includes very few royal charters. As regards distribution over the centuries, the following rough estimates may be given from an examination of J. Kemble, *Codex Diplomaticus Aevi Saxonici* (1839–48), and of W. de Gray Birch, *Cartularium Saxonicium* (1885–93) respectively: 7th century, 60, 98 ; 8th century, 154, 197 ; 9th century, 200, 282 ; 10th century, 567, 905 to Edgar only; 11th century before 1066, 276, nil. Kemble marked some 300 of his documents as being of doubtful authenticity, and still more would be doubted to-day. But some doubted by him are accepted now, and other genuine ones have been discovered. Birch made no attempt to distinguish genuine from false charters in his edition.

which are not in fact charters at all ; and of the residue not_ all are royal charters. Moreover, it by no means follows that because a genuine charter is said to have been promulgated by the king, it was necessarily drafted by clerks in the king's service. For the interested parties themselves might and often did draw up a charter along the lines they desired, and merely presented it to the king for ratification in the approved fashion when he happened to be available. ' The Old English Charter is a religious and a local product. The handwriting is local, the language is local, the formulas are adapted by local scribes from academic models ; the attestation only is official, in as much as the court by which it is ratified followed the king into the locality.'[1]

This statement may be somewhat exaggerated, but it contains a good deal of truth, and it helps to explain why there is no trace of even a rudimentary English royal ' chancery ' before the ninth century,[2] why the royal Household was so slow to evolve anything like a regular secretarial organization much before the tenth century ; and why, although the ' chancery ' of Wessex in the ninth century largely followed Frankish example, the royal ' chancery ' never, in the Anglo-Saxon period, developed any definite notarial system such as came to exist at the Frankish court and elsewhere on the Continent.

Until late in the Anglo-Saxon period, we have few traces of any secretarial organization in the royal Households, but in so far as any writing work was undertaken for the king, naturally it fell to the clerics who were attendant upon him. The king's priests, the clergy of his chapel, supplied whatever ' clerical ' labour was required. In time, they formed the nucleus of a regular *scriptorium* or writing office. From the time of Coenwulf (796–821) at least, some of these king's priests began to figure among the witnesses to charters, but only as some among other and more eminent lay[3] and ecclesiastical personages, and the frequency of their appearance declines during the ninth century.

---

[1] H. Hall, *op. cit.*, p. 177.

[2] Levison, *op. cit.*, p. 221.

[3] There seems no adequate reason for associating, as has often been done, the designation 'pedes sessor' and its variants with any particular secretarial functions. The original meaning of the term as ' sitter at the feet ' does not suggest any such

[It is not until the tenth century that the evidence of the charters themselves suggests that an organized clerical staff, a recognisable *scriptorium* at court had come into existence.] The number of extant royal charters is considerable for the first three-quarters of the ninth century, but they become rare under Alfred, and peter out under Edward the Elder. In Athelstan's reign (925–939), however, they reappear very different in style from those of earlier date, more elaborate and regular in form. [Athelstan's charters display an identity of formulas at different dates, places, and circumstances that can be accounted for only in terms of an established writing office at court.] ' It is at least clear that already in Athelstan's reign a staff of clerks accompanied the king on his progresses, and it is with the appearance of these clerks that the history of the English Civil Service begins.'[1] The charters so produced[2] were solemn documents, invoking the name of Christ, God, or the Trinity, without any salutation of mortals, and after stating the substance of the matter—usually the grant of land or rights in land—conclude with signatures or *signa* of the Cross against the names of the king and the witnesses.[3]

But, as the clerks who drafted these documents themselves often wrote in the names of the witnesses, and in the absence of any notarial device, it was easy to forge such charters, and until better methods of authentication were devised, the royal writing office can scarcely have been a very satisfactory instrument from the administrative point of view. Occasional resort to the chirograph method, which occurred first in England about the

particular association. In the absence of any relevant evidence, it is better to regard these persons as holding indeterminate place, perhaps of high rank, possibly in the Household of Kent. There is nothing to suggest that they were the precursors of the later chancellors. *V.* Asser's *Life of Alfred*, ed. W. A. Stevenson (1904), p. 165.

[1] Stenton, *op. cit.*, p. 349.

[2] The bulk, perhaps about three-quarters, of those extant from the Anglo-Saxon period are in Latin, the rest in the vernacular.

[3] For a convenient, even if perhaps somewhat out-dated discussion of the diplomatics of Old English charters and their differences from the continental equivalents, *v.* Hall, *op. cit.*, pp. 189 ff. The Anglo-Saxon charter, like those of Gaul and Italy, was an offspring of the late Roman charter, showing little connexion with Merovingian charters. ' The history ', writes Levison, *op. cit.*, p. 233, ' of ancient and mediaeval diplomatics to some extent is the history of the acceptance of documentary evidence as a legal means, which passed from the " Hellenistic " countries to the West, and from the Mediterranean world to the North. In this chain of "Receptions", the Anglo-Saxon charter is connected with late Roman and Byzantine Italy.'

end of the ninth century, helped in rather a clumsy way, with the problem of authentication. This, however, was an uneconomic expedient, since it involved copying the document, once at least and often twice, so that the copies on one sheet of parchment could be separated by a zig-zag cut between them, and each copy handed to the parties concerned, and a third copy, if any, deposited in some safe place. Authenticity could then be proved by fitting the parts of the parchment together again. A tedious and expensive process of this kind could have only a limited utility,[1] and the problem of authentication was solved only (and then but partially) with the introduction of a royal seal in the eleventh century. Even so, no genuine royal charter of the Anglo-Saxon period validated by seal is now extant. It is in connection with a different class of document that the use of the royal seal becomes manifest rather earlier.

An innovation of the first importance in the methods of the writing office occurred in the course of the tenth century. Then we begin to get a flow of documents quite different in character from the formal and solemn charters, which they soon supplemented for many purposes at this time, and which were all in the vernacular and apparently of native invention. These novel instruments, writs or writ-charters, as they came to be called, contained no invocations, dispensed with solemn formulas and lengthy lists of witnesses, and were specifically addressed with a bare salutation to some person or persons. They were brief [2] informal notifications of what the king has done or wishes to be done, and are direct and to the point. A written instrument of immense administrative possibilities, without as yet any exact analogy on the Continent, had thus come into existence. The ease and simplicity with which the king could now make his will known meant in time an expansion of administrative action and effectiveness unimaginable in the past. From this device was to spring later on a great variety of royal missives, providing the

---

[1] The principal subsequent use of chirographs was for the recording of agreements or conveyances between parties—final concords, or feet of fines as they were later called. This usage became common in Henry II's reign onwards. *V.* Pollock and Maitland, *History of English Law* (1898), II, p. 97.

[2] *Breve* was the Latin word used to mean a ' writ ' from the eleventh century.

king with a wide choice of instruments for the carrying out of his government.

Writs of an administrative character were being issued to shire courts at least from the time of Ethelred II (979–1016). The earliest *surviving* writ from the reign of Edward the Confessor (1042–1066) bears a two-faced pendent seal, and it seems certain that in his reign a seal was being commonly used to authenticate at least some of the products of the *scriptorium*. There is some evidence that sealed letters were used from the late ninth century at least[1] and the use of a seal under Ethelred II, from whose reign comes the earliest writ resembling in form those common later, seems to be clear.

The use of seals had been very common all over the Roman Empire, but had largely disappeared during the so-called ' Dark Ages ', when recourse was had to various *signa* crosses for witnesses and sometimes to signatures, as some means of validation of documents. Seals came in again at the Merovingian court, and by the time of the Carolingian revival became commonly in use, not only by the royal court but also by bishops and great barons generally. During the eleventh century, sealing became the normal method of authentication for most purposes.

The seal of majesty, or ' great seal ' as its successors came to be called later to distinguish them from smaller seals, used by Edward the Confessor, was not without continental analogies at much the same date, in the Empire and in France. But it was remarkable at the time in being a double-faced pendent seal attached to the document by a tongue cut from the margin, instead of being a single-faced one applied to the surface of the document, as was used in France until the early twelfth century, and in the Empire until a still much later date. The only precedents in the eleventh century for a double-faced seal seem to have been the leaden *bulla* used in the papal and Byzantine courts since the seventh century.

With all this increased activity, the king's clerical staff must have become both better organized and harder-worked. From

---

[1] F. E. Harmer, ' The English Contribution to the Epistolary Usages of Early Scandinavian Kings, in *Saga Book*, XIII (1950) (Viking Society), p. 120. The whole subject has now been fully discussed in Miss Harmer's *Anglo-Saxon Writs* (1952).

the time of Cnut at least we begin to see some of the men who began their careers as scribes in the king's service blossoming forth to be bishops or abbots—a sure sign of their growing importance and favour. Foreigners with continental experience begin to figure among them, and it has been suggested that Cnut and the Confessor may have set themselves to make a chancery after the Continental fashion, but since the formulas of early Anglo-Norman charters and writs remained essentially Anglo-Saxon in character for some time after the Conquest, any such continental influences at this date must have asserted themselves in personnel and organization rather than in the drafting of documents.

But with the introduction of a seal, the problem of its custody and of responsibility for its use must have required solution. There are signs before this time that the secretariat was becoming more coherent, and acting under the supervision of some one officer, whose position among the other staff was outstanding. It is possible to name several individuals in Edward the Confessor's reign who appear to have acted as heads of the secretariat,[1] and we may assume, even if we cannot prove, that these officers were also responsible for the custody and application of the king's seal. In short, the organization and the officer later to be called the chancery and the chancellor were not only in existence but also had had a substantial history behind them before the Norman Conquest. We cannot say that these names[2] were used in the Confessor's reign, but what matters is

---

[1] *V.* H. W. C. Davis, *Regesta Regum Anglo-Normannorum* (1913), p. xiv.

[2] The term 'chancery' was definitely not in use before the Conquest, and probably not before the reign of Henry II. But the question whether the Confessor's priest Regenbald was actually styled 'chancellor' before that event was for long a vexed one. The pre-Conquest texts which use this designation are of very doubtful authenticity, and expert opinion has often been divided on the matter. The better view is that there was no chancellor *eo nomine* before the Conquest. Perhaps the most significant point arising is that the compilers of Domesday Book regarded Regenbald, who survived the Conquest for some years, as having been chancellor under the Confessor, and so designated him. For the controversy *v.* J. H. Round, *Feudal England* (1895), pp. 421–430, and in *E.H.R.*, XIX (1904), p. 92 ; Davis, *op. cit.*, p. xv (both of whom accepted the evidence) ; Larson, *op. cit*, p. 133 ; R. L. Poole, *The Exchequer in the Twelfth Century* (1912), p. 25, n. 2 : Stenton, *op. cit.*, p. 634 (who do not accept it). Further serious doubts have been cast upon the evidence by Miss F. E. Harmer, *Bull. J. Ryland's Lib.*, 22, pp. 349–50. Unfortunately, both Jolliffe, *op. cit.*, p. 137, and Sayles, *op. cit.*, p. 174, appear to accept the evidence without comment.

that the things themselves were already there and were to be carried over into the Conqueror's reign.[1]

[1] *V*. generally Larson, *op. cit.*, p. 137 ff; Tout, *op. cit.*, I, ch. iv, § 1 and 2; Davis *op. cit.*, pp. xi–xiv; Stevenson, 'An Old English Charter of William the Conqueror', *E.H.R.*, XI (1896), pp. 731–44. Cf. V. H. Galbraith, *Studies in the Public Records* (1948), Ch. 2. I am indebted to my colleague Mr. E. E. Barker for scrutinizing this Chapter and making helpful suggestions.

C

CHAPTER II

DEVELOPMENTS IN ADMINISTRATIVE ORGANIZATION DURING THE ANGLO-NORMAN PERIOD

§ 1. The Norman Conquest did not result immediately in any very striking changes in the organization of the central administrative system. William the Conqueror regarded himself as succeeding to and inheriting the attributes of the Old English monarchy, and assumed that its institutions and methods were available to him to use and develop as circumstances and opportunities offered. True, some of the characteristics of the ducal court of Normandy were inevitably transplanted into the court of the King of the English, but in the administrative sphere the general features of the two courts had not been very different in the mid-eleventh century ; true also that Norman feudal conceptions soon worked some changes in various aspects of the royal court, with results which were not and could not have been present at the court of Edward the Confessor. But the feudal characteristics of the Anglo-Norman *curia* supplemented rather than replaced the administrative arrangements of the Old English kings. On the whole, the most remarkable feature of the central administrative history of the Anglo-Norman period is its high degree of continuity with what had gone before. The changes which did occur in this sphere were brought about, in the main, by developing and building upon the foundations that had already been laid in the pre-Conquest period. Elaboration rather than innovation was the key-note for at least a generation after the Conquest, although by the time of Henry I (1100–1135) there are signs that the process of development had been carried sufficiently far to amount to substantial innovation, a result to become very much more apparent in the reign of the Angevin Henry II. Certainly far more evidence survives from the latter reign, but of course this circumstance may in itself make that appearance deceptive.

A new feature of great immediate and subsequent importance, however, becomes manifest from the reign of the Conqueror himself, which, although it can hardly be said to have become institutionalized, exercised potent influence upon the course of administrative history. The circumstances of the post-Conquest era were such as to oblige the kings from time to time to delegate their royal authority to one or more of their subjects. These justiciars, as they came to be called, represent a new executive expedient. They are not comparable with the ealdormen of the Anglo-Saxon days, for these did not attain a viceregal position. The Norman justiciarship, when in existence, amounted to a viceroyalty with a national scope.

The reason for this innovation was clearly enough, in the first instance, the need for the appointment of a responsible and competent executive officer to supervise the government of England during the absence of William I in Normandy. There is no evidence of a justiciar's being in office whilst the king was in England in the reign of William I. The Conqueror, however, was not infrequently absent, and the practice on such occasions seems to have been to appoint one or more justiciars to act for the king until his return. Lanfranc was often so appointed ; various laymen were also chosen at times, apparently on personal grounds, from among men upon whom the king thought he could implicitly rely.

Under William Rufus, the justiciarship became more like a permanent office, unconnected with royal absences from the realm. There was now less occasion for the king to go abroad, and the reasons, apart from Rufus's preoccupations with ungovernmental activities, for a more or less permanent justiciarship can only be surmised. The justiciars seem to have exercised direction, under the king, of the whole financial and judicial arrangements, and no doubt the office was designed as a matter of administrative convenience, calculated to relieve Rufus of the care and burdens of executive business. There may also have been some political motives at work, for none of the justiciars of this time was selected from the ranks of the great hereditary feudatories, so that the machinery of government was kept clear of baronial domination. The employment in the chief executive office under the king of men who in most cases might be described as professional administrators, cannot have been without effect upon the development and efficiency of the governmental machine. There are good reasons for supposing that Ranulf Flambard, the first of this class of men to be justiciar, was an administrator who left his mark upon organization.[1] He had begun his official career about 1083–5 as a clerk under the chancellor, and became *custos sigilli regis* himself before being designated *summus* or *capitalis justiciarius*. The words of a contemporary chronicler describing Flambard's position are significant. He was, says Eadmer, ' *maximus executor voluntatis regiae* '.

The part played by Flambard in applying feudal principles to English society may have been exaggerated, and there is no reason to suppose that he anticipated a later office by becoming treasurer, but there is evidence that as ' executor of the royal will ' he conducted a vigorous administration, especially on the fiscal side. Significantly, all except one of the surviving official documents in which Flambard had a hand, are precepts, not charters. It is not fanciful to attribute to him, and to the most distinguished of his immediate successors, Roger, bishop of Salisbury (the first justiciar to be called ' *secundus a rege* ', and of whom we shall have to speak again later) a large and probably decisive share in the consolidation and heightened efficiency of the secretarial and financial organizations manifest in the later Norman period. Administration was already acquiring a professional, expert flavour, which, even if it was likely to attract public odium, was nonetheless indispensable for future efficiency and expansion.

The justiciars, then, when in office, were the greatest men in the government, under the king. They were not mere household officials utilized for public business, but rather the king's chief ministers, responsible, of course, to no one but the king himself. The office, however, remained purely personal, and was not the nucleus of any organization or department of its own, and perhaps for this very reason, was not in the long run destined to permanency, except perhaps in its judicial aspect. The justi-

---

[1] *V.* especially the valuable essay by R. W. Southern, ' Ranulf Flambard and Early Anglo-Norman Administration ', *Trans. R.H.S.*, 4th ser., XVI (1933), pp. 95–128.

ciars carried out their functions through the existing channels, and gave driving force to the machinery already in being, and improved it in the process.

The centre of administrative routine remained the king's Household, or as it soon came to be called in this aspect, the *Curia Regis*. The essence of the *Curia* continued to be, as before, the king and his entourage, the officers of his Household, the men with whom he was familiar, upon whom he could rely for advice and suggestion and service. The fact that after the Conquest, the old national assembly, the *witenagemot*, became merged in, rather than altogether superseded by, a feudalised council composed mainly of tenants-in-chief holding by military service, made no essential difference to the administrative realities. The great councils of feudatories and prelates which were summoned from time to time were no more than enlargements of the *Curia Regis* for the occasion, and for formal consultative purposes. The core of these deliberative assemblies, themselves devoid of executive functions or powers, remained the king and his officers, who alone were in a position to execute the decisions, if any, reached with the counsel of the baronage and prelates. The *Curia Regis* was still the king's court whether the *magnates* were present or not. Nor as yet is there any trace of a formal king's council for routine consultative purposes. There is perhaps an increasing tendency for certain of the more important of the king's officers to figure regularly as witnesses to charters and writs, and doubtless to act informally as the king's immediate advisers. In any case, the giving of counsel, whether by way of feudal obligation or by way of official duty, is one thing ; the execution of decisions however reached is another and different thing, and it is with this latter function that we are primarily concerned here.[1]

§2. A good deal more is known about the Household of the Anglo-Norman kings[2], especially that of Henry I, than about

[1] The best general account of the early effects of the Norman Conquest is that in ch. xvii of Stenton, *op. cit.*

[2] *V.* G. H. White, ' The Household of the Norman Kings ', *Trans. R.H.S.*, 4th ser. XXX (1948), pp. 127-155. Cf. Round, *The King's Sergeants and Officers of State* (1911).

that of the Anglo-Saxons. Although it may be strictly true to say that ' the great offices of State have their origin in the offices of the royal household of the Norman kings, most of which offices existed in Normandy before the Conquest,'[1] it is also true that these household offices did not differ very materially from those already extant at the court of Edward the Confessor. Their designations became regularised and more closely analogous to those of the Frankish court from which the Normans derived them, and inevitably their personnel largely changed as a result of the Conquest; moreover, the Normans, as we shall see, produced in due course both a chancellor and a treasurer. Nevertheless, the essential administrative organs of the monarchy received little immediate alteration because of the Conquest.

It is not necessary to examine in detail here the offices of the Household which remained primarily domestic in character and functions. Information about the Household remains scanty until very nearly the end of the period, but then suddenly becomes amplified and in certain respects detailed. After the death of Henry I in 1135, and for the information of Stephen, it seems, someone in England[2] set down in writing a statement of the pay, allowances, and commons of the members of the Household as they existed under Henry I. This document, known as the *Constitutio Domus Regis*,[3] although its utility is conditioned by the limited objectives of the writer, provides a good deal of insight into the arrangements and offices, great and small, of the Household at that time.[4] It remains uncertain how far the

---

[1] White, *loc. cit.*

[2] The date and place of composition of this document have been disputed, but Mr. White's opinion, adopted above, is to be preferred. Cf. also his ' The Royal Household under Henry I ' in *Notes and Queries*, CLI (1926), pp. 363–4, 381–4, 399–402, 417–20.

[3] Although hardly of much constitutional significance, the document is printed in translation in C. Stephenson and F. G. Marcham, *Sources of English Constitutional History* (1938), pp. 65–70, where it can be conveniently read. Two copies of the text survive, both defective and differing from each other in certain points. These are printed respectively in the *Black Book of the Exchequer*, ed. T. Hearne (2nd ed. 1774) and in the *Red Book of the Exchequer*, ed. H. Hall (R. S. 1896). Hall's edition has many editorial defects and must be used with caution. Cf. Round, *Studies on the Red Book of the Exchequer* (1898). Cf. A. Lane Poole's recent *From Domesday Book to Magna Carta* (1951). The text with translation is also printed by C. Johnson, *Dialogus de Scaccario* (1950), pp. 129–135.

[4] The best account is that by Mr. G. H. White, *loc. cit.* Mr. White corrects a number of errors in other authorities.

Household had changed since the Conquest, but there is some reason to suppose that Henry I himself had re-organized it and established liveries and allowances for its members, and it is perhaps unlikely that the picture drawn in the *Constitutio* would be applicable in detail to the earlier Norman period.

It is evident from the tariff of pay and allowances shown in this document that the Household had become a large and elaborate assemblage[1] of persons of very diverse rank and services, recompensed on widely differing scales. Three main ranks, with sub-divisions in the second and third ranks, are discernible. The first rank included the chancellor,[2] the stewards, the master butler, the master chamberlain,[3] and the constables. How far the treasurer is to be deemed among these is a matter to be discussed later.[4] Commendable economy is displayed in the fixture of lower pay and allowances for these officers when they happened to be *extra domum* than when they were *intra domum*, except in the case of the chancellor, who apparently was assumed to be always *intra domum*. It is significant that the justiciar is not mentioned at all in the *Constitutio*, and we are justified therefore in assuming that he was not a member of the Household. Among the various officers of second rank figures a master of the writing office,[5] and a host of lesser officers, many of them more or less menial in character, were included in the third rank.

Consciously or unconsciously, the Norman kings seem to have maintained the Anglo-Saxon preference for avoiding palace officers of great standing and potential power. There was never to be a mayor of the palace in England, and none of the household officers of the Norman kings attained to positions comparable with those of their counterparts at the French court. The office of justiciar did not evolve from that of the steward, as used to be thought,[6] and although the steward soon came to

---

[1] It is worth repeating Mr. White's quotation of M. Fustel Coulange's description of the *palatium regis, aula regis* or *domus regia* of the Frankish kings : ' Ce palais n'est pas une demeure, il est un ensemble d'hommes, un personnel qui entoure le roi, et qui, s'il se déplace, se déplace avec lui.'
[2] *V. infra*, p. 25.   [3] *V. infra*, p. 27.
[4] *V. infra*, p. 28.   [5] *V. infra*, p. 25.
[6] This supposition was first disproved by L. V. Harcourt in *His Grace the Steward and Trial of Peers* (1907), pp. 7–18.

be recognized as the principal among the lay officers of the Household, he remained in a very inferior position compared with the stewards of France, who became in the eleventh century chief ministers and commanders of the royal forces. None of the chief offices of the Household held by laymen in the Norman period were given to an earl, and with one exception, no baron who held any of the offices was promoted to an earldom. The practice, continued until late in the twelfth century, of appointing more than one person to the chief offices, must have tended to reduce the personal importance of any one holder. Even the constables,[1] a Norman innovation, did not have much opportunity for aggrandizement, for their military duties were not those of commanders, as used to be thought, but rather those of quartermaster generals.[2] Otherwise, their duties related mainly to horses, hounds, and hawks, and the sporting interests of the kings. The master marshal and the marshals were below the constables, and their duties were of a subordinate character.

For our purposes, however, the primarily domestic offices of the Norman Households are of minor interest. Our concern is with the emergence of a chancellor and the growth of the 'chancery', with the emergence of a treasurer, the separation of the Treasury from the Chamber, and the beginnings of the Exchequer. We turn therefore to examine these developments in more detail.

§3. There is no trace of a chancery in Normandy before the Conquest, and no proof of there having been a chancellor at the ducal court. As we have seen above,[3] there is no conclusive evidence that Regenbald was styled chancellor in Edward the Confessor's time, and although Regenbald remained in the service of William I,[4] it is a Norman chaplain, Herfast by name,

---

[1] It is noteworthy that neither the stewards not the master butlers had seats in what became the Exchequer, whilst the constables and even the marshals at least had certain functions there. *V. infra*, p. 59.

[2] Cf. also G. H. White, 'Constables under the Norman Kings', *Genealogists' Magazine*, XXXVIII, pp. 113–27.

[3] *V. supra*, p. 16 n. 2.

[4] ' His function was to acquaint the new ruling class with old English forms of administration.' (Davis, *op. cit.*, p. xv).

who, from 1068, stands first on the list of chancellors officially so designated. Herfast became bishop of Elmham in 1070, and, with some uncertainties in the early years thereafter, his successors in the office of chancellor can be listed with confidence.[1]

By the time of Henry I and the *Constitutio Domus Regis*, it is clear that the chancellor[2] was not only in the first rank of household officers, but actually the highest paid of all of them.[3] It is true that until 1133 the chancellorship was not given to a bishop, and that each chancellor who was rewarded with a bishopric resigned his office without delay, and probably on his nomination to the bishopric.[4] But the fact that nearly everyone of the Anglo-Norman chancellors became bishops after comparatively short terms in office, shows that the chancellorship had become an office of major importance and a ready channel for preferment.

The chancellor was responsible for the king's seal, supervised the secretarial work of the chaplains, as well as being the head of the royal chapel. By the time of Henry I, the *scriptorium* had greatly increased in status and importance. The master of the writing office, who was responsible for the secretarial work under the chancellor and who had the actual custody of the seal, is recorded in the *Constitutio* as being at first only very moderately remunerated. But, it goes on to say, Robert of the Seal's pay was greatly increased[5] by King Henry, and the master of the writing office now figured among the officers of second rank in the Household. Both Robert and his predecessor Richard of the Chapel eventually became bishops, and the office of *magister*

---

[1] *V. Handbook of British Chronology*, ed. Powicke (1939), pp. 64 ff. Cf. Stenton, *op. cit.*, p. 634.

[2] The name ' chancellor ' is said to derive from the ' *cancelli* ' or screen in the Household behind which the clerks performed their secretarial duties.

[3] White, ' The Household of the Norman Kings ', *loc. cit.*, p. 129. The chancellor's pay was 5s. per day, and his allowances one lord's simnel and two salt simnels, one sextary of clear wine, one sextary of ordinary wine, one thick wax candle, and forty pieces of candle. The editors of the *Dialogus de Scaccario* (*v. infra*, p.51) were mistaken (pp. 191–2) in giving a different account.

[4] *Cf.* White, *loc. cit.*, pp. 131, 135, whose view on this point is preferable to that of Stubbs, *Const. Hist.*, I, p. 353, and of Poole, *op. cit.*, p. 185.

[5] The increase was from tenpence a day plus allowances to two shillings a day plus allowances.

was the origin of the later vice-chancellorships. Under the immediate supervision of the masters, the royal chaplains were employed part-time in writing writs and records, and with them were associated sergeants of the chapel and other staff.[1]

Whatever changes in the organization and personnel of the *scriptorium* may have occurred after the Conquest, it is evident that there was no drastic change in its methods. If the extant specimens are genuine, the Old English element seems to have remained strong in the writing office of William I. Some of his charters have many Old English features ; many writs of his were Old English in form and language. Charters were still sometimes drawn up by the grantees. As late as 1069 his solemn charters were in all respects comparable with Old English productions. Before very long, however, the character of charters and writs changed. The clerks themselves began to draw a distinction between *carta* and *breve* ; Latin replaced English in the writs, although sometimes bilingual writs were used, and the charters began to be drafted less on Old English and more on French lines. But there was no sudden break in continuity ; Old English forms still survived for a time. For administrative purposes the clerks were tending to adopt a stereotyped form of writ in which the Old English valediction was replaced by a short list of witnesses and a note of the place of issue.

The chaplains of the Conqueror do not often appear as witnesses to his charters, and some important charters are not attested even by the chancellor. The witnesses to these documents still include a miscellaneous number of *curiales*, officers of the Household, magnates, and prelates, and sometimes members of the royal family, including the king himself. The frequency with which writ-charters or writs of various kinds were issued in the Anglo-Norman period testifies to the growing flexibility of the administration and its growing interference in local affairs. The writ-charter, combining some of the features of the solemn charter and the informal writ, and often sealed with the royal seal, was to have much influence on the diplomatic forms of the next generation and of the thirteenth century. The growing

[1] Cf. Round, ' Bernard the King's Scribe ', *E.H.R.*, XIV (1899).

adaptability of the *scriptorium* by the end of Henry I's reign is manifest, and it was going to be utilized to the full before the twelfth century was over.[1]

§ 4. By the end of the reign of Henry I, important developments occurred in the sphere of the royal financial organization,[2] developments which were to prove decisive for the future administrative system. These developments included the separation of the Treasury from the Chamber, the establishment of the office of treasurer, and the beginnings of the organization of the Exchequer as the financial bureau of the *Curia Regis.* Much, but by no means all, of the evidence for these conclusions comes from the *Constitutio Domus Regis*, and some from the earliest surviving account roll of the Exchequer itself.

In Henry I's time, it seems, if not earlier, the original Chamber evolved into three departments ; the *Camera* or Bedchamber itself, under a master chamberlain,[3] usually represented by two or more chamberlains serving in rotation ; the *camera curie*, which dealt with what later came to be called the privy purse expenses and the expenses of the Household, managed by one or more chamberlains who were presumably the deputies of the master chamberlain ; and the Treasury, managed in the early years of the reign by two chamberlains known then as chamberlains of the Treasury, who at first were probably also deputies of the master chamberlain, but who, before the reign was over, came to be under an independent officer styled the treasurer, equal in rank with the master chamberlain.

The first two of these departments remained parts of the Household. The *camera curie*, or the Chamber as a financial office, continued to be an office in which affairs of State were transacted. It received payments, which were recorded and acquitted by clerks in the Treasury, and it made disbursements of

---

[1] *V.* generally, Tout, *op. cit.*, I, pp. 127–131 ; Stenton, *op. cit.*, p. 633 ; Davis, *op. cit.*, p. xvi ; Hall, *op. cit.*, pp. 208–226 ; C. Johnson, ' Some Charters of Henry I', in *Essays in Honour of James Tait* (1933), pp. 137–43.

[2] *V.* G. H. White, ' Financial Administration under Henry I ', *Trans. R.H.S.*, 4th ser. VIII (1925), pp. 56–77.

[3] For further discussion of this office, *v.* White, ' Master Chamberlains under the Norman Kings ', *Notes and Queries*, 13th ser., I, (1923), pp. 223, 245, 263.

various kinds. Following the king as it did, a place of its own was assigned to it at each stage of the king's itinerary.[1] The Treasury remained fixed at Winchester,[2] and the weight of evidence suggests that it was not regarded as a part of the Household.[3] In part of the later Norman period, the Treasury had become far more than the storehouse it had originally been and was to become again, and for a time it acted as a financial bureau with a wide range of business. It received direct a substantial proportion of the revenue, and disbursed it to the king's creditors ; it kept elaborate accounts which were audited by external auditors chosen from among the magnates of the realm ; it was served by officers who had their official residences in Winchester and their supporting manors in Hampshire. Its premises were extensive enough for general legal and administrative business to be transacted therein from time to time.[4]

At the beginning of Henry I's reign, the Treasury appears to have been in the charge of two chamberlains, who have been identified.[5] The exact origins of the office of treasurer remain obscure; it may have come into existence by gradual evolution, or may have been an entirely new office created by Henry I. Uncertainty still prevails as to the date of its origin and the identity of its first holder. But it seems to be established that it existed before 1130, and the balance of the argument is in favour of a layman, William de Pont de l'Arche, as being the first identifiable holder of the office, at that time and until the end of the reign.[6] The *Constitutio* is definite in asserting that the treasurer was to be remunerated on the same basis as the master chamberlain—in certain circumstances. Exactly what those circumstances were remain indeterminate, owing to ambiguity in the *Constitutio* and

[1] Tout, *op. cit.*, I, pp. 84–5. In 1139, Roger of Salisbury was arrested by Stephen *in camera curie*, then at Oxford.

[2] There was a branch of the Treasury for Normandy, probably at Rouen, but Mr. White does not accept the view of Professor Haskins (*Norman Institutions*, pp. 106–7) that there was a separate treasurer for Normandy under Henry I. *V.* White, ' Treasurers in Normandy under Henry I ', *Notes and Queries*, CL (1926), pp. 59–60.

[3] White, *Trans. R.H.S.*, (1925), p. 58, *et infra*, p. 29. The editors of the *Dialogus*, p. 18, and Tout, *op. cit.*, p. 86 took a different view.

[4] Tout, *ib.*, p. 83.

[5] White, *op. cit.*, pp. 60–64.

[6] *Ib.*, pp. 64–72. Mr. White recognizes that the evidence is insufficient for conclusive argument, but his examination of the problem has not been bettered.

divergence between the two texts of it.[1] It seems, however, quite clear that the/treasurer is not there regarded as in any way subordinate to the master chamberlain,/that the treasurer might, in at least some circumstances, be regarded as an officer connected with the Household, but that the treasury officers who were subordinate to him, who were not mentioned at all in the *Constitutio*, were not regarded as members of the Household for any purposes.

But the Treasury was not destined for long to be a financial bureau as well as a storehouse of treasure. From a date early in Henry I's reign we begin to get substantial evidence that the centre of financial control and account was shifting to a third organization which rapidly outgrew the Treasury, was located differently from it, acquired a different name, and which speedily absorbed the Treasury itself into its own control. The process whereby the Exchequer, as this new organization came to be called, evolved out of the Treasury in the early twelfth or late eleventh century, remains very obscure.[2] There are good grounds for believing that the process preceded the adoption of the chequered table method of computation from which the organization ultimately derived its name. Obviously the adoption of the method must have been the result of some definite decision at some definite date, but, as Liebermann pointed out, the essence of the Exchequer was not the method of computation. It was, he says, rather ' the permanent board of royal officers, commissioned with a function reaching far beyond that of a mere treasurer . . . with the duty of examining that all the sources of royal revenue should really flow into the Treasury, and of judicially determining what was due to the king.'[3] There is

---

[1] White, *ib.* The *Constitutio* says that the Treasurer is to be treated like the master chamberlain ' si in curia fuerit et servierit in Thesauro (Red Book) / ut Thesaur [arius] (Black Book). As the Treasury was fixed at Winchester, whilst the court followed the king, the first of these two versions seems to mean that the Treasurer was not paid as a member of the Household except when the king was at Winchester. The second version might either mean the same, or that the Treasurer's duties as such were intermittent, or that he was only so paid when actually serving at court—presumably as treasurer of the *camera curie*. As Mr. White observes, there seems to be no satisfactory way of resolving this ambiguity.

[2] Cf. Tout, *op. cit.*, pp. 93–99 ; Round, *The Commune of London* (1899), pp. 62–96 ; Poole, *op. cit.*

[3] In his review of Poole's *op. cit*, E.H.R., XXVIII (1913), p. 155.

reason to suppose that this ' pre-exchequer treasury-court ' was functioning before the exchequer method of computation had been adopted, and Liebermann was disposed to place it as early as 1085, and certainly before 1113. In any event, it is clear that the financial board and the chequered table had been in existence long enough to give rise to the term ' barons of the exchequer ' (*barones de scaccario*) in a royal writ issued before May, 1118, and and it is a very safe assumption that both the organization and the chequered table were extant some time before that date. The terms of the writ imply that the Exchequer was already clearly differentiated from the Treasury. It has been surmised that this fresh administrative organization is to be attributed largely to the work of Roger of Salisbury and his kinsfolk. ' Its effect was to transfer gradually all important financial and financial-judicial business to the Exchequer and reduce the Winchester Treasury to its original position of a storehouse.'[1] The adoption of the accounting method of the abacus,[2] worked out on the chequered cloth, which gave the Exchequer its name, now supplemented, without superseding, the more primitive method of the tallies.[3] As a result, the Exchequer acquired a sphere of its own, and was rapidly becoming the chief accounting branch of the financial system. Moreover, it is certain that in Henry I's reign, if not sooner, the recording of accounts reached the high level of detailed entry on a roll. The earliest surviving Pipe Roll of the Exchequer dates from the thirty-first year of the reign.[4] The surviving rolls in this great series are continuous only from the second year of Henry II, but the portions of the Roll of 31 Henry I which still exist are not only proof that the Pipe Rolls were being written up as early as 1130, but also suggest that the same or similar records were being kept well before that date. For the Pipe Roll of 31 Henry I is no tentative experiment in the craft of

---

[1] Tout, *op. cit.*, I, p. 94.

[2] There is good reason to suppose that the royal clerks were familiar with the abacus at the beginning of the twelfth century, and it may have been known to members of the *curia* under William Rufus, perhaps under William I. *V*. Haskins, ' The Abacus and the King's Curia ', *E.H.R.*, XXVII (1912), pp. 101–6.

[3] *V. infra*, p. 56, for more explanation.

[4] For a facsimile, *v. The Pipe Roll of 31 Henry I*, (Pipe Roll Society, 1929). Portions may be read in translation in Stephenson and Marcham, *Sources*, pp. 49–54. Cf. C. H. Walker, ' The Sheriffs and the Pipe Roll of 31 Henry I ', *E.H.R.*, XXXVII (1922), pp. 67–79.

account-keeping, but is as fully-fledged as those of Henry II's time. Undoubtedly the fact that this Roll is the earliest of the kind we have, is due to the accidents of survival, not to the omission of the officials to compile them from an earlier date.

Thus by some date early in Henry I's reign, a third financial organization, the Exchequer, came into being alongside the Treasury and the Chamber, and was destined soon to primacy in the financial sphere. But there were not as yet, nor for long after, any sharp distinctions among them. Close relations, especially between the Exchequer and the Chamber, persisted ; all the principal officers of the Exchequer at this time were derived from the Chamber, which seems to have continued for a long time to be the nursery for budding financial administrators. 'At the Exchequer they might be called "barons", just as on the judicial side of the *Curia Regis* they might be called justices, but by whatever name they went, they were in origin officers of the Chamber.'[1] The treasurer and the master chamberlain became the official heads of the Exchequer, but it was doubtless inevitable that the treasurers, when clerics, should soon become predominant over the lay chamberlains, and become the heads of the Exchequer.

The originally close ties among these three financial organizations, soon, however, became loosened. The Chamber perambulated with the king and the Household ; the Treasury lingered at Winchester until the reign of John, and in time degenerated into a mere local office under the supervision of the sheriff of Hampshire, whilst the main Treasury appeared in London, and in the thirteenth century in the form of the Treasury of the Exchequer, whose storehouse for cash, archives, and records it remained.

But the Exchequer had already become fixed in location, and the meetings of the barons of the exchequer became periodic, at Easter and Michaelmas. The place of meeting was usually London,[2] and by the end of the century, if not sooner, West-

---

[1] Tout, *op. cit.*, p. 95.

[2] There is evidence of a subordinate Exchequer in Normandy by 1130. *V.* Round, *E.H.R.*, XIV (1899), pp. 425 ff.

minster. The great financial department, with its ramifications into almost all branches of administration,[1] was by then firmly established substantially in the form and the position which it was to occupy for centuries. From the reign of Henry II, much more evidence survives as to its operations and methods, further consideration of which is postponed to the next chapter.

[1] Cf. W. A. Morris, ' The Sheriffs and the Administrative System of Henry I, *E.H.R.*, XXXVII (1922), pp. 161–172.

CHAPTER III

THE CONSOLIDATION OF THE ADMINISTRATIVE CURIA REGIS IN THE ANGEVIN PERIOD : THE AGE OF THE JUSTICIARS, 1154–1232

§ 1. Notwithstanding the numerous outstanding events and the many diverse developments of the reigns of Henry II, Richard I, John, and the early years of Henry III, it is possible and convenient to regard the eight decades from the accession of Henry of Anjou in 1154 to the fall of Hubert de Burgh in 1232 as forming substantially a distinct period in administrative history. Despite all the changing circumstances of these fruitful years, and despite the impossibility of rigid adherence to any clear-cut divisions in administrative as in other kinds of history, the period as a whole presents some features which tend to give it a certain degree of cohesion, and a certain degree of differentiation from the periods which preceded and followed it. It was essentially the period which saw the zenith of the early mediaeval forms of government and administrative methods ; the culmination of administrative organization that was primarily household in character and basis. The expansion of administrative machinery during this period was to be enormous, but essentially it was to be expansion of and within the *Curia Regis* itself. Before the period ended, or at least early in the ensuing period, the expansion became so great as to exceed in some respects the feasible limits of a unified curial organization, and to give rise to organs of administration, which, although of course in theory and in practice they were the king's, were nonetheless sufficiently specialized in function, sufficiently self-operative and competent within their own sphere, and sufficiently removed from the king's personal intervention, as gradually to cease to be primarily departments of the Household, and to become slowly what later were to be called departments of State. Naturally this process was exceedingly slow and unconscious, the result of natural developments and needs which no one foresaw or

D

planned, but nonetheless a process which was destined in time to modify profoundly the basic character of the government and indeed of the monarchy itself.

But in the period now under consideration, this process had not gone very far, and broadly speaking, the administrative system of the Angevins until the early thirteenth century was unified and centred in the *Curia Regis* itself, and remained in close relations with the king and his Household, or with the king's personal representative when the king, as was so frequently the case until late in the period, was absent from the realm.

Nor in this period was administrative organization much affected by what we should call politics. The keynote of the period in the administrative sphere was still essentially constructive—the construction by the monarchy and its agents of the administrative machinery itself, rather than disputation about the control of the machine or parts of it. The politics of the period—and where there is government, there are bound to be politics of some sort—were still essentially feudal politics, and at whatever objectives they were aimed, they were not directed primarily, if indeed at all, at the control of the administrative machine. The Great Charter, which may justly be regarded as the culmination of the feudal politics of the period, certainly sought to prescribe certain limits to the scope of the king's administrative discretion by defining specific points of law, but did not otherwise interfere with the administration. Only if the king infringed these limits was the question of administrative intervention by the baronage raised—in the security clause 61 of John's Charter. That famous clause did not reappear in the subsequent issues of the Charter, but never again would it be the case that administrative history would be unaffected by politics. The thirteenth century was to see the beginnings, and more than the beginnings, of political repercussions upon administrative organization. Influences other than those of the king and his agents were to be brought to bear upon the administrative machinery, and the strains and stresses resulting therefrom were to play their part in moulding the structure itself.

Another feature tending to give the period a certain unity—

indeed perhaps the principal feature in this connection—is the frequency and duration of royal absences from the realm in the earlier part of the period, and the consequently great importance in practical administration of the justiciarship and of the justiciars. Of the thirty-four and a half years of his reign, Henry II was absent from England for a total period of twenty-one and a quarter years, spread over at least fourteen occasions, twice for more than four years at a time, twice for more than two years at a time, eight times for the best part of a year at a stretch. Richard I was absent for all but five months of his reign of nine and a half years. John was out of the realm for a much smaller proportion of his reign, but even he during the seventeen and a half years of his kingship, was away nearly five years in all, on at least six occasions, and once for nearly two and a half years. There can be no doubt that the long absences of the first two Angevins profoundly affected the character and development of administration at home.

The great reign of Henry II is justly famous for its administrative and legal developments, but it is obvious that all but the ultimate issues and major questions of policy must have been dealt with and worked out by others than the king himself during at least two-thirds of the reign. It was even less feasible in those days for the king to maintain intimate contact with the details of administration *in absentia* than it is for a Minister of the Crown to-day to have the same grip upon his department when he is abroad as he could have when at home. Most of the creative administration of the reign must have been initiated, and certainly carried out, by the great justiciars and other officials.

As for the reign of Richard I, from the administrative point of view, there can scarcely be said to have been a king at all, and it is to his delegates that we must look for the practical administration of the realm. There can be no doubt that during these long periods of royal absenteeism, experience was gained and seeds of administrative initiative and self-sufficiency were sown that were to bear much fruit later on. During these periods, the core of the Household, the king himself and his immediate entourage, were not readily accessible, or perhaps not accessible at all for detailed administrative purposes. Inevitably, therefore, organs of government that had originally sprung from the Household and had remained in intimate relation with it, attained a self-sufficiency and acquired a degree of bureaucratic assurance earlier and more quickly than otherwise would have been possible. The Continental possessions, campaigns, and ambitions of the Angevin monarchs had consequences upon English administrative history which were not the less profound because they are incalculable.

But, from another point of view, the inevitable delegation of royal power to a succession of justiciars at home tended perhaps to maintain a degree of unification of administration that might not otherwise have continued for as long as it did. For the justiciars, under the king's authority, concentrated in themselves the direction of executive, financial, and judicial business to an extent never afterwards equalled by any of the king's subjects. This circumstance lends colour to the description of this period as the 'Age of the Justiciars', and, granted the usual reservations and qualifications proper to the use of historical labels, this description has its justification. Inevitably, the continuance of a high degree of concentration of power in the hands of one or sometimes two officials tended to delay, or at least to impede, the process of specialization of function and the growth of departmentalism. Whilst most of the undefined executive discretion of the king remained for substantial periods to be exercised by one or two active administrators, ranging over the whole field of administration, the self-sufficiency of the various branches of the machine could not reach a very high level. The force of circumstances, including royal absenteeism, and the pressure of business tended to encourage the growth of departmentalism, but the justiciarship, whilst it lasted, prevented the ripening of this process.

But apart from occasional revivals in special circumstances in the later years of the thirteenth century, the old justiciarship ended with the fall of Hubert de Burgh in 1232, for the tenure of the office by Stephen de Segrave until 1234 was little more than nominal. The degree of administrative unity until then characteristic of Angevin government was not, presumably could not, thereafter continue to be maintained. ' In the administrative field, the events of 1234 quickened a development that had long been in progress, and henceforward there is no mistaking the separate identity of the several departments of government— household, chancery, exchequer, king's bench, common bench— overlapping perhaps, but self-contained ; the concentration of functions, administrative, judicial, and financial, which had been implicit in the justiciarship, disappeared with the office.'[1]

If this be so, then it is fitting that we turn next to take some account of the justiciarship and the justiciars of the period as a whole, before beginning an examination of Henry II's administrative system.

§ 2. 'The central fact in the administrative history of England and Normandy under the Angevins ', it has been said,[2] ' is the delegation of authority to the justiciars, who acted as viceregents in the king's absence. They held courts in the king's name and issued writs in their own. It was through the exchequer that the justiciar exercised his viceregal authority '.[3] The detailed administrative work falling to the justiciars, and the secretarial needs involved, became very great, especially as the judicial innovations of Henry II's reign, and the fiscal innovations of Richard I's, began to take fuller effect and to require from the centre an ever-increasing number of administrative decisions, writs to be issued, and documents to be drafted and preserved. It is evident that the justiciars could not discharge their duties without the assistance of a substantial clerical staff, and although there seems to be no doubt that these clerks were what we should call ' seconded ' from the royal Chancery, there is some justification for speaking of a ' justiciars' Chancery ', even if perhaps only to emphasize the extent to which chancery work necessarily gravitated around the justiciar during the king's absence.

---

[1] H. G. Richardson, in *The Memoranda Roll for the Michaelmas Term of i John* (Pipe Roll Soc., new series, XXI, (1943), p. lxxxvij). For much of what follows in this and subsequent chapters, cf. generally, V. H. Galbraith, *An Introduction to the Use of the Public Records* (1934), and *Studies in the Public Records* (1948).

[2] Richardson, *ibid.*, p. xi. For some illustrations of the work of the justiciars in the judicial sphere, *v.* G. O. Sayles, *Select Cases in the Court of King's Bench* (Selden Soc., 55 (1936), vol. I, p. xxvij).

[3] Cf. *Dialogus*, p. 67, ' Illic enim resident capitalis domini regis iustitia, primus post regem in regno ratione fori . . . '

It is tempting to think that Henry II began his reign with some personal experience of an office equivalent to that of justiciar of the realm of England. The attribution by a chronicler[1] of the title ' justiciar ' to Henry to describe his position under the terms of the Treaty of Wallingford of November, 1153, may have had no technical justification, but serves at least to remind us that Henry certainly had some few months' experience of English administration before he succeeded to the throne in October, 1154. There had been no justiciarship since the death of Roger of Salisbury in 1139, nor was the office to attain quite the same magnitude until the appointment of Ranulf de Glanville in 1180. The viceregal aspect of the office was diminished in the early years of the new reign by the appointments, as at least titular regents, of Queen Eleanor and of the king's son Henry, who was associate-king from June, 1170. But the time came when neither of these members of the royal family could be trusted, and the young Henry died in 1183. From that time onwards the way was clear for the unrivalled pre-eminence of the justiciars until the fall of de Burgh in 1232. Recourse to a virtual or actual *rector regis* for a short time under Richard I and in the early years of Henry III temporarily interrupted the titular supremacy of the justiciarship, but scarcely affected its administrative importance.

In the early years of the reign, the office of justiciar was made a joint one, and the growth of its actual importance was somewhat impeded not only by that fact but also by the fact that at times other personages of great weight with the king influenced the administration. Thomas Becket's intimate relationships with the king during his tenure of the chancellorship (1155–62) greatly enhanced the importance of that office for the time, and the survival of Nigel, bishop of Ely, as a dominant influence in the financial sphere for some years before his death in 1169, tended to restrict the scope of the first two justiciars of the reign, Robert de Beaumont, earl of Leicester, and Richard de Luci.

The background of Robert, earl of Leicester, was feudal

---

[1] *Roger of Hoveden*, I, p. 212, ' Rex vero constituit ducem justitiarium Angliae sub ipso et omnia regni negotia per eum terminabantur '. Stubbs, *C.H.*, I, p. 360 n. 3, minimized the significance of this remark; D. M. Stenton, *C.M.H.*, V, p. 554 seems rather to magnify it.

rather than official, but he had been trained and favoured in the service of Henry I, and although he had given support to Stephen, he maintained relations with the Angevins during the troubles, and became justiciar by January, 1155. It is possible that Richard de Luci was already filling such a position before the death of Stephen, and henceforth the two acted jointly for some thirteen years. There is some evidence, not perhaps very conclusive, that Leicester was recognized as the superior officer of the two, and it may be that de Luci was his subordinate and deputy rather than his equal, at any rate until 1167.[1] However that may have been, Leicester was in the position of viceregent during Henry II's long absence from December, 1158, to January, 1163, and subsequently played an important part in the Councils of Clarendon and Northampton in 1164, and was intimately concerned in the business of the Constitutions of Clarendon and the consequential negotiations with Archbishop Thomas Becket. To him fell the unenviable task of attempting to pronounce the sentence of the Council of Northampton upon the recalcitrant archbishop. He was again in a viceregal position in early 1165, and from late 1166 till his death in 1168.

Richard de Luci thereupon came into his own and remained sole justiciar until his retirement probably in late 1178. He too had been intimately concerned with the affairs of Becket ; indeed, he had been the king's instrument for securing the fateful election of Thomas to Canterbury in 1162 ; he too, shared in the drafting of the Constitutions of Clarendon, and twice was subjected to excommunication by the archbishop. Viceregal duties fell to him during several royal absences, and he played an important part in defeating the Scots invasion of 1174. He was strong enough to oppose Henry II's unscrupulous proposals to enforce the forest laws during the troubles of 1174 despite his own previous grant of dispensation for that period. De Luci, it seems, resigned before Michaelmas, 1178, and spent the last few months of his life in retirement in his abbey of Westwood.

The vacancy in the justiciarship for about a year after de Luci's resignation may have been due to the difficulty of filling it rather than to any relative unimportance of the office during

---

[1] Richardson, *op. cit.*, p. lxxvj, n. 2.

his tenure of it.[1] Nor was there much in the past career of Ranulf de Glanville to suggest that he would become sole justiciar for the remaining nine years of the reign. His early life remains obscure, but he began to appear prominently first as sheriff of Yorkshire from 1163 ; his chance came when as sheriff of Lancashire he organized resistence to the Scots invasion of 1174, won the battle of Aln-wick, and personally received the surrender of William, King of Scots. From that time on he entered more closely into the service of Henry II, becoming a justice in eyre, ambassador to the court of Flanders, a king's justice, and in 1180, justiciar, and remained the most trusted officer of the king for the rest of the reign. It is true, no doubt, that the most constructive measures of the reign had already been taken, but it was from that time onwards that their full effect was being felt, and enormously increasing the administrative activity of the king's court. The successful handling of this work is the true monument of Ranulf de Glan-ville, and it is rather as a practical administrator than as a lawyer or jurist that he should be regarded. Doubtless he was adept as a king's justice, but there is no suggestion that he ever had any legal training as distinct from experience, and nothing could be more improbable than that he was in reality the author of the *De Legibus et Consuetudinibus Regni Angliae* commonly attributed to him. That he had a major share in creating the system revealed in the *De Legibus* is not open to doubt, but there never has been any genuine evidence for the now well-worn tradition that he was the author of the treatise.[2]

So intimate and trusted an officer of Henry II could scarcely be left to rule England in Richard I's absence, and hence it came about that he was included in Richard's entourage on the Crusade, and that he ended his life in the incongruous environment of Acre in 1190.

Richard I, it seems, did not contemplate a sole justiciarship or viceregency to carry on the government during his absence on

[1] *Ibid.*, p. lxxvij.

[2] It is hardly too much to say that a remark in Hoveden and the form of the title of the *De Legibus*, which appear to comprise the only supports for the tradition, are not in fact evidence of the authorship at all. The suggestion that Hubert Walter was the author has much probability, although again there is no direct evidence. *V. De Legibus*, ed. G. Woodbine (1932), p. 183 ; Pollock and Maitland, *H.E.L.*, I, pp. 163-5.

Crusade. William de Mandeville, earl of Essex, and Hugh Puiset, bishop of Durham, were to be joint justiciars, but in major affairs were to act with the advice of four specified persons, who had been justices during the previous reign, whilst William Longchamp, bishop of Ely, was appointed chancellor. The history of the next two years was largely taken up with the consequences of the breakdown of this arrangement, caused partly by the early death of the earl of Essex, partly by the struggles of Longchamp to monopolize power for himself. On Essex's death, Longchamp as chancellor was soon able to make such use of his command of the seal and of his influence at the Exchequer as to reduce the justiciarship of Hugh of Durham to futility.

Longchamp's supersession of Hugh was approved by Richard I, and although his appointment as justiciar followed, he continued to emphasize his position as chancellor, and tried to evade as much as possible the co-existent authority of the four justices, and sometimes authenticated acts of government with his own private seal instead of the king's seal. This personal aggrandizement, however, was not destined to last very long. It was contrary to Richard I's intentions, and out of harmony with contemporary ideas of how government ought to be carried on in the king's absence. The crisis of 1191, which resulted in Longchamp's displacement from power at the hands of a baronial council under the guidance of Walter of Coutances, archbishop of Rouen, who had been sent over by Richard I with a secret commission as justiciar for use if need arose, forms a very remarkable episode. Its constitutional implications cannot be considered here, but in the administrative sphere it meant mainly a return to normality, with Walter of Coutances as sole chief justiciar, but acting in association with the four justices and the barons of the exchequer.[1]

Walter of Coutances had served his administrative apprenticeship as a clerk of Henry II, had been vice-chancellor in 1173,

---

[1] An excellent account of these events is contained in Jolliffe, *op. cit.*, pp. 229–237. A more detailed study is provided by B. Wilkinson, ' The Government of England during the absence of Richard I on the Third Crusade ', in *B.J.R.L.*, 28 (1944), pp. 485–509, but not all scholars will follow this learned writer in his sharp distinction between *negotia regis* and *negotia regni* at this time, and his belief that responsibility for the two was divided. Cf. A. Lane Poole, *From Domesday Book to Magna Carta* (1951).

and became bishop of Lincoln in 1183. His justiciarship may therefore be regarded as maintaining the Henrician traditions. The new financial problems arising from the need to raise large sums for the payment of Richard I's ransom were partly dealt with by him, and the end of his justiciarship in 1193 saw his acting as a personal hostage left in Germany as security for the residue of the ransom money.

It fell to his successor in the justiciarship to take the further steps required to pay off the debt. It is probable that when the life of Hubert Walter comes to be written with the care that it deserves, it will be found that he was the greatest of the justiciars and the most striking personality of the Angevin period. The range and variety of his services and abilities were exceptional. His rise from a clerkship in Ranulf de Glanville's household to the archbishopric of Canterbury, to the justiciarship, to the chancellorship thereafter, in the service of Henry II, Richard I and John successively, betokens no ordinary official career, and his achievements in high office were no ordinary achievements. If in addition he was the true author of the *De Legibus* attributed to Glanville, as he probably was, then, indeed, in Hubert Walter we have the most remarkable man of his day in England.

Trained in the Glanville circle, he became a baron of the exchequer in 1184-5, and a justice of the *Curia Regis* before the end of Henry II's reign. Becoming bishop of Salisbury soon after Richard I's accession, he accompanied the new king on the Crusade, and later visited him in captivity. He was sent to England in April, 1193, as a commissioner for raising the ransom, was elected archbishop in May, and before the end of the year he succeeded Walter of Coutances as justiciar. It fell to him to officiate at Richard I's second crowning in the following April, and from May, 1194, he exercised power during Richard's second prolonged absence. During these four years the pupil of Henry II and Glanville successfully administered the realm on the principles he had learnt from his masters, and in some respects, especially the fiscal, carried these principles further. He resigned the justiciarship in 1198, but accepted the chancellorship after the accession of John, and not only retained that office till his death in 1205, but was probably responsible for highly important developments in Chancery practice during those years.[1] The consolidation and maintenance of the Angevin system of administration owed much to Hubert Walter.

The successors to Walter in the justiciarship were of a different calibre, and it may be that the constructive work of the office came to an end in 1198. Soon royal absenteeism ceased to be a fundamental factor in government, and after the loss of Normandy in 1204, the viceregal quality of the justiciarship was much less in evidence. True, the long minority of Henry III gave rise to circumstances in which the power of Hubert de Burgh attained a high level, but the growth of the administrative machine and of departmentalism had by now proceeded apace, and it is doubtful whether even de Burgh was ever the cornerstone of the administration in the way some of his predecessors had been.

It might indeed be argued that the older style of justiciarship ended with John's first justiciar, Geoffrey Fitzpeter, earl of Essex. Fitzpeter had been sheriff of several counties and a justice of assize and of eyre in the last years of Henry II, had figured in the central administration from the days of Richard I's first absence, was associated with Walter of Coutances in the crisis of 1191, and had laboured in the formidable task of raising the king's ransom. It was perhaps symbolic of the passing of the old order that Fitzpeter should be found promising the maintenance of the laws of Henry I at the council of St. Albans in August, 1213, and that when in October he died, King John should be reported as saying that he himself was now for the first time king and lord.

Peter des Roches, bishop of Winchester since 1205, had been associated with Fitzpeter as co-viceregent, and now became justiciar. He had not been of the school of Henry II, and his Poitevin origins introduced a train of consequences that were to leave their mark upon English administrative history in the early thirteenth century, and in part perhaps in the long run were to help to bring about the end of the justiciarship itself. In John's reign, not much time was vouchsafed for des Roches to reveal himself as an administrator at the highest level, for after a

[1] *V. infra*, p. 74.

short period as guardian of the realm in John's absence in early 1214, he was mainly engaged in the support of the king prior to, during, and after the episode of the Great Charter. In due time it fell to him to crown Henry III, whose personal guardian he became. But the new régime had no room for des Roches at the head of affairs. With William Marshall, earl of Pembroke as *rector regis et regni*, Hubert de Burgh became justiciar and the effective head of the administration for more than sixteen years. De Burgh had served Richard I, been sheriff of several counties, and had supported John at Runnymede. His services in securing the succession of Henry III were great, and his naval victory over the French proved decisive, and paved the way for the Treaty of Lambeth and the pacification of the realm. After the death of the Marshal in 1219, and the withdrawal of Pandulf, de Burgh remained the most powerful figure. On the whole, his administrative policy was on traditional lines, with some tendency to magnify the justiciar's office. But his political difficulties were great ; his rise to power made him many enemies, and his own actions were often violent and unconciliatory. Peter des Roches and his Poitevin friends were not easily ousted, and bided their time.

For years, however, de Burgh maintained his supremacy. The confirmation of the Great Charter in 1225 is a tribute to the justiciar's sagacity ; his declaration of Henry III's coming of age in 1227 enabled him to procure the dismissal of Peter des Roches from his place as the king's guardian. For the next four years des Roches was out of the country and out of the justiciar's way, but his return in August, 1231, bent upon revenge, heralded de Burgh's ruin ; for Peter still enjoyed much influence with the king, and possessed great capacity for intrigue. De Burgh's dismissal on 29 July, 1232, marked the end of the Age of the Justiciars. For Peter des Roches did not take on the office, but remained nonetheless the power behind the throne. True, one of his supporters, Stephen de Segrave, was put into the office for a period, but with his dismissal in May, 1234, the office lapsed. Its temporary revival during the troubles of 1258–61 was in quite different circumstances and does not belong to the continuous history of the office. The keys of administrative

power passed elsewhere, and the *capitalis justiciarius regis* of the
Angevins became but a memory of the past.

§ 3. ' The unity of the king's court, whether it be attendant
upon him or upon his *alter ego*, the justiciar, is an idea that persists
over all the administrative contrivances that seem obviously,
to our view, to be making for departmentalism.'[1] The *Curia
Regis* of the reign of Henry II, and indeed for long after, was the
centre of administrative action of all kinds, and the channel of the
king's will. Whatever manifestations of the king's executive
may occur, whether falling in the sphere of what we should
call judicial, fiscal, or simply administrative action, they occur
within the *Curia*. No matter whether custom or expediency,
convenience or routine, determines that some action shall
normally be taken within a particular organization within the
Curia, in the Exchequer, the Chancery, or Chamber, or elsewhere,
it is all action within the *Curia Regis*, and all is the application
of the king's will and power. In so far as the king has competence, the *Curia Regis* has competence, and every part of it has
equal competence, at least in theory. It is only expediency that
determines that certain classes and types of business are better
dealt with in one section of the court rather than another ; but
practice long continued hardens into routine, and routine
becomes customary, and out of customary routine sprang in
time clearly differentiated organizations which, although of course
still all the king's and the king's alone, and still part of the all-
embracing *Curia*, became more and more remote from the
Household, until at last they had little or nothing in common
with it, save a common origin and a common duty of service to
the king.

The *Curia Regis* might, and often did, consist of more, much
more, than what we should call the king's servants and officials.
To it are summoned from time to time the magnates of the
realm, lay and ecclesiastical, the feudal tenants-in-chief who owe
to the king, among other obligations, the service of giving
counsel. When summoned and present, they too are part of the
Curia for the time being, rendering to the king advice, acceptable

[1] Richardson, *op. cit.*, p. xv.

or unacceptable ; aiding him in reaching judicial decisions which for one reason or another are too difficult or too embarrassing for the king and his officials to reach on their own ; co-operating with him in sanctioning some declaration of law ; or perhaps considering and consenting to some expedient for meeting the king's financial needs that cannot be met by the existing sources of revenue. In these advisory, consultative, and consentient ways, 'the feudal council' participated in the work of the *Curia Regis*, but it was not and could not itself be an executive or administrative body. It could not, in the nature of things, itself take steps to carry out into effect any decisions that might be reached at its meetings. It was for the king and his officers to apply the judgments, to promulgate the decrees, to raise the money, and perhaps to shape policy in accordance with the advice given and the views expressed.

The whole point with which we are concerned at the moment has never been better put than in the words of Mr. Charles Johnson as follow : ' If we reduce the system of government to its simplest elements, we may conceive of it as consisting of two only, the King and his subjects. The executive powers are all concentrated in the former ; he commands, the others obey. This simple constitution differentiates itself in two ways ; by association in responsibility and by delegation of powers. On the one hand, the great ones of the realm are called to aid the King in his decisions and form his council, or *Curia* ; on the other, the duties of state, judicial, financial, and military, are distributed among the members of his household, the Steward, the Butler, the Chancellor, the Treasurer or Chamberlain, and the Constable with his subordinate the Marshal. The Exchequer, as we find it under Henry II, is not a mere department of state, but is a combination of these two elements of the administration acting together at stated times for purposes of finance.'[1]

But it is not to be supposed that the Exchequer of Henry II was merely a financial organization. It was that, but also far more than that. It was the principal administrative agency of the *Curia*. ' It was through the exchequer that the justiciar exercised his

---

[1] *The Great Roll of the Pipe*, 2 *Richard I* (Pipe Roll Soc., new ser. 1 (1925), pp. xiii–xiv).

viceregal authority. To regard the exchequer merely, or even primarily, as a court or office of finance, is to misconceive its nature. The exchequer was a court of universal competence, an office of general administration . . . Doubtless finance constituted the bulk of the work of the exchequer until the later years of Henry II, but, with the development of the writ system and the extension of the immediate jurisdiction of the royal justices, an immense accession of business came to the exchequer. Finance and litigation were kept, on the whole, apart, but the personnel of the court of law was not specialised ; its members might be termed indifferently barons or justices. Gradually it became convenient to speak of the legal side as the Bench, while the financial side retained the name of the exchequer ; but that Bench and exchequer were identical terms admits of no doubt . . . The exchequer, or Bench, or the "*magna curia*", call it what we will, is omnicompetent at this period.

The justiciar then is supreme over finance and the administration of justice, which are centralised at the Exchequer, and he may use the Exchequer seal, or his own, for the many writs that must be issued for these and other purposes of government. Now all these functions are functions of the *Curia Regis*. There are not distinctive names for the place where the litigant obtains his writ and the place where his action is tried : both are the curia, and even the exchequer in its financial aspect may be termed *curia regis*. . . The king's justices sit at the exchequer at Westminster : their head is the justiciar and he often presides over them, but they are in the king's court, whether the king is in England, or as he more often is, overseas.'[1] The law-book which goes under Glanville's name was designed to describe the laws and customs observed ' *in curia regis ad scaccarium et coram iustitiis ubicumque fuerint* '.[2]

It was only gradually that the Exchequer came to be thought of as a place rather than as an occasion. The two annual audits at Easter and Michaelmas loomed largest in the activities of the Exchequer on its financial side, and tended to attract to themselves the main focus of attention, but even under Henry II, the

---

[1] Richardson, *op. cit.*, pp. xiij–xv.
[2] These words are used in the *Incipit* to the *De Legibus*, cited *ibid.*, p. xiv.

Exchequer was beginning to be thought of as a place and conceived of as an institution with a location and a duration of more
permanence than was implied by the half-yearly audits. In the
earlier years of the reign, the audits might not be held near
London, but in one of half-a-dozen towns. By 1172, however,
the Exchequer was settling down at Westminster, even though
the Easter session might still sometimes be held elsewhere.
Inevitably the Exchequer acquired a more or less permanent
staff of officers apart from the *barones de scaccario* whose presence
was needed for the solemn audits and other major activities ;
and these lesser officers seem to have taken up permanent
residence near what came to be called Westminster Hall before the
end of the twelfth century.[1]

' The more minutely the institutional history of the twelfth
century is studied, the more it has become evident that there are
few elements of the administrative system of Henry II that were
not already in existence in the days of Henry I '.[2] But the great
expansion of royal justice resulting from Henry II's judicial
innovations, the writ system, and the opening up of the resources
of the king's justice to a wider public, inevitably wrought changes
in the *Curia Regis* on its judicial side, and consequently upon its
financial side as well. In the old days, the demands upon the
judicial function of the *Curia* were not very great. It was one
thing to have to deal with pleas of the Crown, pleas between
tenants-in-chief, and occasionally pleas arising from default of
justice elsewhere ; it was quite another and a far more difficult
thing to have to deal also with pleas of property and possession
from an unlimited number of parties who might have recourse
to the king's justice by virtue of paying for the appropriate
writ. In the early days of this development it was natural enough
that much of this judicial business should come to be handled by
that part of the *Curia Regis* that had already become centred at
the Exchequer—*in curia regis ad scaccarium*. The barons and
officials of the Exchequer had already acquired experience of
settling questions of property and possession arising out of their
revenue business, much of which was necessarily judicial in
character, and the exchequer audits themselves resembled a

[1] *Ibid.*, pp. xij–xiij.   [2] Tout, *Chapters*, I, p. 100.

judicial operation. There was not, of course, as yet, anything like a professional judiciary ; all who administered justice in the king's name were either magnates commissioned by him for the occasion, or household officials put to that kind of work. It was neither fitting nor feasible for the king himself or the feudal council to deal with an ever-increasing mass of pleas between subject and subject—common pleas as they came to be called. Moreover, at the time when the new need began to be seriously felt, there was no likely place available as a centre for the transaction of this kind of business, except the Exchequer. There was the great hall of Rufus in the palace of Westminster, but this had many uses, and in any case was the place where the king or his justiciar from time to time heard the pleas that were not common pleas or at any rate not common pleas of first instance. But nearby was the Exchequer, with its staff of skilled and capable officials, and upon whose premises there were no great demands except at the half-yearly audits. To the king's court at the exchequer therefore went much of the business of common pleas, not as a matter of any precise specialization of function, but as a matter of convenience. Whoever did the work, and wherever it was done, it was all equally in *curia regis*. The very same men might, and often did, act indifferently as barons of the exchequer for financial business, justices for common pleas, and as justices *coram rege* for crown and other pleas, as well as in a variety of other ways. But manifestly litigation between subject and subject, and the royal financial affairs were not exactly the same kind of business, and so far as practicable, they were kept apart, and gradually differentiation between the two grew. The legal side began to be called the Bench, whilst the financial side retained the name ' Exchequer '. In the course of the early thirteenth century, the Bench was to separate from the Exchequer altogether, and to pursue its own development, with its own plea rolls and justices and staff, and become the court of common pleas.

But we are not here concerned with the development of the litigious side of the Exchequer, nor of the court of common pleas and its relations with the jurisdiction *coram rege*.[1] We must

---

[1] It is a mistake to regard the famous commission of five justices of the *Curia* to hear pleas in 1178 as itself marking the origin of the later court of common pleas.

E

turn to examine the work of the Exchequer as an office of finance and administration.

We have already seen that the essential features of the Exchequer system were in existence in the reign of Henry I, and the accident that far more information about the system of Henry II is available than there is about the system of Henry I must not blind us to the fact that the early rather than the middle and late years of the twelfth century were the most creative period in the development of the Exchequer as a financial organization, and that Roger, bishop of Salisbury was ' to all seeming, the principal architect of Anglo-Norman administration '.[2] Roger and his kinsmen of the second and third generations dominated the Exchequer during several decades of the twelfth century, and together comprised the most remarkable family in administrative circles in the mediaeval period.

Roger, a native of Caen and a humble priest, became a chaplain to Henry I, who made him chancellor at his accession, and procured for him the bishopric of Salisbury in 1102. Roger thereupon ceased to be chancellor and became treasurer instead, and being in the king's highest confidence, was several times, as *iusticiarius totius Angliae*, the greatest man in the government during the king's absences. To the period of Roger's high office belong the re-organizations of the *Curia* resulting in the formation of the Exchequer board, the development of the annual audit of the sheriffs' accounts, perhaps the adoption of the *scaccarium* itself, and the systematic compilation of the accounts later called the *magnus rotulus pipae* (or Pipe Roll). Little direct evidence of Roger's personal initiative in these matters survives, but that he

This was only one of a series of similar experiments, and cannot be regarded as of permanent importance. There is no doubt that the Bench which came later to be the common bench or court of common pleas was at first synonymous with the Exchequer, and that the later court evolved out of the king's court at the Exchequer. *V*. R. L. Poole, *op. cit.*, ch. viii ; Richardson, *op. cit.*, p. xiij ff ; Sayles, *op. cit.* I, Introduction. For general discussion of the judicial work of the *Curia* in the following period, C. T. Flower, *Introduction to the Curia Regis Rolls* 1199–1230 (Selden Soc., 62 (1944)). For the early records of pleas, *Rotuli Curiae Regis*, ed. Sir F. Palgrave, (1835), and the series of *Curia Regis Rolls* (1923–) published by the Public Record Office, covering the years from 1194 to early Henry III, together with Pipe Roll Society, vols. XIV and XXIV. For the history of exchequer jurisdiction proper, H. Jenkinson and B.E.R. Fermoy, *Select Cases in the Exchequer of Pleas* (Selden Soc. 48 (1932)).

[2] Richardson, *op. cit.*, p. lxxxiij.

was a great administrator is not open to doubt, and his name was held in veneration by the officials of the next generation.

His nephew Nigel or Neal followed in the service of the king from 1126 or 1127, becoming bishop of Ely in 1133, and was probably treasurer before the end of the reign. At one time, Roger was justiciar, a son or nephew of his was chancellor, and his nephew Nigel was treasurer; the family between them thus wielded great influence over the administration. The jealousy evoked by their dominance brought about their temporary eclipse in 1139, in which year Roger himself died, but Nigel, though not again treasurer, continued to serve as a baron of the Exchequer, assisted in the restoration of the administrative machinery after the accession of Henry II, and retained great influence at the Exchequer for many years. Moreover, his son Richard, known as FitzNigel or Fitz Neal, carried on the tradition, occupied the office of treasurer for some forty years, and immortalized himself and the exchequer system of Henry II by composing the *Dialogus de Scaccario*, the earliest treatise upon the working of a government 'department' in England, and the principal source of our information about the Exchequer of the period. It has commonly been believed that his father purchased the office of treasurer for him in 1158, and that he obtained possession of it in 1160, but the evidence for this story is very flimsy.[1] He was however treasurer in 1160, and may have been so before the end of 1156. He gave up the office shortly before his death in 1198, and became bishop of London in 1189.

Recent investigation has not revealed any very striking developments in exchequer practice during his long tenure of the treasurership, the continuous history of which is commonly dated from his appointment. His earlier years of office were probably overshadowed officially by his father; as treasurer his work was to carry on the system which had been developed by his famous great-uncle and restored by his father, and it may be that he tended to adhere to that system with an excess of veneration. But his great achievement and chief monument to fame is in

---

[1] The accounts of the details of the official careers of Roger and his family in the standard works differ from each other materially. Corrections and a valuable contribution are furnished by Richardson, ' Richard Fitz-Neal and the Dialogus de Scaccario ', *E.H.R.* XLIII (1928), pp. 161–171, 321–340.

the literary rather than the purely official sphere. It is remarkable that as early as the 1170's an official should have been able to conceive and compose such a work as the *Dialogus de Scaccario*,[1] envisaging as it does the routine and practice of the Exchequer on its financial side as a whole, setting it down in literary form, dedicated to Henry II, ' *rex illustris, mundanorum principum maximus* '.

The exact date of its composition cannot be determined, but there is no doubt that it was originally completed in the late 1170's—probably some years before the author of the *De Legibus et Consuetudinibus Angliae* was at work on the other great literary memorial of Henry II's government. There is some reason for supposing that the extant text of the *Dialogus* represents a first edition which was subsequently, about 1189, partly revised by the author himself.[2] Whether this be so or not, Richard Fitz-Nigel in this work reveals intimately the processes of the Exchequer of his day, the minds of himself and of his fellow-officials, and so helps to span the centuries. ' In the twenty-third year of the reign of King Henry II ', he begins, ' while I was sitting at the window of a tower next to the river Thames, a man spoke to me . . .' The dialogue that ensued was the result of this conversation, imaginary or otherwise.

It has been said[3] that the Exchequer of Henry II ' consists of the " Curia " imposed upon the " Treasury " as a court of control ', and this is a fair enough description of the organization upon the financial side. As a financial bureau, the Exchequer was organized in two distinct parts, the origins and nature of which were different.[4] The Upper Exchequer was in effect a

---

[1] The work does not, of course, have a contemporary title. The author speaks of it as ' *de necessariis observantis scaccarii* '. The best edition is that edited by A. Hughes, C. G. Crump, and C. Johnson (1902), Oxford, to which reference is made in the following pages. A useful translation is provided in E. F. Henderson, *Select Historical Documents of the Middle Ages* (1925), pp. 20–134. Mr. Charles Johnson has published an admirable new edition with text and translation for the *Medieval Classics* series (1950).

[2] Richardson, *op. cit.*, pp. 336–40.

[3] *Dialogus*, p. 28.

[4] Much the best short account is that by Mr. Charles Johnson, in his Introduction to the *Pipe Roll of 2 Richard I* (P.R.S., N.S.1, 1925). For what follows *v.* generally, Poole, *op. cit.*, and the Oxford Edition of the *Dialogus*. For a valuable bibliography of the whole subject *v.* A. B. Steel, ' The Present State of Studies in the English Exchequer in the Middle Ages ', *A.H.R.*, XXXIV (1928–9), pp. 485–512.

session of the *Curia* charged with the oversight of the financial business ; the Lower Exchequer was in effect a central office of the Treasury set up to serve and assist such sessions of the *Curia*, and in particular to handle and store the moneys received during the course of the business of those sessions. As we have seen above, the Treasury was of course very much older than the exchequer organization, pre-Norman in origin, whereas the ' exchequer-court ' was an innovation of the early twelfth century, and there is therefore some justification for regarding it as ' an imposition of the *Curia* upon the Treasury '.

It is convenient to consider the Treasury part of the organization first. The *Dialogus* itself calls this the Lower Exchequer, or the Receipt. The term ' Lower Exchequer ' never became official, and various names came to be applied to it—Treasury of Receipt, Receipt of the Treasury, and later, Exchequer of Receipt, or Receipt of the Exchequer. By whatever name it was called, this Receipt, in the twelfth century, only existed as such in connection with the exchequer sessions at Easter and Michaelmas. For those sessions, the Treasury at Winchester ' detailed off ' a squad of staff equipped with ' departmental ' apparatus, such as chests and bags for storage and custody of coin and other receipts, and sent them up to the place appointed for the meeting of the Exchequer. After the session, these returned to the Treasury, and the receipts added to the Treasury's store. During the sessions, naturally the Exchequer required a temporary ' strong-room ' or treasury in which to store its cash and valuables, its seal and its archives (including perhaps Domesday Book for ready reference, as well as many other records). There was, therefore, a ' temporary treasury ' attached to the Lower Exchequer. The treasurer and chamberlains, as heads of the Treasury, were of course also heads of the Receipt, but being themselves pre-occupied with the session of the *Curia* in the Upper Exchequer during the sessions, they dealt with the less dignified work of handling the money in the Receipt through deputies.

The principal of these deputies was the treasurer's clerk. It was his duty to seal up the bags of money received, to record in writing the amounts received, the name of the payer and the reason for the payment. He also inscribed the tallies of the receipt

—wrote out the receipt, as we should say. Next in the hierarchy came two chamberlain's knights, who carried the keys of the money chests, supervised the weighing of the money after it had been counted and placed in wooden skippets by hundreds of shillings, and finally put the money in forels (leather cases) by hundreds of pounds. They supervised also the cutting of the tallies, and, in common with the treasurer's clerk, they paid out money on the order of the king or the barons of the exchequer. These three, the treasurer's clerk and the chamberlain's knights normally accompanied the treasure on its journeys from the Exchequer to the Treasury at Winchester, and as the deputies of the treasurer and chamberlains, these were the only officers of superior rank engaged in the Lower Exchequer. The other more subordinate, technical or menial staff, the silverer or weigher, and the fusor (or meltor), who were concerned with the assay of the coins,[1] the four tellers to count the coins, the usher and the watchman, and the details of their duties, need not concern us here.

In addition, there was the tally-cutter, who was a servant of the chamberlain. A tally was simply a receipt for money paid in, consisting not of a written record in the ordinary sense, but of a piece of wood specially cut and knotched in such a way as to indicate the amount involved even to illiterate persons who could not read the brief description of the transaction written upon the tally itself. The tally was usually a small stick of hazelwood about eight inches long. It was bored at one end for convenience in filing. The size of the sum involved was indicated by the number and depth of the cuts made on two edges of it. A thousand pounds was shown by a deep cut (the thickness of the palm of the hand), a hundred by a cut less deep (the breadth of the thumb), twenty pounds by a cut still less deep (the breadth of the little finger), single pounds by a cut the size of a ' swelling barleycorn ', and shillings by a little cut big enough only to take out a piece of wood, pence by incisions not large enough even to take out any wood. When the cuts had been made in the proper places, and a brief record of the transaction inscribed upon it, the stick was split through its length almost to the bottom, so that one part

[1] For details of this process, *v.* Poole, *op. cit.*, pp. 76–78.

retained a stump, and the other and shorter part remained flat. The longer stumped half was the tally proper, which was handed to the sheriff or other ' accountant ' as his receipt ; the other half or counter-tally was retained at the Exchequer.[1] Doubts as to the authenticity of a tally could thus be settled by matching it with its counter-tally.

This brief description indicates the principal type of tally, a receipt for each payment into the Treasury of Receipt, for use as a voucher, which when produced later at the audit in the Upper Exchequer, was accepted as proof of payment without question. But the tally-cutting procedure was not necessarily so simple as this, in the case of the sheriffs' accounts. At the Easter term, the sheriff paid in a portion of his farm, but no accounts were then enrolled ; as an acknowledgment for the sum then paid, he was given provisionally a short tally, called a ' memoranda tally ' ; moreover, another small tally, called a ' combustion tally ', was also cut to record the deduction made from his payment on account or ' profer,' because of the proportion of bad money revealed in the assay of the coin paid in.

Later on, when accounting at the Upper Exchequer the sheriff produced these tallies, and after their comparison with the counter-tallies that had been retained and brought forward at the appropriate moment, and all necessary adjustments made at the close of the account, a full-length tally was cut and substituted for the memoranda tallies, which were then destroyed. Thus at the end of the account, the sheriff's clearance depended upon his being in possession of all the appropriate verifiable tallies. So large did these sticks loom in the eyes of those concerned, that the sessions

---

[1] For fuller details on tallies, *v.* references in p. 52, n. 4 above. For additional information and photographs of tallies, *v.* H. Jenkinson, ' Exchequer Tallies ', *Archaeologia*, LXII (1911), pp. 367–80, H. Hall, *Introduction to the Study of the Pipe Rolls* (P.R.S., 1884). With the subsequent use of exchequer tallies as instruments of credit we are not here concerned, but the subject may be pursued in Jenkinson, ' Mediaeval Tallies ', *Archaeologia*. LXXIV (1925), pp. 289–357, or briefly, in Tout, *Chapters*, II, pp. 99 ff. Tallies were commonly used in transactions between private parties, and continued to be used at the Exchequer for some seven hundred years, not being finally abolished until 1834. Six days afterwards, on 6th October, an attempt at reducing what must have been a vast store of counter-tallies by burning them, led to the destruction of the Houses of Parliament. A bag containing Exchequer tallies of the thirteenth century found its way into the Public Record Office in the twentieth century, and these are the subject of Sir Hilary Jenkinson's articles mentioned above.

of the Exchequer were often called by contemporaries simply 'At the Tallies', and this name indeed was very commonly used in the days before the term 'Exchequer' had become enlarged to mean more than the chequered cloth or table.

The foils or counter-tallies, were, as we have noted, retained in the Exchequer and together constituted a record of payments made by the sheriffs and other debtors at the Receipt, but by Henry II's reign at least, the Lower Exchequer was resorting to the practice of making a written record, the Receipt Roll, to facilitate reference. A fragment of what seems to be something of this kind survives from Easter, 7 Henry II, and a fragmentary roll of 31 Henry II shows that the receipt roll had developed into a complete statement of the payments from each county on all accounts for the term with which the roll dealt.[1]

The audit branch of the Exchequer is called in the *Dialogus* the greater or Upper Exchequer, but in the records it is usually called simply the Exchequer (*scaccarium*). It is 'the king's court for matters of finance', and its staff is with some exceptions ' the staff of the household put to financial tasks '.[2] It was essentially a court of account, of which the treasurer and the chamberlains were members, but which included a number of others who had no connection with the Treasury. The king himself might and sometimes did preside ; certain great officers are always there, and other persons holding no other specific positions in the *Curia* might be ordered by the king to attend. Normally the justiciar presided at these meetings ; the chancellor, treasurer, chamberlain, constable, and the marshal normally attended in person or by deputy, and these, together with such others as might be ordered to attend, comprised the *barones de scaccario*. These constituted the *Curia ad scaccarium* ; to them the decision of difficult questions was entrusted, for, as the *Dialogus* says, ' the special science of the Exchequer consists not in accounts, but in judgments of all sorts.'[3]

---

[1] The fragment of 7 Henry II is printed in *P.R.S.*, N.S. 1. (1925), pp. xxiv–xxv, and that for 31 Henry II was printed and edited by H. Hall (1899). It should be noted that from the skin on which the roll was written, it came to be known as the Pell, and that the treasurer's clerk was called the clerk of the Pells, an office continuing to exist until 1834.

[2] *Dialogus*, Introduction, p. 14.
[3] Ibid., p. 67.

But some of the great officers were not always able to be present, and some had their deputies and assistants to deal with the more mechanical processes of business, and some of these lesser officials, as we shall see, steadily grew in importance and ultimately superseded their superiors.

The work of the Exchequer as a financial court centred on the half-yearly audits of the accounts of the sheriffs and others of the king's debtors. In essence, the purpose of these sessions was to get all the sheriffs and debtors or their accredited representatives before the barons of the exchequer, to decide what sums they owed to the king, after due allowance for authorized expenses and previous payments, etc., and to see that in each case the balance was paid in, and to record these transactions.

With these objectives, obviously the Exchequer officials had a great deal of preliminary work on hand preparatory to the actual commencement of the two sessions at Easter and Michaelmas. In the intervals between sessions, the officials were much occupied with the preparation of the writs of summons to be issued in good time to all the ' accountants ', or persons who were to render account. These writs were not a mere summons to attend, but included a meticulously detailed statement of the precise items and amounts for which the recipient was to account. The labour of preparing such statements was very great ; no corrections in the writs as issued were permitted ; every detail of the allowances and off-sets had to be included. One can imagine the perturbation of the sheriffs and other debtors on receiving one of these formidable writs of summons, and the anxiety with which its itemized demands must have been scrutinized. The formulas of the writ were sufficiently intimidating : ' Henry, king of the English to the sheriff of . . . greeting. See as you love yourself and all that you have that you be at the Exchequer . . . and have there with you whatsoever you owe. . . .'[1]

Nor was it an easy matter to compile such itemized writs ; mistakes would not do, for no corrections were allowed, and the recipients could not be made to answer at the ensuing session for anything not included in their writ of summons. At the same

[1] For discussion of these writs, *v. Introduction to the Study of the Pipe Rolls*, ed. H. Hall (P.R.S., 1884), and Poole, *op. cit.*, pp. 138.

time, the business was complicated. It was not only a question of accounting for the sheriffs' farms (roughly the annual value of the king's manors in each shire or other bailiwick less the costs of collection) ; there were various other sources of revenue to be considered, and for which the sheriffs were responsible— receipts for encroachments, the profits of royal justice, portions of special levies, Danegelds, scutages and aids ; authorized allowances and deductions of various sorts had to be calculated and off-set. Besides the sheriffs, a variety of other accountants had to be dealt with : bailiffs and stewards of honours, reeves of towns, custodians of temporalities of vacant bishoprics and abbacies, of escheated baronies and fiefs, and sundry other debtors, all had to be summoned to render account.

No doubt partly because of the complication of the sheriffs' accounts, and partly because of the need for getting cash into the Treasury more than once a year, the sessions of the Exchequer were not annual but half-yearly. The proceedings at the two sessions were not by any means identical. At the Easter term, the sheriffs were required to pay in a lump sum equal to half their annual farms, and to make a verbal statement of what allowances and discharges were due to them, without at this stage producing the warrants for these in the form of writs and quittances. At Michaelmas, the completion of the account was made, and the whole balance of the debt paid, less the allowances for which warrant could be produced, and usually less also a sum allowed as a ' carry-over ' for current expenses. Both sessions thus began with what came to be called a ' profer ' of cash by the accountant, which at Easter term was followed by a ' view ' of accounts, and at Michaelmas term, by the *summa* or completion of the account.

The writs of summons having been issued, and the appointed day having arrived, the barons of the exchequer, themselves summoned by writ to attend, their deputies and assistants, assembled at the place appointed, and formed themselves into a kind of tribunal around the *scaccarium* or chequered table itself. The *Dialogus* gives a full description of the arrangements made on these occasions.

One has to picture the sheriff or other accountant entering the room in which the court is sitting, and taking his seat (along with his clerk) at one of the narrower ends of a large rectangular table, upon which the *scaccarium* itself was placed. Opposite to him, at the other end of the table, sat the justiciar, who had the oversight of all that went on in the Upper and Lower Exchequers, and who had authority to issue a writ by his sole witness, or in his own name. On the justiciar's right some high-ranking additional member of the court might sit, whose attendance had been commanded by the king. On the justiciar's left sat the chancellor, ' without whose consent or counsel nothing of importance is done or ought to be done '. To him belonged the oversight of the exchequer seal, which was a duplicate of the king's seal, and which was kept in a bag sealed with his seal in the treasury attached to the Lower Exchequer and brought out for sealing exchequer documents when required ; to him also belonged the chancellor's roll, a duplicate of the treasurer's roll ; but, as we shall see, the actual application of the seal and the compilation of the roll was the work of his assistants who also sat around the table. The chancellor was supposed to be equally responsible with the treasurer for the record kept, but in fact his other duties often kept him away from the board, so that in practice his representatives who were actually present were of more practical importance in the proceedings than he was.

On the chancellor's left, on the same line of bench but beyond the edge of the table, sat the constable, the two chamberlains, and the marshal, if present. These officials had no concern with the details of the business at the board, but might be called upon to assist in various ways ; any of them might be used to witness documents ; the constable was probably seldom present in person ; the chamberlains had oversight of the Lower Exchequer; the marshal was responsible for the oversight of the counter-tallies, and for the custody of defaulters ordered by the board to be arrested, and at the ' sum of the account ' administered the oath to the sheriff, who was required to swear on his conscience that he had rendered his account according to law.

At the long side of the table, to the justiciar's right and the sheriff's left, sat some of the officials most intimately concerned with the proceedings. At the end nearest the justiciar sat the treasurer, and on his right, his scribe, then the chancellor's scribe, the chancellor's clerk, and the constable's clerk. The justiciar, if present, was the president of the board, but the treasurer naturally played the most active part in the proceedings. He conducted the business, interrogated the ' accountant ', received the accounts, and dictated the terms in which the record of the business was to be written down. He had to dictate with complete accuracy, and the record authorized by him could not be challenged ; if a manifest error was made, it might be corrected only with the common counsel of the barons, in their presence and during the session ; the record of a previous year or session might be altered only by the king.

The treasurer himself, however, did not, of course, write the record, the Great Roll of the Pipe, as it came to be called, and of which we must speak later ; that was the business of his scribe, who sat next to him (this was the official later called the clerk of the pipe, and later still clerk of the pells). Next sat the chancellor's scribe (later called the comptroller of the pipe), whose business it was to compile an exact duplicate of the treasurer's roll, for the chancellor's use ; it also fell to him to write up writs of issue, allowance, or discharge authorized by the barons during the session,[1] as well as at the appropriate time to write out the writs of summons for the following term.

His neighbour at the table, the chancellor's clerk, was his overseer, who also had important duties of his own which made him the key man in the proceedings, and in the long run were to make his office the most important of all, at the Exchequer. It was for him to check the sheriffs' accounts, to demand from them at the board satisfaction for each item of debt, and to assure himself that the writ of summons was responded to in every particular, and which he checked and sealed before issue. Other duties also fell to his lot, and no wonder the *Dialogus* says that he had ' infinite labour ', chiefest after the treasurer. But the labours of the office were destined to have their compensation, for in the

---

[1] The principal writs were writs of *liberate*, authorizing payment or issue out of the treasury, and writs of *computate* or *perdono*. These writs were made out in duplicate, and the counter-writs were retained by the chancellor's clerk. At the audit, the writs had to be produced as vouchers by the accountants.

absence of the chancellor, his clerk rose to eminence, attracted to himself the title of ' the chancellor of the exchequer ', and became set on the path which eventually was to make him the sole effective financial Minister of the Crown.

Last on this bench was a place for the constable's clerk, whose main function seems to have been to bring into the Upper Exchequer the counter-writs from elsewhere for the purpose of verifying the writs that might be produced in the course of business. Opposite to this bench, on the other long side of the table, on the chancellor's left and the sheriff's right, sat first, a cutter of tallies, then the calculator, and finally, when present, the chancellor's second-in-command, the *magister scriptorii*.

The tally-cutter at the board was concerned with the tally-cutting work done there, with the adjustment of tallies in the light of the final account, with the checking of the counter-tallies, and their transference to the marshal for safe custody. The master of the writing office was not concerned with the calculations at the board, but with the provision and supervision of the writers acting on behalf of the chancellor. But his duties in the Chancery were far more important and onerous, and his attendance at the Exchequer, if it occurred at all at this period, was probably only occasional and formal. In between the tally-cutter and the *magister scriptorii* was the calculator's place, and consideration of his duties brings us to the use of that *scaccarium* which had come to give its name to the whole organization.

The *scaccarium* was a large rectangular board, measuring ten feet by five feet, with a raised edge around it, on which was placed a black cloth ruled with white lines a foot apart, certainly in columns, probably in squares. There were seven of these columns, which were used for calculating, from right to left facing the calculator, pence, shillings, pounds, scores of pounds, hundreds, thousands, and tens of thousands of pounds, respectively. By the placing of two sets of counters, one set above the other, in the appropriate columns, the calculator displayed the state of an account. On the side of the board furthest away from him he set out in counters the sum due from the sheriff or other accountant, and below, on the side nearest to him, the sum

received. By the simple process of removing counter for counter
from each level, a credit or debit balance was at length revealed
for all to see.

The ' game of the Exchequer ', in the late Dr. Hubert Hall's
vivid description,[1] was played something like this : ' The
Treasurer speaks first, slowly and distinctly ', and asks his adver-
sary if he is ready to render his Account. The latter replies in
the affirmative, and is immediately challenged upon the first item
of his reckoning. Hereupon a general commotion ensues. The
clerks turn the membrances of their rolls to compare the entries
of previous years, and the Chamberlain's sergeants heap upon the
table rouleaux of silver, counter-tallies, and warrants, representing
the accountant's credit in the Treasury. Then the Calculator,
rising in his place, prepares to make the moves of the game as
they are dictated from the contents of the Great Roll.

The sum of each separate entry of the Farm of the County
being announced, he leans over and arranges on the side farthest
from him, the amount quoted, in specie or in counters within the
appropriate columns. Next, he sorts out the credit before him
in heaps in the same columns below this dummy treasure, and
when everything is complete, subtracts pence from pence,
shillings from shillings, and pounds from pounds, till the corresponding pieces on both sides are exhausted by the exchange.
Then, unless the Accountant is quit, so much as is left on either
side represents the advantage or loss of each, respectively ; he
making good the deficit, or being allowed the surplus, as the case
might be.

Meanwhile, the tallies held by the Sheriff's servants have
been carefully compared with the foils preserved in the Exchequer, to guard against a forgery or even a slip of the knife—
and woe betide him if any such flaw be discovered, for then he
would be handed over to the Marshal for safe custody . . . unless
he could fasten the fraud upon his deputy or attorney.

And so the contest is slowly waged, the piles of silver, gold
and metal counters, sticks, and scrolls, being marshalled,
advanced, and swept off the board, just as the pieces or pawns of
the real game would have been played, till the Account of the

[1] H. Hall, *op. cit.*, pp. 40–42.

Farm is concluded, and the mimic warfare terminates in a truce between the parties for another six months at least.'[1]

The Great Rolls of the Pipe, or Pipe Rolls, as they came to be called, were the record of the Upper Exchequer, and they survive in almost unbroken succession from 2 Henry II to 1 William IV, and until the beginning of chancery enrolments in the early years of John, they are the sole consecutive series of official records.[2] They do not record the annual balance of the royal revenue, but merely the annual states of account of the sheriffs and some other accountants. The Exchequer was not, of course, the only place in which payments to the king might be made; there was always the king's private treasury—the Chamber— able and willing to receive payments, and in some cases persons not accountable at the Exchequer habitually paid their debts into the Chamber. Debts so paid by Exchequer accountants might be pleaded in discharge of debts due at the Exchequer in due course, and such payments were eventually noted on the Pipe Rolls as having been made *in camera regis* or *in camera curiae.* The balance of payments actually paid in and out of the Lower Exchequer does not appear in the Pipe Rolls, and if such a record was kept in the Lower Exchequer, it does not survive. The Pipe Rolls are not therefore a comprehensive statement of the royal revenue, but are essentially a record of the sheriffs' accounts, entered county by county, item by item, year by year,[3] in accordance with book-keeping principles, which, though remote from modern methods, are intelligible, and doubtless served their purpose

[1] This description is somewhat simplified; for fuller details see the works referred to above, and in addition H. Hall's ' The Dot System at the Exchequer ', in *Pipe Roll of* 10 *Henry II* (P.R.S., 1886).

[2] Extracts from the Pipe Roll of 33 Henry II may be read in Stephenson and Marcham, *op. cit.*, pp. 91–95. H. Hall's *Introduction to the Study of the Pipe Rolls* is useful. A large number of Pipe Rolls and cognate documents, have been printed, the earlier ones in facsimile, by the Pipe Roll Society. For the name ' Pipe Roll ', *v.* Sir J. H. Ramsay, ' The Origin of the name " Pipe Roll " ', *E.H.R.*, XXVI (1911), pp. 329–30, 749.

[3] It should be borne in mind that the older theory, adopted by Stubbs and Poole, that there was an ' exchequer year ' different from other methods of reckoning, has been abandoned. As Mr. H. G. Richardson has shown in ' The Exchequer Year '. *Trans. R.H.S.*, VIII, IX (1925, 1926), the Exchequer used the ordinary regnal year for dating purposes, but the Pipe Rolls naturally looked back over the whole year of account, whilst the Receipt and later Issue Rolls, were made up more or less day by day. ' If " Exchequer Year " means anything, it means merely the period from one Michaelmas to the next '.

adequately ; at any rate they continued in use, with modifications, until 1 William IV. Until the end of the twelfth century, the gross farm of the shire was not entered on the Pipe Roll, but only the balance between that and the sums paid in, plus authorized disbursements. The gross amounts were recorded in what was called the *rotulus exactorius* retained in the hands of the treasurer, but of this no specimen survives and nothing is known of its actual contents.

Enough has been said in this general description of the Exchequer of Henry II to indicate the nature of its activities and the extent of its development. Clearly the Exchequer on its financial side had come to be very much like a department of public finance. Of course all its financial business is the king's business, but it was the more public part of the royal revenue with which it dealt—largely, though not exclusively, the part for which the sheriffs of the counties were responsible. The calculation, payment, and accounting for this had largely become matters of routine ; difficult questions and legal decisions that might arise could best be dealt with and usually disposed of by those experienced in the routine. The work could go on, and indeed must go on, whether the king was present or absent, at home or abroad. The Exchequer was still essentially a part of the *Curia Regis*, and some of its important officials were still household officials, but it was rapidly becoming, if indeed it had not already become, something like a department ' of State ', with its own methods and practices, largely self-sufficient, in which, although of course the king was the ultimate authority, the first principle was its own custom, the custom of the Exchequer (*lex scaccarii*), which, because it was developed so thoroughly and so early, was to prove exceedingly tough and long-lived.

The Exchequer of Henry II, then, was well on the way to a departmental independence of its own, but this cannot be said in this period of the other two principal organs of royal administration, the Chamber, and the Chancery.

The Chamber, by its very nature, was essentially, and always remained a household department,[1] very close to the king. The great development of the Exchequer as the ' public ' finance

---

[1] *V.* generally, Tout, *Chapters*, I, ch. iii, §v.

department, becoming fixed in one place and largely fixed in routine, necessarily enhanced the importance of the Chamber as the king's personal financial bureau, as, in later parlance, his 'privy purse', travelling as it did with him wheresoever he might go, dealing with his personal expenses and those of his Household, and with any immediate financial needs that might arise close to the king himself. But there was not as yet any sharp distinction, if indeed, any distinction at all, between the king's private and public capacities and finances, or between private and public business. Organization was determined, not by any such theoretical considerations, but by convenience and expediency. All the revenue was the king's, whether it came into the Exchequer or into the Chamber. Nor was there any hard and fast rule as to which class or part of the revenue should be paid into the one or the other. The amounts and the sources of Chamber receipts varied greatly from time to time, and we do not know what they all were ; we know little at this time of chamber receipts apart from the items for which quittance was granted afterwards in the Exchequer, and entered on the Pipe Rolls. Sums were paid into the Chamber in response to writs, which might divert from the Exchequer parts of the sheriffs' farms, aids of various kinds, farms of castles, manors, fines, or rents. Many chamber receipts seem to have been casual, and it may be that there were already certain 'chamber manors' accounting regularly and solely to the Chamber as there were later on in the fourteenth century. Certainly there were some chamber receipts which were not accounted for at all at the Exchequer and which are not therefore reflected in the Pipe Rolls, and of which we know little at this time, for the rolls of the Chamber, which were kept from about 1164, do not survive.

From whatever sources the Chamber derived its funds, it was concerned, not only with the purely financial business of the king and his Household, but also with a certain amount of other administrative business and secretarial work. It is possible, though not probable, that even at this time, the Chamber had a seal of its own distinct from the 'great' seal and the exchequer seal. The clerks of the chamber, as we shall see, were not only financial clerks, but the trusted agents of the king, and might

F

be put to handle various sorts of business, especially confidential business, on the king's behalf, and many a chamber clerk who served the king well climbed to high office and exalted position. It was not exactly a case of the Chamber's doing ' some work of the chancery as well as some of the work of the exchequer ', as Tout wrote.[1] Such words imply that the Chamber was in some way trespassing on the domains of the other two organizations, but nobody thought of the matter in that light then. All the business was the king's business ; all the organizations were merely parts of the one *Curia*, and it was merely administrative convenience and routine, and the king's will, that determined whether any particular piece of work should be done in one part or another.

The treasurer had by now ceased to be concerned with the work of the Chamber, and the master-chamberlain is no longer much in evidence. Indeed, not much evidence of the internal organization of the Chamber at this period is available. There seem to have been two, perhaps three chamberlains, who by now were quite distinct from the chamberlains of the Exchequer, and these *camerarii* were normally laymen and knights ; there were various subordinate officers *de camera*, but the backbone of the organization very soon became a very important group of clerks, the *clerici camerarii*. The growing accountancy and writing work of the Chamber required more letters and skill than the lay chamberlains could provide, and there was therefore an imperative need for a class of experts in writing and finance. A group of skilled clerks of the Chamber sprang into prominence after the first ten years of Henry II's reign. The Chamber rapidly became a nursery of clerical administrators, many of whom, like Walter of Coutances, began careers in the Chamber that were to end in the highest offices in State and Church.

The Chamber of Henry II was thus a ' solidly organised institution, competently staffed, and always likely to extend its functions.'[2] As a factor in administration it was a potent force, for it was very close to the king himself, very responsive to his wishes, and with its financial resources and capable confidential clerks, it remained a ready and elastic instrument for implementing the king's will.

[1] *Ibid.*, p. 108. [2] *Ibid.*, p. 119.

The Chancery[1]—the term was in use before the end of the reign—in the time of Henry II, although a well-organized and developed office, still remained a household office and nothing more. Its development in this period was by way of consolidation and improvement of methods rather than in increased importance in relation to other parts of the administrative system. The high standards of drafting, diplomatic technique, and the great activity characteristic of Henry II's Chancery laid firm foundations for chancery traditions, and placed an efficient secretarial organization at the king's disposal. But it does not appear that the chancellor's office was as yet regarded as one of the first importance, and indeed it is possible that the office receded somewhat at this time. The existence of the justiciarship would naturally tend to keep the chancellorship well below the first rank. As yet the normal preferment held by a chancellor was an archdeaconry, and those elected to bishoprics resigned the chancellorship before consecration. Indeed there were but three chancellors in Henry II's reign. The great influence of the first of these, Thomas Becket, chancellor, 1154–62, was due not so much to his office, but to his personal intimacy with the king at that time. Henry II's experiences with Thomas may have caused him to be wary of too powerful chancellors, and at Thomas's resignation on becoming archbishop, no fresh appointment to the chancellorship was made for eleven years, the keepership of the seal being accorded to Geoffrey Ridel without the title of chancellor. From 1173, however, Ralph of Warneville became chancellor, and in 1182, Geoffrey, the king's bastard, later archbishop of York, succeeded him. Neither of these regularly discharged the duties of the office in person, and it seems that both found in Master Walter of Coutances an admirable deputy to act for them at court, if not formally as vice-chancellor, at least informally as *sigillifer*. More formally, there was still the *magister scriptorii*, who was the *clericus qui preest scriptorio* who attended at the meetings of the Exchequer and looked after chancery work there. These, and the chancery clerks who worked under them, were concerned in the developments in diplomatic and office routine that took place in this period.

[1] *Ibid.*, pp. 135–139.

During the reign, the royal acts emanating from the Chancery begin clearly to fall into three main categories evolving from the earlier writ-charters, which gave more elasticity and therefore more efficiency to Chancery's work.[1] In time these categories came to be distinguished not only by their inherent differences, but also by the methods by which the king's seal was applied to them. The most formal type, the ' charter ', retained the list of witnesses and was couched in formal terms, but with less pomposity than formerly, and was issued with pendent seals impressed upon strips of parchment or of leather of threads or silk. Writs were framed in much less formal, terser style, with a number of witnesses that was to be reduced to one only, the king himself, if not in Henry II's time, then very soon after. These writs were becoming at this time distinguished into two types—' letters patent' and ' letters close '. The former term was used in Henry II's time, and although the term ' letter close ' does not yet appear, the thing itself was already in use, in the form of letters addressed to individuals and issued closed up. Moreover, technical sub-divisions of letters close, such as writs of *liberate*, *computate*, and *perdono*, were familiar to the author of the *Dialogus*, and must have been in common use before that treatise was composed.

Henry II's Chancery was distinguished for its clear business-like methods, its economy of phraseology, and its ability to cope with the vastly increased amount of work with which it had to deal. But it did not as yet enrol records, though it probably already kept copies of the documents issuing from it. Consequently its documents of this period are much scattered. Of the numerous orders issuing from Chancery to Exchequer, only one survives from this time, although the existence at the time of great numbers of such orders is shown by the tell-tale entry ' *per breve regis* ' on the Pipe Rolls as warranty for action.

The relations between the three principal organs of Henry II's administrative system were thus close and intimate and the system itself coherent and effective. The Chamber was primarily concerned with the finances and supplies of the Household and

[1] For full details of Chancery diplomatic at this time, *v.* L. Delisle, *Recueil des Actes de Henri II* (Paris, 1909–27).

the king himself, and did not as yet play any large part in governmental administration. The principal secretarial work was still mainly centred in the Chancery, which sent its officials to do the writing work at the half-yearly sessions of the Exchequer, most of whose responsible officers were themselves household officers, whose sessions were essentially meetings of the *curia ad scaccarium*. There is still only the one king's seal, nominally in the custody of the chancellor, actually often in that of the *magister scriptorii*; and it is only a matter of administrative convenience that a duplicate of it is kept in the Treasury for exchequer business. As yet there is little to detract from the basic unity of the administration. The supreme direction is in the king or his justiciar; the administrative personnel are still based upon the Household in one way or another. But the time would come, and come soon, when this high degree of unity would no longer be maintained, and when parts of the administrative organization would move further away from the king's own Household.

§ 4. The full effects of the judicial innovations of Henry II's reign, with their vast repercussions upon the administration, were not fully felt in his lifetime, nor hardly perhaps until the early years of the thirteenth century. A good many years elapsed before the implications of the new writ system and the expansion of royal justice, involving the issue of many writs, the collection of the fees for them, the organization of the requisite judicial machinery, the collection and handling of the profits of justice, and the like, inevitably put a great strain upon the administrative system as operative at the date of Henry II's death. The strain of the eventually vast increase of detailed business to be dealt with in the king's court produced results which could hardly have been foreseen in Henry II's time, but his administrative machine had been built upon sound foundations, and, once consolidated, proved itself capable of almost limitless expansion. It is perhaps the greatest tribute to the work of the great Angevin and his ministers to say that their machine never broke down under the weight of the burdens which, as time went on, it had to bear. The vitality and toughness of the Angevin system was to endure indefinitely. But the huge increase of business was to have many consequences in the administrative sphere, as well as in other spheres, both political and constitutional.

Inevitably among those consequences was the growing impersonality of the kingship in a widening range of administrative business. Whatever may have been the case in the past, from now on, many parts of the administrative machine were to work with less and less reference to or intervention by the king himself. ' The machine of government has, in fact, grown so complex by the end of the twelfth century, the operations to be performed have so multiplied, that personal government is out of the question.'[1] Only a bureaucracy of officials, able and willing to take responsibility, could keep such a machine operative. All government was still, of course, the king's in theory and practice, and the king's alone, but more and more of it came to be government in the king's name, rather than by the king himself.

Moreover, the greater the multiplicity of business, the greater the need for increased specialization of function, and for adaptation of methods. As we shall see, the time came as the thirteenth century passed when, no matter what the theory continued to be, much administration in fact was carried on in organizations which could no longer be regarded as primarily part of the Household. The greater the degree to which departments emerged from the Household, the greater their self-sufficiency, the deeper their bureaucratic complexion, the remoter they became from the king's personal influence, and consequently the less immediately responsive they became to his wishes in so far as these might encroach upon routine. The extent to which this kind of development produced a reaction and a revival of administrative initiative in the Household is one of the most important and difficult questions in the administrative history of the thirteenth century, and will have to be considered later on.

There can be no doubt that these tendencies at the end of the twelfth century and the beginning of the thirteenth century were enhanced and complicated by the simple facts that Richard I was an absentee king for all but a few months of his reign, whereas John was active within the realm for three-quarters of

---

[1] Richardson, *Memoranda Roll*, 1 John, p. lxxxviiij.

his, and that after the loss of Normandy in 1204 all the kings of England, broadly speaking, found their interests centred primarily upon England and English administration, no matter what foreign enterprises they might enter into from time to time. Richard I's reign was almost wholly a period of administration without the king, but thereafter, except for short periods and during minorities, the administration was never to be without the king, until 1649–1660.

The immediate effect of Richard I's long absence can only be conjectured. The period was, in the circumstances no doubt inevitably, not one of any marked innovation in the central administration. We have to envisage the system of Henry II carrying on under the general direction of the justiciars and the advisers appointed under the varying arrangements authorized by the king.[1] Longchamp's rise and fall, the crisis and baronial council of 1191, the intervention of Walter of Coutances, Hubert Walter's fiscal innovations, are important in political and to some extent constitutional history, but there is not much to show that Henry II's administrative system was thereby modified to any significant extent. The important thing was that the system could and did cope with the situations arising, continued to function and to perform its principal tasks under the several justiciars, with very little contact with the king himself, without the Household, and with a Chancery that was more like a justiciar's Chancery than a king's. The fillip to the self-sufficiency of the Exchequer and of the Chancery must have been very considerable, and some fresh orientation in these organs must have resulted, even though kept in bounds by the at least theoretical omnipotence of the justiciar. Under Hubert Walter, from the end of 1193, we are told, ' the traditional system of government, by which a chief justiciar executed the commands of an absent but accessible king, and supervised the administration of justice and finance, was restored.'[2] On the whole, therefore, the impression given by Richard I's reign in the administrative sphere, is one of quiet consolidation, of a system learning to grapple with the increase of business resulting from Henry II's reforms, but

---

[1] *V. supra*, p. 41, and references therein.
[2] F. M. Powicke, *C.M.H.*, VI, p. 214.

remaining essentially the same system at the end of the reign as it was at its beginning.

But the general impression of John's reign in the same sphere is very different. It is impossible to survey the evidence of this period without at once perceiving that a fresh spirit is being given to the administration. The restless, impulsive energy, spasmodic drive, the intemperate will and sporadic initiative of the king himself, become apparent. Moreover, the full implications of Henry II's reforms were by now making themselves felt on the administrative machinery. Adaptation to meet both the king's wishes and the increased routine business was necessitated. Congestion of business at the Exchequer induced some simplification of its procedure; pressure of work involved better methods in Chancery; the king's requirements produced complications in the Household, particularly in the Chamber and the Wardrobe, and the employment of an additional seal, the small or privy seal, closer to the king and more immediately responsive to his wishes than the 'great' seal in the custody of the chancellor. 'The reign of John is, to a degree found in no period of previous history, a commentary upon the development of the *Curia Regis*.'[1]

The developments were along the old lines in the main, resulting in improved methods to cope with the pressure of business, greater specialization in some respects, and a certain difference in the relative importance of the several administrative organizations. The Exchequer devises a better procedure, Chancery begins its great series of enrolments (or at any rate they begin to survive from this period), but the nerve-centre of the higher administrative activity, the source of initiative is no longer so much *in curia ad scaccarium* as *in camera regis*. The Chamber, with its small seal, and its subsidiary the Wardrobe, very close to the king, becomes the pivot of the administration, the immediate instrument of the king's executive power, when he chooses to exert it.

Of the administrative organisms, the Exchequer felt most the consequences of Henry II's judicial expansion. The ever-increasing volume of business in the royal courts brought extreme congestion of work. A steady stream of writs issued from

[1] *Ibid.*, p. 218.

Chancery; acting on these the justices amerced officials, juries, plaintiffs, and defendants for defaults of every kind. Fees were seldom more than half-a-mark, and amercements on individuals were usually similar, and the result was a vast number of small debts that had to be accounted for at the Exchequer. 'Even before the end of Henry II's reign', as Miss Mills says, 'it must have been clear that new machinery was needed to cope with the new type of revenue. In the early thirteenth century the question of reform became urgent.'[1]

The old methods of accounting at the Exchequer could not continue indefinitely. It became impracticable to cut a tally for each separate item of debt and to enter every item on the Pipe Roll year by year until the debt was eventually paid off in full. A system which, for example, involved the cutting of 1,094 tallies for as many debts amounting to £610 in one county,[2] was obviously in much need of reform. From 1199 the increase in the number of fees, fines, and amercements was rapid. By 1200 the Pipe Roll was commonly compiled in long double-column entries; by 1215 it was hopelessly clogged with long lists of fines and amercements with which the Exchequer was failing to cope.[3] Not even the keeping and retention in the Exchequer of Memoranda Rolls[4] to assist the officials in their tasks sufficed to keep the Pipe Rolls in manageable proportions; some substantial simplification of procedure was needed.

After some tentative experiments, two principal methods of easing the situation were found, but some years passed before they became the regular practice. Both followed from the

[1] Mabel Mills, 'Experiments in Exchequer Procedure', *Trans. R.H.S.*, 4th ser. VIII (1925), p. 153, Cf. Richardson, 'William of Ely, the King's Treasurer,' ?1195–1215, in *ibid.*, XV (1932), pp. 45–90.

[2] Mills, *ibid.*, p. 154.

[3] *Ibid.*, p. 155.

[4] It is probable that memoranda rolls of some kind were kept in Henry II's time, but the earliest surviving example is dated 1 John. *V.* the edition published by the Pipe Roll Society, n.s. XXI (1943). Cf. H. Jenkinson, 'Financial Records of the Reign of John', *Magna Carta Commemoration Essays*, ed. H. C. Malden (1917), pp. 244–300. Miss Mills, *op. cit.*, p. 135, poses the very interesting questions whether this rapid development was the natural result of Henry II's assizes, or of John's acquisition of a grip upon the administration. Probably it was the result of both. Whatever the cause, the irritation felt in the country at the constant exaction of small sums came to be reflected in the terms of the Great Charter. Of still greater importance in this connection was a large increase in the amounts exacted on account of the 'increment and profits' of the sheriffs' farms. *V.* Miss Mills, *loc. cit.*

principle of making the sheriffs responsible for the collection of all debts due to the Crown in their bailiwicks. About 1206, the idea was at last hit upon that a single tally could be issued to cover a multitude of debts included in a sheriff's profer. The invention of these *tallia dividenda* much reduced the work involved at the Receipt, even though full particulars still had to be entered on the Receipt Rolls. Moreover, this arrangment facilitated in the Upper Exchequer the use of grouped entries in the Pipe Rolls, which had already been partially resorted to. More and more debts were entered in groups, whilst the record of individual items was left to subsidiary rolls, such as the *Originalia*, Estreat, and Receipt Rolls. These devices went far to solve the problem of congestion at the Exchequer, but they were not to become regular practice without difficulties. For the political circumstances of 1215–17 were to produce a complete breakdown at the Exchequer. The audit in the autumn of 1214 was the last to be held before the Treaty of Lambeth, and when the Exchequer re-assembled on 12 November, 1217, three years' accounts required auditing, and the first problem was not reform, but making the normal machinery work once more.

The relations of Exchequer and Chancery were still very close, and although their functions were distinct, both were but aspects of one and the same *Curia*, and in some respects their activities overlapped. It must be remembered, too, that even taken together, their joint activities did not exhaust either the financial or the secretarial work of that *Curia*. As we shall see, the Chamber and the Wardrobe had their parts to play in these matters.

The outstanding development in Chancery in John's time is the beginning (or survival) of a continuous series of enrolments. The Chancery Rolls that begin in 1199 have continued to be made and preserved in one form or another ever since. But there is no doubt that the practice of enrolment—the copying of documents on to parchment sheets sewn together end to end and subsequently rolled up to form a roll[1]—originated a good deal earlier

---

[1] Usually of about 30 membranes, size 12 ins. by 24 ins. Exchequer records were kept on the different principle of fastening membranes together all at the head. The English Chancery method was unique at the time. The Papal and French Chanceries, which were maintaining records at much the same time, preferred the book or register form.

than the accession of John. The prime (but hardly the only) motive for adopting such a practice seems to have been a financial one—to facilitate the work of the Exchequer in collecting the king's debts. It may well be that Hubert Walter, as chancellor 1199–1205, brought his great administrative experience to bear upon the problem of chancery archives, and that as a result, the practice of enrolment became far more extensive, systematic, and permanent, but it is certain that enrolment in Chancery had its origins further back.

There is some evidence that a form of Fine Rolls, recording promises of payments to the king for grants of land and other favours, were being kept in the time of Henry II, probably from 1175.[1] Some form of transcripts of this record were being sent for information and action to the Exchequer, and the roll of these extracts (or estreats) soon became called the Original Roll, and before long the *Originalia* Roll (presumably because they originated action in the Exchequer). Later on, the *Originalia* Roll was confined to debts arising in Chancery, and the rest were entered on what were called Estreat Rolls. A fragmentary *Originalia* Roll exists for 7 Richard I.[2] and some kind of Fine Roll (at first called Oblate Roll) must then have existed, though none survives from earlier than 1 John.

These Rolls were intended to record debts to be collected and accounted for at the Exchequer, and the motive for their compilation is sufficiently obvious. In part, but only in part, other Chancery Rolls were made and preserved with a view to recording charges upon the Exchequer ; partly also to facilitate the work of Chancery itself, primarily, in all instances, in the interests of the Crown, but eventually also with some reference to the interests of private persons.[3]

From the late twelfth century, the Chancery had found it necessary to keep duplicate copies of many of the writs which it issued ; these *contrabrevia* were kept on files. In the second year of John, these files gave place to enrolments. Two series were

---

[1] Richardson, *op. cit.*, xxi–xxxiij.   [2] Printed, *ibid.*, pp. 85–88.

[3] ' That royal records might and should serve the private interests of the king's subjects was clearly an afterthought and it was likely to be a conception of slow growth ', Richardson, *op. cit.*, p. lj. As early as the reign of Henry I reference in private litigation was allowed to Domesday Book.

maintained at first, one for the king's French domains, one for England and Ireland, concerned mainly with the Norman and English Exchequer interests respectively.[1] These Rolls, which may be described as an early species of what was to become the wider class of Close Rolls, were mainly concerned with charges upon one or other of the two Exchequers, notifications of which were sent by writ to the appropriate Exchequer for action, but other documents and memoranda were sometimes included in them by the Chancery clerks. The need for recording matters of more than financial interest was evidently growing, for miscellaneous documents are included in the other Chancery rolls of the period ; as time passed, non-financial matters predominate on the Close Rolls ; by 1226, the financial items were relegated to separate *Liberate* Rolls, the Close Rolls then becoming more strictly rolls of letters close.

From 1199, the first Charter Roll was initiated. Hitherto, no systematic record of charters issued from Chancery had been kept, and the charters surviving from an earlier date, survive among the archives of outside bodies, cathedrals and monastic houses, or of private persons, or in the Exchequer[2] or sometimes in exemplifications by Chancery. The reasons for this new departure are the subject of debate. It may be that ' the word went forth from Hubert Walter, immediately on John's accession, that the king's court was to keep copies of its outgoing letters,'[3] but there is no direct evidence of this. It is true that on 7 June, 1199, King John issued a decree regulating the fees to be charged for instruments under the great seal, but it is going too far to argue that the Charter Roll was henceforth kept so as to facilitate the exaction of these fees.[4] More pertinent was John's instruction to the justices of the Bench that they should recognize his predecessor's charters only if confirmed by him.[5] Such a requirement would inevitably encourage the keeping of a systematic record of its charter work by Chancery itself. By 3 John, separate

[1] A fragment of the English *Liberate Roll* for 2 John is printed in Richardson, *op. cit.*, pp. 88–97.
[2] For various reasons, charters were sometimes enrolled in the Exchequer, on the Pipe Rolls, or on the rolls that came to be called the *Cartae Antiquae* Rolls.
[3] V. H. Galbraith, *Studies in the Public Records* (1948), p. 74.
[4] Richardson, *op. cit.*, p. xliij.
[5] *Curia Regis Rolls*, I, 331.

rolls for the less solemn but still formal letters patent, the Patent Rolls, were being kept.[1]

With these developments, an enormous step forward in the administrative efficiency of the *Curia* had been taken. For the first time, the government secured a comprehensive written record of its actions. These chancery enrolments, exchequer records, the rolls of the justices,[2] and the archives of the Chamber and Wardrobe,[3] afforded the government a mass of written record without equal at the time, from which it could draw information and data, and check administrative action at will. A source of stability and efficiency had been created which never thereafter was to be lacking—but more effective government did not, of course, necessarily mean more good government, as John's use of his power was to show.

The new archives of the Chancery gave further impetus, no doubt, to the process of differentiation in the *Curia*. The Exchequer had long had its own records ;[4] Chancery now had its own. But Chancery was still primarily a household department, and the chancellor a household officer. It did not, however, follow that the whole of the Chancery, nor the chancellor himself, nor even the keeper of the seal, would always be with the king. The ceaseless perambulations of John perhaps made such proximity impracticable, or at least, very inconvenient. What mattered was that the king should have to hand the means for initiating administrative action whenever he wished, and these means were now supplied by the Chamber.

[1] The Charter, Patent, and Close Rolls for John's reign are printed in full in the Record Commission's publications.

[2] The *Curia Regis* Rolls—plea rolls of the *Curia*, the predecessors of the later *de Banco* and the *Coram Rege* Rolls, date from 1194, and the Feet of Fines (documents made in triplicate recording the compromises or 'final concords' made in the king's court, the foot (*pes*) of which was filed in the Treasury) from 1195.

[3] *V. infra*, p. 79.

[4] It should be remembered that the Treasury remained for centuries an important depository for records of many kinds, irrespective of place of origin. Not only Domesday Book, returns of knights' fees, records of enquiries, but also various other documents were stored there. *Magna Carta* was not enrolled on the Charter Roll, but copies were kept in the Treasury. Chancery enrolments were retained in the Chancery, and from the early thirteenth century, a keeper, later called *magister rotulorum* was appointed. The modern judicial Master of the Rolls remains responsible, through a Deputy Keeper, for the archives deposited in the Public Record Office, which was built on the site of a building (the *domus conversorum*) which housed chancery clerks in the fourteenth century.

The origins of the small seal which soon became known as the privy seal, are not clear. There is some far from conclusive evidence that a small seal was already in use for administrative business as early as Henry II's time.[1] The seal left behind in England by Richard I when he went on Crusade may have been simply the exchequer duplicate of the king's seal, or possibly some other, ' small ' seal.[2] But the use of a small or privy seal only becomes certain after the accession of John, when acts enrolled in Chancery are specifically stated to have been issued under the *parvum* or *privatum sigillum*, or authorized by warrants under such a seal. As yet there is nothing to show that the small and privy seals were identical, but soon the evidence becomes conclusive on this point, and there is no reason to doubt that the two terms applied to the one and the same seal from the start. In contradistinction, the older king's seal soon came to be called the ' great ' seal.

It is also clear that from the early years of John the privy seal was particularly used for chamber business, and that normally it was in the custody of chamber officials, some at least of whom would always be with the king. The king now, therefore, whatever may have been the case earlier, had to hand a ready instrument for administrative action ; a letter or writ under the privy seal was sufficient to move the great seal, wherever it might be, or to carry instructions to any part of the *Curia*, and indeed, outside of it. An effective secretariat grew up in the Chamber, which, although perhaps not as yet wholly distinct from the general household secretariat presided over, at least nominally, by the chancellor, nonetheless afforded the king an ever-ready channel for the expression of his will.

But, though the use of the privy seal doubtless enhanced the effectiveness of the Chamber, it was in any case the principal centre of administrative activity around the king himself. The supreme executive was wherever the king was ; his instructions must be carried out somehow, in whatever way was convenient at the moment ; he must have cash available for current expenses, whether for his personal needs, or for the Household, or for his

---

[1] Delisle, *Recueil*, Introduction, p. 235.
[2] Tout, *Chapters*, I, pp. 148–150.

immediate enterprise, be it a hunting expedition or a military campaign or some other undertaking requiring cash. Elasticity, adaptability, and immediacy were the qualities required to meet these needs, and no theories of division of labour, departmental routine, or any such considerations entered into the matter. ' Wherever the king came, a score of latent duties might leap into activity, in the stable, or in the kitchen, at the gate or in the forest; and all would be under the supervision of the royal Chamber. Every kind of activity, from matters of State to the trivial details of domestic life, were within the cognisance of the Chamber, and of its financial department, the Wardrobe.'[1]

The Wardrobe had hitherto been little more than a place of deposit, closely connected with the Chamber, but the term soon became applied more to the things deposited than to the place of deposit. As such the Wardrobe was essentially a part of the king's baggage which usually travelled about with him, and as such was capable of indefinite expansion. Important archives, charters, correspondence with foreign princes, and other documents which, for whatever reason, were to be kept close at hand, were added to the Wardrobe, and it was found convenient to add also stores of ready cash. As the Wardrobe grew in this way, the custody and care of it became a more and more responsible task, requiring capable officials and records of its own ; since it stored ready cash, it was convenient that it should also pay it out as needed. A busy office, closely associated with the Chamber thus came into being. Their association was so close that perhaps it is an exaggeration to call the Wardrobe ' the financial department of the Chamber ' at this time ; it was rather the Chamber's organization for storage and disbursement. In that sphere its activities in John's reign were great and increasing, and are revealed in much detail in the records of expenditure kept in its own *Misae* Rolls.[2] Usually, its expenditure was

---

[1] Powicke, *op. cit.*, p. 222.

[2] The *Misae* Rolls were a kind of day-book of the Household, anticipating the *jornalia garderobae* of a later period. They were sent into the Exchequer and enrolled on the *praestitia* rolls. The earliest surviving are those for 11 and 12 John respectively, and are printed by the Record Commission in *Rotuli de Liberate ac de Misis et Praestitia regnanti Johanne* (1844). The mise roll of 14 John, with the *praestitia* roll, are printed in H. Cole, *Documents illustrative of English History in the 13th and 14th centuries* (1844).

of a routine nature, for the current expenses of the king and
the Household, but on occasion, when a military enterprise
was on hand, the outlay might increase enormously, and embrace
such items as payments to foreign allies, wages for mercenary
soldiers, the cost of a campaign.

It was the business of the Chamber to see that funds sufficient
to meet the needs of the moment, whatever they might be, were
available in the Wardrobe. As we have seen, portions of the royal
revenue were habitually diverted to the Chamber,[1] and the
Exchequer could be drawn upon as might be necessary. Funds
out of the Treasury, whether at Winchester, or later, at Westminster, were transmitted by servants of the treasurer, under
guard, to the Chamber and stored in the Wardrobe. But the
Treasury was in a fixed place, whereas the Chamber and Wardrobe
normally travelled all over the country (often outside of it) with
the king, ' and to get the king's money to the king's administration was a major undertaking upon which the whole safety
and order of the nation must turn.'[2] The ceaseless perambulation
through the realm of King John and his entourage after the loss
of Normandy added to the difficulties inherent in the problem.
From about the summer of 1207, it seems, the normal arrangements were breaking down. The Exchequer could not adequately
meet the king's demands for ready cash ; the royal progresses
became held up for lack of funds; the dangers of transmitting cash
over long distances became more apparent. But the resourceful
Chamber was ready with improvisations and adaptations. 'The
camera was to hand always, free to ignore or anticipate the
exchequer terms, taking up the king's debts where they fell
due, a place of payment *ipsi domino Regi*, under the king's eye,
where debtors could be more profitably dealt with than in the
courtroom setting of the Exchequer under the restrictions of the
lex scaccarii.'[3]

The use of the Chamber as a travelling treasury of receipt
was not, of course, new in John's reign, but was now greatly
extended. Moreover, further drastic steps were taken to ensure

---

[1] *V. supra*, p. 65.
[2] J. E. A. Jolliffe, ' The Chamber and the Castle Treasuries under King John,'
in *Studies in Medieval History presented to F. M. Powicke* (1948), p. 120.
[3] *Ibid.*, p. 122.

that adequate local funds should be available. The Treasury itself came to be partly dispersed and localized by the establishment of provincial treasuries in the king's castles at such places as Bristol, Devizes, Nottingham, Marlborough, Corfe and Exeter. It is possible that this striking piece of adaptation was resorted to in 1207 as the result of friction arising between the Chamber and the Exchequer, and if this is so, then perhaps a new stage in administrative history had been reached—a stage in which disharmony between a household department and a department outside the Household could occur, nowithstanding that both were parts of the same *Curia*. As the thirteenth century passed, more was to be heard of this kind of problem.

But for the time being, the situation is admirably summed up in Mr. Jolliffe's words : ' There is nothing public or private in the governing institutions of the early thirteenth century, and if the king be there, all the powers of the kingdom may be packed within the small compass of the *camera regis*. Under John, in practice and in temper, the greater part of executive government had in it the authoritarianism of military organization and borrowed easily from the precedents of war, and we can hardly exaggerate the extent to which the power and order of the kingdom was in this age a creation of the king. Where he did not infringe common right—and that is a large qualification—his strong executive government was an acting out of the full implications of kingship, partly as he had received it from his father and brother, partly as he himself remade it. That there was violence and abuse in his handling of the law the complainants of the Charter tell us, and we cannot question their verdict : but the general scope of John's kingship they accept in silence. They have known and can conceive no other. Law and exceptional affairs of state may come within the scope of a baronial *universitas*—*ideally* they may do so—but the executive is still the king's. It is there that we may look for the creativeness and strength of monarchy, and in doing so, understand that paradox of historians which speaks of John as " the strongest of the Angevins ".'[1]

[1] *Ibid.*, pp. 141-2. Cf. H. Jenkinson, *op. cit.*, p. 300 : ' We seem to see working a single very powerful administrative brain. Was that brain King John's? '

G

§ 5. The period from the accession of Henry III in 1216 to the fall of Hubert de Burgh in 1232 shows no marked innovation in the administrative sphere as it was in 1215, which remained substantially the system of Henry II, as modified in some respects during John's reign. From 1232, however, marked changes occurred which can best be regarded as inaugurating a fresh phase of administrative history.[1] In 1232, Hubert de Burgh's dismissal virtually ended the administrative justiciarship. True, Stephen de Segrave was to hold the office for nearly two years thereafter, but the office was no longer the same as it had been; it was never again in ordinary circumstances the centre of administrative power; during Segrave's tenure of the office, the location of power under the king was not with the justiciar but with Peter de Rivaux, whose accumulation of household and other offices eclipsed the justiciarship, and for a time concentrated in his hands a degree of administrative power, central and local, of enormous and unprecedented scope. His use of this power opens a new chapter in administrative history.

The accession of a minor to the throne was unprecedented in England in 1216, and various legal and political difficulties required to be overcome. But in the administrative sphere, the situation in the earlier years was not very different from that arising from the prolonged absences of the kings in the then recent past. Once the troubles of the civil war were over, and the Treaty of Lambeth concluded, the principal problem was to get John's administrative machinery to work again. It was mainly the business of William Marshal, the earl of Pembroke, as *rector regis et regni*, to procure the pacification, assisted by Gualo and Pandulf, the papal legates, and by Hubert de Burgh, who had been made justiciar by King John at Runnymede. So far as ordinary administration was concerned, it may be safely assumed that the main burden fell to the justiciar. After the death of the Marshal in May, 1219, and the retiral of Pandulf in 1221, Hubert de Burgh 'had the realm of England in his hand',[2] and for about ten years exercised his justiciarship very much in the

---

[1] F. M. Powicke's view indicated in *Henry III and the Lord Edward* (1947), p. 84, is preferable to Tout's choice of 1234 as the best dividing line (*Chapters*, I, p. 239).

[2] Powicke, *op. cit.*, 43, citing Bracton's Notebook, pl. 1221.

traditional, Angevin style, in susbtantial co-operation, however, in matters of policy, with Archbishop Stephen Langton until the latter's death in 1218. To a very large extent, the justiciarship of Hubert de Burgh meant a revival and continuation of the old administrative system.

A prime necessity was naturally to get the exchequer machinery working again. The Exchequer re-assembled in November, 1217, and set the wheels revolving once more.[1] Only a partial audit for the war-years was feasible, but steps were taken to revive normal working for the year 1217–18. The volume of business soon became very great, and the number of fines and amercements to be dealt with very large. For a time these were coped with by a liberal resort to dividend tallies and grouped entries on the Pipe Rolls, and between 1218 and 1223, clause 25 of the 1215 Great Charter forbidding the exaction of ' profits ' on the farms of the counties was observed, although this clause was in fact omitted in all the re-issues of the Charter in Henry III's reign.

But after this promising start, a period of apparent reaction set in—largely coincident with the attainment of his maximum power by Hubert de Burgh. Between Michaelmas, 1223, and Michaelmas, 1228, dividend tallies and grouped entries are much less in evidence, whilst very large profits on the farms were exacted. The reasons for this reversion to older and less satisfactory methods can only be surmised, but presumably it was due to de Burgh's predilections. About 1228, the reaction ceased —if indeed it had been reaction—and by then de Burgh's grip on the administration was beginning to fail. His final fall in 1232 was to be followed by extensive financial reforms under the impetus of Peter de Rivaux.

The fact of Henry III's minority naturally gave rise to difficulty in the matter of providing a seal for the authentication of acts which normally would have required the king's ' great ' seal. The difficulty was overcome at first by the use of the Marshal's own seal, but a great seal came into partial use in October, 1218.[2] By a decision of the great council, however,

---

[1] Miss Mills, *loc. cit.*

[2] For details, *v.* Powicke, ' The Chancery during the Minority of Henry III, *E.H.R.*, XXIII (1905), pp. 220–235. Cf. L. B. Dibben, ' Chancellor and Keeper of the Seal in Henry III's Reign ', *E.H.R.* XXVII (1912), pp. 39–51.

this was not to be affixed to charters or grants in perpetuity, because of the nonage of the king, and this restriction remained even though Henry III was declared by Pope Honorius to be of age in 1223. The great seal did not come into full use until January, 1227, when Henry III declared himself to be of full age, and began to issue charters and to require that those of his predecessors should be submitted for confirmation. From 1218 to 1226, the seal was in the custody of Ralph Neville, bishop of Chichester, who was appointed chancellor in 1226.

Inevitably, the minority had reduced the administrative importance of the household departments to small or negligible proportions. The Chamber and Wardrobe of an infant king could not play any part in the general administration, and there was not, of course, during the minority, any privy seal. But as the king grew older, and began to assert his own will, these instruments began to revive. As we shall see, the key-note of Henry III's assumption and exercise of royal power was to be not only a revival but also an expansion of the place of the household departments in the administrative system.

There is no evidence of the revival of a privy seal before December, 1230, and the only comparable seal until then was the justiciar's own seal and the seals of other responsible agents of the royal power. It is possible that the policy of withholding a privy seal from the king for some three years after he had attained his majority was a part of de Burgh's deliberate policy for maintaining Henry III's dependence, and that this was one among other reasons for the king's growing animosity towards the justiciar. However, from early December, 1230, Henry III acquired a privy seal of his own, and its use was to play some part in later developments.[1]

As early as 1219, soon after the death of William Marshal, renewed activity in the Chamber and Wardrobe becomes apparent, and before long a more distinct differentiation between the two occurred, although they continued to overlap in various ways. But the major revival came in the Wardrobe, which in the years to come was to outgrow and to overshadow the Chamber itself, at any rate as the financial department of the Household.[2] The

[1] *V.* Tout, *Chapters*, I, ch. iv, § iii.   [2] *Ibid.*, ch. v, § ii.

reasons for this rather lop-sided development remain obscure, and at first perhaps it was due to merely personal factors, and principally to the fact that Peter de Rivaux, who was to assume so great a place in the financial and administrative developments of the ensuing years, was closely associated with the Wardrobe.

Peter de Rivaux, a nephew or son of Peter des Roches, was a Poitevin clerk who began his official career in the king's service about 1218, and for some five years figured as the principal financial officer in attendance upon the king, employed in receiving moneys from the Exchequer and elsewhere for the defrayal of the king's household expenses. His official designation at this period is obscure ; sometimes he is called the chamberlain, and the payments to him are *in camera* or sometimes *in garderoba*, but from 1223 he seems more specifically to be regarded as clerk of the wardrobe, jointly with Walter of Brackley. His responsibilities there, however, ceased by January, 1224, no doubt as a result of de Burgh's ascendancy. But during his term, the magnitude of wardrobe finances increased rapidly, and the department seems to have been well on the way to the position of importance[1] which it was to occupy under Henry III's personal rule. It was able to finance the king's expedition to Brittany and Poitou in 1230, for which purpose it became temporarily expanded on a large scale.

It was the failure of this expedition that was probably decisive in determining Henry III, eager to assert his own powers more fully, to rid himself of de Burgh, and to recall the Poitevins to his service. By July, 1232, Hubert de Burgh lost his office of justiciar, and Peter des Roches was back at the king's side, without office, and his kinsman Peter de Rivaux was accumulating so many administrative offices, that it mattered little who was justiciar.

[1] The earliest surviving wardrobe account presented to the Exchequer is dated 5 January, 1224, to 10 April, 1227, and is printed in Tout, *Chapters*, I, pp. 233–238.

CHAPTER IV

CONTINUITY AND CHANGE IN THE ADMINISTRATIVE SYSTEM : THE BEGINNINGS OF POLITICAL REPERCUSSIONS, 1232–1307

§ 1. ' In bringing all officers of State and all departments of government under the Crown's immediate control, Henry III was not devising tyrannical or unconstitutional innovations ; he was simply perfecting the Angevin system of government.'[1] This statement summarizes the soundest interpretation of the general nature of the administrative history of the reign of Henry III from 1232 onwards. There was no material change in the structure of the administration in the years 1232–1258—no material change that is sufficient to differentiate it in kind from that of the Angevin period. It is true that in two important respects Henry III's administration differed from that of his predecessors : the Angevin justiciarship ended with Hubert de Burgh's fall in 1232, and the king himself, being seldom absent from his realm, could be and often was in effect his own justiciar. In other words, the difference essentially arose from the fact that the potential direction of the administrative machinery in this later period rested in the king himself more continuously, more intimately, and for longer spells, than it had for at least a hundred years, if not indeed than it ever had at any time since the Norman Conquest. The culmination of Angevin administrative development, combined with a much higher degree of personal royal direction, or at any rate presence, gave to these years their basic character in the sphere of administration. It was essentially this combination that eventually evoked a baronial opposition which, whilst it can hardly be said to have been aimed at any substantial modification of the central administrative system as

---

[1] R. F. Treharne, *The Baronial Plan of Reform*, 1258–63 (1932), p. 23. The firs t chapter of this work provides the best introduction to the administrative history of this period. Cf. the same writer's brief survey ' The Personal Rule of Henry III and the aims of the Baronial Reformers of 1258 ' in *History* XVI (1932), pp. 336–340.

such, certainly aimed at modifying the king's exclusive control of it.

The contrast between the administrative history of the period 1232–58 and what had come before, relates not to the Angevin period proper, but to the minority of Henry III himself. The years from 1216 to 1232 saw no effective royal control; the executive power had necessarily been exercised by others than the king himself. Hubert de Burgh had begun his administrative career as a royal officer pure and simple in the days of King John, but his prolonged justiciarship during the minority and beyond, inevitably tended to give the office a flavour of independence; his elevation to the earldom of Kent, on the basis of which much of his personal influence rested, tended to make him look something like a 'baronial' justiciar, responsible in a vague way to the great council; his great position seemed to come about independently of the reigning sovereign. The chancellor, Ralph Neville, bishop of Chichester, who succeeded Richard Marsh in that office in 1226, was, if anything, in a still more independent position, being in effect appointed by the great council, and having obtained a grant of the office and the issues of the great seal for life. William Mauclerk had also obtained a life-grant of the office of treasurer. The circumstances of the minority thus tended to encourage the ideas that the great offices in the administration had a strong position of their own, were vested with an initiative that emanated only nominally from the king himself, and were actually responsible (if responsible at all), in a vague and loose way to the great council. In this sense, and with these large limitations, there had been a measure of 'baronial' influence, perhaps even of ultimate control, over the administration, because of, and only because of, the minority of Henry III.

But the Angevin traditions gave no countenance to such ideas. No Norman or Angevin king had favoured baronial tenure of important administrative office; none except royal nomination to office had occurred; from 1179 to 1232, with two insignificant exceptions, all the justiciars had been king's men trained in the *Curia Regis*. The treasurers and chancellors had sprung from the same source. Before the accession of Henry III, none of the great offices had ever been in any sense a baronial office or the perquisite of an independent prelate ; on the contrary, their occupants had nearly always been 'professional' experts trained in the king's court. Never had they been in any way responsible to the great council, the baronage, or the Church, but always wholly dependent upon the king.[1]

But there can scarcely be any doubt that the circumstances of the last phase of John's reign and the conditions of the minority fostered the notion of the possibility and desirability of some degree of 'baronial' influence upon the government, and went far to determine the form eventually taken by the baronial opposition to Henry III's régime. Equally without doubt 'in seeking to assert his individual authority over his officials, Henry III was simply attempting to restore the conditions which had characterised the reigns of his predecessors.'[2]

It is in this light that the administrative history of the period 1232 to 1258 is best interpreted, and on this interpretation it is clear that Henry III not only attained a high degree of success in his administrative policy, but also did much to determine that the Angevin conception of the central government was to prevail for a century thereafter, and indeed to remain basic to English administrative history until Tudor times at least.

The revival of the Household as the centre of administrative initiative, inaugurated by the concentration of many offices and powers in Peter de Rivaux, a wardrobe official, and the lapse of the administrative justiciarship in 1232, signified no more than a return to the traditions of the past, and was, one might almost say, the inevitable result or even the very manifestation of, the revival of the personal kingship itself. Once the king was in a position to exercise executive power himself, inevitably the centre of administrative activity gravitated around him and the organs of administration close to him in the Household. It was not a question of seeking to circumvent the Chancery and the Exchequer, even if departmentalism in these quarters was growing ; these were just as much the king's organizations as the Household itself, of which they were only off-shoots. Any inconvenience from personal considerations that might have

---

[1] Treharne, *op. cit.*, p. 17.   [2] *Ibid.*, p. 18.

arisen in consequence of the survival of a treasurer and chancellor
from the minority was overcome as far as possible : the treasurership was made too uncomfortable for Mauclerk to dispose him
to stand upon his life-grant ; chancellor Neville, it seems, readily
resumed, if indeed, he had ever really lost, his character as a
royal civil servant.[1] With the heads of the ' departments of
State ' reduced to their normal relations towards a ruling sovereign, with the administrative justiciarship terminated, and the
Household revived, there was no question of the king's wishing
or needing to circumvent the ' great departments ', or to play off
the household organs against them. All in the last resort were
equally under his thumb ; executive power was once again
restored to the monarchy, and once again it was only a matter of
administrative convenience whether one organ or another was
utilized for this purpose.[2] In all this, ' Henry III was simply
resuming the processes begun by his grandfather as a natural and
essential part of the Angevin policy of administrative centralisa-
tion . . . The administrative developments of the reign of Henry
II were at last brought to completion.'[3]

The question how far the baronial opposition to Henry III's
government, as manifested in the ' draft constitution ' of 1244,
the Provisions of Oxford and Westminster, and the *Forma
Regiminis* aimed at temporarily or indefinitely modifying what
must be called the Angevin conception and structure of the
central administrative system is a very difficult question to
answer with precision. Varying answers have in effect been
given to it by historians of the period, and opinions differ
considerably upon it. Consideration of this question is for the
present purpose better postponed until a later section[4] ; for
whatever the aims of the baronage may have been in this respect,
it can hardly be said that they did in fact procure any permanent
modification of the traditional conception or structure of the
central administration. When the Barons' Wars were over, when
Simon de Montfort's revolutionary régime had collapsed, and
normal government was resumed, the central administrative

[1] On this point, *v. infra*, p. 109.
[2] A statement by the present writer in a different sense in his *English Constitutional History* (1948), pp. 101–2, needs revision.
[3] Treharne, *op. cit.*, p. 23.   [4] *V. infra*, pp. 120 ff.

system was essentially the same as it had been before 1258. All the organs of administration, whether in the Household or outside of it, were still the king's alone ; the officials were his and responsible to him alone. True, the four decades between 1232 and the end of the reign did not pass without developments in the administrative sphere that were durable, but these were almost wholly the result of organic growth, not of political pressure from outside the *Curia*. In short, the political repercussions of this period were not such as to produce substantial modifications in the administrative system as inherited from the Angevins and as developed in Henry III's time. Edward I succeeded to an administrative organization that was traditional ; nor was it to be much modified in his reign. From the administrative point of view, therefore, the reigns of Henry III and Edward I, from 1232, notwithstanding the diversity and complexity of the events that took place, are best considered as one period.

§ 2. ' There seems to be no doubt . . . that the fall of Hubert de Burgh was an incident, though a very dramatic incident, in an effort to overhaul the system of royal finance and to define the responsibility for its administration.'[1] It is indeed clear that the importance, even perhaps the permanent importance of the so-called ' Poitevin régime ' of 1232–34 lies primarily in the sphere of finance. As Sir Maurice Powicke goes on to say, these short years laid down the lines of development in the administrative sphere which earlier historians have ascribed to the ordinances and statutes of Henry III's son and grandson. Moreover, although the political crisis of 1233–34 produced some modification of the arrangements introduced after the fall of Hubert de Burgh, nevertheless, there was no reversal of the basic administrative reforms which had then been set on foot ; what followed was not a reaction, but a continuation. The fall of Peter de Rivaux from office was not by any means the end of his financial reforms, nor even the end of his influence upon administration. It is indeed very doubtful whether, from the standpoint of administrative history, there is any justification for regarding

[1] Powicke, *Henry III and the Lord Edward*, p. 84.

the short period 1232–34 as distinct from the twenty-four years
that were to ensue to 1258 ; the crisis of 1234 was doubtless
real enough, but it made little difference to the course of administrative history, and it is only a matter of convenience of exposition
that suggests treatment of the ' Poitevin régime ' in a separate
section.[1]

Sir Maurice Powicke is no doubt right to emphasise the
importance of the financial motive and aspect of the changes of
1232–34, for in the sphere of reform this was the outstanding
feature. But it was not simply a question of reform and innovation ; it was from the broad point of view also a question of
restoration—the restoration of the Angevin conception of royal
administration, without the justiciarship, involving a distinct
revival and development of government centred in the Household. As a result, the duality of English administration—based
partly upon departments of the Household and partly upon
' departments of State '—was perpetuated. If this duality had
not been confirmed after the first royal minority in English
history, we may take it for granted that subsequent administrative and also constitutional developments would have been
decidedly different from what they were.

The pressing need for the reform and improvement of financial administration determined much of what was done in these
years, and was the reason for the enormous concentration of
financial power in the hands of Peter de Rivaux, whose career
hitherto had been confined to the Chamber and Wardrobe of the
Household. The reforms that were made came from a household
official, not from some high-ranking magnate selected to be
justiciar. Therein lies much of the significance of the régime
of 1232–34.

Peter des Roches, bishop of Winchester, who since his return
to England and to the king's good graces in the summer of 1231,
was instrumental in procuring the downfall of Hubert de Burgh,
whose dismissal came on 29 July, 1232. Des Roches remained
close to the king till 1234, but, taking no office for himself, he

[1] For this section generally, *v.* Powicke, *op. cit.*, I, ch. iii, ' Reform at the
Exchequer ' ; Tout, *Chapters*, I, ch. v, § iv, ' The Position of Peter de Rivaux, 1232–
1234 ; M. H. Mills, ' The Reforms at the Exchequer, 1232–42 ', in *Trans. R.H.S.*,
4th ser. X, pp. 111–134.

exercised his influence in an advisory capacity only. Indeed there is not much evidence that he at any time displayed outstanding administrative ambition or ability. Doubtless it was sufficient that his kinsman Peter de Rivaux should be selected as the man in whom administrative power was to be concentrated to an unprecedented degree.

The new justiciar, Stephen de Segrave, was essentially a lawyer, not an administrator, and his tenure of the office until his dismissal in May, 1234, when the office lapsed, marks the degeneration of the old Angevin executive vice-royalty into a specialized office of judicial eminence. The next, and last administrative justiciarship was to be a product of the baronial plan of reform of 1258, with the justiciar responsible to the baronage—a revival of the ' good old days ' highly coloured by the exigencies of the politics of 1258.

The services of the other great officers of the Hubertian régime, the chancellor and treasurer, were retained. Both Ralph Neville, bishop of Chichester, and Walter Mauclerc, bishop of Carlisle, had been placated before de Burgh's dismissal, by grants of their offices for life. Neville, as we shall see later,[1] seems to have acquiesced readily enough in the new arrangements. The position of the treasurer was soon reduced to nominal importance by the accumulation of real financial powers in Peter de Rivaux, who, notwithstanding the life grant in favour of Mauclerc, replaced him as treasurer in January, 1233.

No serious difficulties arose, therefore, from justiciar, chancellor, or treasurer, and the administrative arena was clear for Peter de Rivaux to exercise all the executive power accruing to him from the huge array of offices put upon him. Already on 11 June, 1232, he was granted for life the offices which he had hitherto held only during pleasure, namely, the custody of the Wardrobe, the Chamber, and the Treasury of the Household—offices sufficient to give him authority over the whole Household. On 15 June, he received also for life the custody of the king's small seal, and thus became the first keeper of the small seal known to us by name, and indeed the first keeper of a royal seal definitely withdrawn from the chancellor. In each office he was

---

[1] *V. infra*, p. 109.

empowered to appoint a deputy if he himself should be called to higher office in Church or State. To complete his control of household finance, on 28 June he was appointed king's chamberlain of London and king's buyer in all fairs and markets.

To this concentration of household administrative power, it remained to add a large number of offices outside the Household, so as to assure to him authority large enough to enable him to overhaul the whole system of royal finance. With this end in view he was made sheriff for life of twenty-one counties.[1] He was also made constable of many royal castles, chief justice of the English forests, and keeper of all escheats and wardships. A number of similar offices in Ireland were added. On 6 January 1233 he became treasurer of the exchequer. In short, he was appointed to every important financial office in England and Ireland.

The motive for such an intensive concentration of power in the hands of one man cannot be regarded as ' simply to play a new move in the game of winning power for the Poitevins.'[2] Nor, as Tout goes on to suggest, was it a question of an almost conscious struggle between the ministers dependent on the court and the holders of the great offices of State, who considered themselves the mouthpieces of baronial policy. In 1232, all ministers were dependent upon the court ; there was not as yet any baronial policy in these matters ; and only by anticipation can it be said that there were any ' great offices of State '. Consequently there was not any struggle between one set of ministers and another. The motive was clearly the desire for a thorough overhaul of the financial system, which had been producing very poor results, was riddled with abuses and corruption, and stood in need of reform such as could only be got by unprecedented and drastic measures.[3] What was wanted was not a triumph over a

---

[1] Four other *curiales* were appointed sheriffs of nine counties : des Roches of one, Segrave of five, the two stewards of the household of two and one respectively. Thirty out of the thirty-seven shires were thus entrusted to five *curiales*. Of the remaining seven, one was held by an ex-treasurer ; London and Middlesex was elective ; three were hereditary, and two were becoming so.

[2] Tout, *Chapters*, I, p. 218.

[3] Mills, *op. cit.*, pp. 111-112. There is evidence that the need had not been entirely overlooked in Hubert de Burgh's time. The liabilities of the sheriffs had received attention in 1223-4, and investigation had been made into the liberties and customs of the Crown with reference to the fixed part of the ' profits ' of the shires. In 1223-4 the sheriffs were required to pay in the profits in excess of the farm. Cf. Powicke, *op. cit.*, I, p. 95.

non-existent baronial administrative policy, but more cash in the royal coffers.

The grant of twenty-one shrievalties to de Rivaux, although nominally for life, was not intended to be permanent and he did not, of course, achieve the impossible task of discharging the duties of these offices in person. The object was to give him authority over the existing sheriffs, who continued to perform their duties as his deputies unless and until they were replaced, as very nearly all of them were between May, 1232, and April, 1233. But all the existing sheriffs answered at the Exchequer for the whole year 16 Henry III (1231–32), and Peter de Rivaux resigned nearly all his sheriffdoms by Michaelmas 1232.

The year 1232–33 was one of great activity at the Exchequer, ' especially with regard to summoning officials to account, enquiries into outstanding accounts and into the local receipt of money not handed in to the central exchequer. Special attention was given to distraint of recalcitrant debtors.'[1] ' *Debet respondere* ' was the key-note of these proceedings. The frequency of *loquele* with the king, council, or chief ministers reveals the close attention given by the government to financial questions. A careful, detailed, and critical survey of the Pipe and Memoranda Rolls, such as Miss Mills has made, shows that these records were better and more carefully kept after Michaelmas, 1232.

Investigation into the financial administration of the shires and plans for reform were in progress when, in the spring of 1234, a baronial reaction brought about the termination of Peter de Rivaux's official career and the end of the ' Poitevin interlude '. But the political crisis of 1234 did not by any means terminate the process of financial reform, which, as we shall see, continued to bear fruit in the years following. As Sir Maurice Powicke has observed, ' the fact is that the reforms at the Exchequer and in the shires between 1223 and 1241 must be regarded as a whole.'[2]

It is not necessary here to enter into the circumstances of the crisis of 1233–34. Professor Wilkinson is fully justified in saying[3] that its real nature has been obscured by a tendency

---

[1] Mills, *op. cit.*, p. 117.   [2] *Op. cit.*, p. 97, n. 2.
[3] ' The Council and the Crisis of 1233-4' in *Bull. John Ryland's Lib.*, 27 (1943–4), pp. 384–93 ; cf., the same author's *Constitutional History of England. 1216–1399*, I, ch. ii ; Powicke, *op. cit.*, pp. 129–147. The constitutional significance of the episode

to regard it as the first example of a constitutional opposition to the domination of the household officials fortified by the possession of the small seal. As he goes on to say, it was too early for any sharp distinction to be drawn between household and other officials, and there is no evidence that the baronial and episcopal opposition at this date was directed towards the administrative structure as such, nor even to the Poitevins as such. Sir Maurice Powicke has reminded us that there were only two Poitevins of importance in the government at this time, the two Peters themselves, and these were scarcely mentioned in contemporary accounts of the crisis.[1] There is no evidence that the household or small seal were the subject of discussion at the *colloquium* of Gloucester. All the evidence goes to show that the crucial question in the eyes of the opposition was not one of administrative structure or method, but a question of the composition of the king's advisory council. ' The great men of England, after they had welcomed or acquiesced in the downfall of the great justiciar (Hubert de Burgh), found themselves faced by an entirely unexpected situation. They were cold-shouldered at court.'[2]

Under the political pressure brought to bear, and in the course of his somewhat temperamental reaction to that pressure, Henry III got rid of Peter des Roches from his counsels, and by the end of June, 1234, Peter de Rivaux lost his numerous offices. Some, at least nominal, changes were made in the king's advisory council ; but the council as such had no executive powers, and in fact the administration went on after 1234 very much as it had before. De Rivaux, it seems, continued to exert important influence on financial policy,[3] and the reforms so much accelerated in 1232–34 were soon resumed and became incorporated in

is likely to remain the subject of controversy, but one may perhaps doubt whether Powicke's view that this crisis was more important than that of 1258–63 is generally acceptable.

[1] Powicke, *op. cit.*, p. 122.   [2] *Ibid.*, p. 123.

[3] Peter des Roches's influence on government seems to have terminated in 1234. He retired to his diocese for about a year, was abroad in 1235 and returned in broken health in 1236, and died in 1238. Peter de Rivaux was restored to some measure of influence, and, although it cannot be proved, it is very probable that he was concerned in the financial reforms of 1236 that carried further the policy he had adumbrated in 1232–34. Many years elapsed before he attained any important office again ; but in 1250 he was twice temporary keeper of the great seal, in 1253 a baron of the exchequer, and finally keeper of the wardrobe once more from

96 *Administrative History in Mediaeval England*

administrative method. In this, and in other important respects, especially in the predominance of the Wardrobe among the Household departments,[1] Peter de Rivaux's short term of power was to have lasting consequences.

§ 3. So far as administrative history is concerned, it can hardly be said that the crisis of 1234 caused any marked break. It is true that there was not again such a concentration of powers in one man as Peter de Rivaux had enjoyed, or at any rate possessed. On the other hand, the great fillip given to the Wardrobe by his short spell of power was not spent by the changes of personnel which were the main result of the crisis ; on the contrary, for at least a century, if not longer, the Wardrobe was to be by far the most important of the administrative departments of the Household, and with its custody of the small seal and its substantial finances, it provided the king with an administrative organization that could easily be expanded or contracted according to circumstances, and could be adapted to a great variety of executive business. Furthermore, the financial reforms which had been set in train before 1234 were continued and absorbed into exchequer practice and eventually formulated in legislation.

The principal developments in administration that occurred in the period 1234–58 were not the result of political pressure, but of organic growth. The Exchequer was to pursue its financial reforms and to be organically separate from the Household ; the Chancery was to improve its organization and to become less essentially a household organ. The judicial organizations, with which we are not concerned here, were likewise to be further differentiated, departmentalized, and even to some extent professionalized. This period was the Age of Bracton, in which great progress in the development of the common law was made.[2]

Michaelmas 1257 to July 1258. He died in 1263. *V. Tout, op. cit.*, I, pp. 280–2, 298–300. Tout's account of Peter de Rivaux's work was written before Miss Mills's valuable paper on ' The Reforms at the Exchequer ' (*loc. cit.*) appeared, and his account scarcely did justice to its subject. It would hardly do now to speak of de Rivaux's ' personal incapacity ' as Tout did (p. 281), and possibly Tout was too much influenced by what Powicke (p. 97, n.2) calls the ' Poitevin legend '.

[1] *V. infra*, p. 101.

[2] As E. F. Jacob observes in what is the best short survey of the reign (England : Henry III) in *Cambridge Mediaeval History*, VI (1929), ch. viii, p. 272) : ' The great consolidating factor of the first forty years of Henry III's reign is the steady increase in the number of original writs '. In Glanville this number was 39 ; by 1259 it was 121.

In all respects the Angevin system of government came to fruition. Administrative development had by now proceeded so far that it could be largely self-subsisting, and although very likely Henry III's administrative ability, as distinct from his political acumen, has been traditionally under-estimated,[1] it is difficult to identify him personally with any of the particular developments of the period in the administrative sphere. But for the general administrative scheme he must receive some credit. The relations between the Household and other departments, even if becoming more complicated, remained harmonious, and the general impression of the administrative structure at this time is not unfavourable. 'In this sphere of central government, these years witness great advances in organization, always directed towards greater technical efficiency and a higher degree of adaptability.'[2] Viewed simply as a bureaucratic machine, the administrative system of Henry III attained a higher level of skill than ever before. 'Never before had the Crown wielded such power, nor had the reality of royal authority ever been so closely brought home.'[3]

Singularly little criticism was directed towards the central administrative system as such at any time in Henry III's reign ; and when baronial opposition came to a head in 1258, its object was to control the system at the centre and thereby to reform the abuses in local government. The very effectiveness of the central organization was a source of trouble, for with the expansion of business, opportunities by local officials for abuse and corruption multiplied. The weakness of Henry III's system was not in its central structure, but in its failure to supervise and curb the activities of its local agents. Henry III's failure was in ensuring that his great administrative machine was used to further the ends of good government. His system lacked the inspiration and driving force of high ideals, and it was this lack, rather than technical incompetence, that gave rise to the political opposition

[1] A general effect of Sir Maurice Powicke's picture in his great work *Henry III and the Lord Edward* is to give a more favourable and better balanced impression of Henry III than has hitherto been usual. Professor Wilkinson's recent *Constitutional History of England*, I, is even more pointedly to the same effect. A similar note was struck by E. F. Jacob, *loc. cit.*
[2] Treharne, *The Baronial Plan of Reform*, p. 38.
[3] Treharne, in *History*, XVI (1932), pp. 336-40.

H

leading to the baronial plan of reform of 1258. What that plan was to reveal was primarily lack of confidence in the king's own executive capacity, not in the administrative machinery as such. The plan therefore was mainly directed to substituting a baronial for a royal executive, at least for a time—a baronial executive which would use the royal administrative system for carrying out its own policies.

' The government [of Henry III] could not have lasted twenty-four years had it not been for the direction and control supplied by that undefined but omnicompetent body, the king's council, the centre of initiative and co-ordination in the *Curia Regis.*'[1] We may perhaps reject the word ' omnicompetent ' from this quotation, for as Professor Treharne is well aware, the king's council was not as yet vested with any executive power of its own, and indeed ' can hardly be described as a body at all.'[2] This small group of ' *consiliarii regis* ' was naturally regarded by the king as ' his instrument for ruling the kingdom, and he treated its personnel, scope, and powers as matter for his sole discretion, and the fact that it was not a body of definite constitution, permanent standing, and known powers, made it all the more acceptable and useful to him.'[3]

This clear and intelligible formulation of propositions about the council helps to clarify our minds on the subject, but is perhaps couched in terms that are too modern to be wholly apt for the period in question. Professor Treharne himself furnishes the corrective by admitting to a temptation to deny the existence of the king's council at this time, and to translate the words ' *consilium regis* ' by ' king's counsel '—' the sum total of advice taken by the king on each separate matter of discussion, great or small.'[4] This admission does not militate against the fact that at this time identifiable *consiliarii regis* appeared, some at least of whom were sworn to give good counsel. They remained essentially counsellors, not councillors.

There was not, of course, anything new in the king's having about him more or less intimate advisers to aid and counsel him in the discharge of his executive duties. Such a phenomenon

---

[1] Treharne, *The Baronial Plan of Reform*, p. 30.
[2] *Ibid.*   [3] *Ibid.*   [4] *Ibid.*, p. 31.

was natural and inevitable, and clearly present from the earliest days of the kingship. Such informal, almost daily advice, as distinct from the formal and periodical consultations with assemblies of *witan* or *magnates* was a necessity to any king, however simple his administrative machinery, and all the more needful as that machinery grew more complex. What was new, or appears to be new, in Henry III's early years, was the specific appointment (we may perhaps call it) of persons to perform this particular function of rendering counsel—as yet a function rather than an office. Such persons might or might not hold actual administrative office under the king, in the Household or outside of it. Whether they did or not, obviously as *consiliarii* their position might be one of importance and influence. For by their advice they might move the king—the sole repository of executive power in the ultimate issue ; the king and his *consiliarii* could co-ordinate administrative action, formulate administrative policy and measures, decide on steps that could not be taken by any one administrative organ, nor even perhaps by the king alone in the absence of information and more-than-departmental advice. It was not a question of the king's being obliged to accept the advice of his *consiliarii*, nor of the *consiliarii*'s being able to dictate to the king, nor a question of the *consiliarii* as such possessing executive power ; such ideas as these did not belong to the early thirteenth century. The king was the executive, and it was for him to select his *consiliarii* as he chose, and to accept or reject their advice as he thought fit.

The rapid growth of the practical importance of the *consiliarii* in the early thirteenth century was probably due primarily to the growth in the complexity of the administrative system. However that may have been, certainly very soon the question of who should figure among the *consiliarii regis* became the principal bone of contention between the king and those magnates who opposed or disliked his policies. As later on, ' counsel ' became at least in part institutionalized into a council, and as this acquired at least some executive powers of its own, the question of the composition of the king's council became the burning question in mediaeval politics—the question whether it should be determined wholly by the king or wholly or partly by others than the king. For eventually ' control of the Council meant the power to direct the entire system of government, without any necessity for fundamental changes in the structure or working of the administration ; hence the steady continuity of mediaeval administrative development in England, in spite of the frequent reversals of the mastery during the long political struggle. The constitutional conflict thus begins with the first attempt of the magnates to criticise the composition and working of the King's Council, and to demand some representation in its ranks and some control over its action.'[1]

Further discussion of the manifestation of this conflict is better postponed to the following section. Here it is sufficient to note that the *consiliarii regis* played their part in assisting Henry III in the direction of the administration, that his preference clearly was for *curiales, familiares,* or *ministri* as his counsellors, with as few baronial figures among them as possible—a preference that might be described as in the best Angevin tradition ; that the question of the composition of the ' council ' was the main issue raised in 1234, 1237, 1244, and above all, in 1258 ; and finally that although there is unofficial evidence of an oath's being taken by counsellors before 1234, and although the baronage proposed or imposed such an oath on each of the occasions of crisis, we do not possess anything like a text of the counsellors' oath until 1257, nor any very reliable information on the subject until Edward I's reign.[2]

The king with his *consiliarii* controlled the affairs of State, and in this period the ' council ' became more professional in character. ' It included a few barons, the chief officers of the realm and household, who in this period were not sharply distinguishable, some of the royal justices, and a little group of king's clerks and others who were honoured by such designations as counsellor, familiar, ' special ', and secretary. This last element, rooted in the household, was the most significant and frequently the most important, for the king usually chose able men for intimate duties.'[3]

[1] *Ibid.*, p. 32.
[2] *V.* Baldwin, *The King's Council in the Middle Ages* (1913), pp. 16–37, 345–347 ; Treharne, *op. cit.* ; Powicke, *op. cit.*, ch. viii ; Wilkinson, *Studies in the Constitutional History of the* 13*th and* 14*th Centuries* (1937), pp. 112–120.
[3] Powicke, *op. cit.*, p. 293.

Little is heard of regular meetings or records of the council at this time. A few memoranda of proceedings survive,[1] but until the council became more definitely institutionalised, little of this kind is to be expected. The counsellors, as Powicke observes,[2] 'were not royal favourites, nor on the other hand did they direct an institution. They were diplomats, soldiers, judges, experts in chancery or exchequer practice, officers of the household, as the case might be . . . The counsellors were familiar with the world of magnates and bishops, and with administrative life in diocese and shire. They maintained and developed that remarkable tradition of oversight and investigation which is perhaps the most persistent feature of Henry's reign and which found such a rich expression in the reign of his son. They were able, as members of the royal household, to supervise activities which they understood. Some could devise new writs or draft new statutes, others could suggest ways of raising money and see that financial expedients were enforced. They could help to revise the heads of a judicial commission or the articles of an administrative enquiry.'

But the counsellors as such were only advisers, and the carrying out of decisions necessarily fell to the administrative organizations. ' In abandoning the Poitevins, Henry III in no wise gave up the policy of making his household the centre of his administration of the State,'[3] and within the Household, the Wardrobe was to be the chief administrative organ. ' The central administrative fact of the Minority is the growth of the king's domestic treasury, his Wardrobe, with its staff of clerks and its own traditions and methods.'[4]

It is not easy to see[5] why the Wardrobe should have come to the forefront and should have overshadowed the Chamber in the way that it did in these years. Nothing is known of the Wardrobe in the years 1216–1219, but the Chamber was at work as a place

---

[1] *V.* references in *ibid.*, p. 295 n.1 : cf. E. F. Jacob, ' The Reign of Henry III : Some Suggestions ' in *Trans. R.H.S.* 4th ser. X (1927), pp. 21–53.

[2] Powicke, *ibid.*

[3] Tout, *Chapters*, I, p. 240.

[4] Jacob, in *C.M.H.*, VI, p. 261.

[5] *Supra*, p. 79. The explanations given by Tout, *op. cit.*, p. 230–232 are not perhaps very convincing, being mostly descriptions of what things happened rather than of why they happened.

of receipt of money from the beginning of the reign. From 1220, the Wardrobe was again operative, and for a time the relative positions of the two organizations seem to have been much the same as they had been under John ; there was much overlapping of functions, with the Wardrobe apparently subordinate to the Chamber. The growing differentiation between them in the ensuing years is a very obscure process, and seems to have been connected with the official career of Peter de Rivaux, who sooner or later as the principal financial officer in the Household became identified with the Wardrobe rather than the Chamber, without however losing his connection with the latter ; ' the chamberlain of 1219 became the clerk of the Wardrobe of 1223.'[1] Peter de Rivaux, in association with Walter of Brackley remained responsible for wardrobe finance until a date not later than 4 January 1224, when he disappears from the records, and probably from England, for seven years, in consequence no doubt of the strengthening of Hubert de Burgh's power following from Honorius III's declaration of the king's being of sufficient age to govern.

During Peter de Rivaux's time at the Wardrobe, a rapid development in its finances occurred, derived partly from what appears to be a new source—direct payments from the Exchequer.[2] After the withdrawal of Peter, the principle of a joint clerkship of the Wardrobe was maintained ; Walter of Kirkham was now associated with Walter of Brackley, and the joint account of these two, for the period 5 January 1224 to 10 April 1227 is the earliest wardrobe account proper which survives.[3] ' It is clear that by then the wardrobe had become responsible for the whole finance of the king's household, and therefore had become the accounting and directive department of the palace, and met also its own departmental expenses. Most important of all is the fact that it was the wardrobe which managed all great extraordinary expenses, whether of court festivities . . . of expeditions to put down domestic rebels . . .or of armies sent abroad. . . . The wardrobe was not only becoming upon occasion a second treasury, but a war office and admiralty as well.'[4]

[1] Tout, *op. cit.*, p. 191.
[3] *Ibid.*, pp. 233–238.
[2] *Ibid.*, pp. 191–2.
[4] *Ibid.*, p. 195.

It is not, however, entirely clear that the Wardrobe was without some supervision from the head of the Chamber,[1] and it is significant that on his return the first office to which Peter de Rivaux was appointed was that of treasurer of the chamber (September, 1231),[2] and Kirkham and Brackley were soon afterwards removed from the Wardrobe. By 11 June 1232, as we have seen,[3] Peter combined the custody of the Wardrobe, Chamber and Treasury of the Household with numerous other offices, and during his ascendancy in all the financial offices, the relative positions of Chamber and Wardrobe became immaterial. In the meantime, as we have mentioned above,[4] a privy seal had been revived. From December 1230, Henry III had a privy seal of his own, which was kept in his own custody or that of a household officer. It was no accident that in June 1232, the custody of the privy seal was accorded to Peter de Rivaux, for henceforth its custody was to be associated with the Wardrobe.

The result of Peter de Rivaux's ascendancy in this sphere was a better consolidation of the household offices.[5] For whatever precise reason, the Wardrobe from now on rather than the Chamber became established as the accounting and financial department of the Household as a whole, and the household treasurership became annexed to the office that was soon to became the keepership of the wardrobe. Some of the old designations, such as ' treasurer of the chamber ' continued in vogue for a time, but ' after the years 1232–34 the king's personal treasurership was definitely dissociated from the chamber and united with the custody of the wardrobe. We may believe, too, though we cannot as yet prove it, that the custody of the small seal was henceforth a function of the wardrobe and not of the chamber.'[6] The custody of the Wardrobe was no longer to be a joint office; a single great officer of the Household was permanently set apart to govern the Wardrobe, called for a time indifferently keeper, clerk, or treasurer of it.

As a consequence of these developments, the Chamber, although retaining its identity and independence of other depart-

---

[1] Cf. Tout's remarks (*ib.*, p. 195) on Luke the Chaplain, by whose view and testimony Kirkham and Brackley's account was tendered to the Exchequer.
[2] *Ibid.*, p. 200.   [3] *V. supra*, p. 92.   [4] *V. supra*, p. 84.
[5] Tout, *ibid.*, pp. 218–232.   [6] *Ibid.*, p. 228.

ments, receded in administrative importance, and left few or no records behind it for this period. Later on in the fourteenth century, as we shall see,[1] it was to revive again and resume a position of great importance in the administrative system.

Thus, by the time of the fall of Peter de Rivaux, the Wardrobe had become an effective organ of administration, very close to the king. It was financed by direct payments from the Exchequer, and its financial resources could therefore be indefinitely expanded within the capabilities of the Exchequer, as occasion required. It accounted to the Exchequer, which remained the ultimate accounting authority. It found room on its staff for the literate knight as well as the clerk, and its administrative potentiality was accordingly strengthened. Its custody of the privy seal gave it effective secretarial capacity, and brought it, as we shall see,[2] into intimate relations with the Chancery. In utilizing the Wardrobe in these ways, Henry III had to hand a practical and ready instrument for centralizing administration in the Household, and for carrying on government according to methods and principles which were essentially Angevin, and which by now were traditional for a ruling sovereign.

The period in wardrobe history from 1234 to 1258 has been divided into two periods :[3] the years 1234–40, when the Wardrobe was in English hands, and the years 1240–58, when it was in foreign hands. But it is doubtful whether the change in the provenance of the officials made any substantial difference in the administrative position of the department, and although the earlier period may have been a time of ' moderation, economy, and prudent counsels,' and the later period may have been marked by a ' régime calamitous and unpopular which culminated in the great catastrophe of 1258 ',[4] these differences can scarcely be attributed to changes in the personnel of the Wardrobe. In both periods the officials naturally had to carry out the king's instructions, and the differences between the two phases arose from the circumstances that in 1234–40, Henry III was not concerned with overseas expeditions, whereas he was twice so

[1] *V. infra*, p. 184.
[2] *V. infra*, p. 113.
[3] Tout, *op. cit.*, pp. 241–242, 244–259, 260–283.
[4] *Ibid.*, pp. 241–2.

concerned in the years 1240-58. Inevitably the organization, financial and otherwise, of these expeditions fell to the Wardrobe, and would have done so whether it had been in English or foreign hands, and the change of personnel made little or no difference to the Wardrobe as such. The calamitous result of the king's policies is another question altogether, and belongs to the political rather than the administrative sphere.

The fact is, as Tout observed, that the whole period witnessed the consolidation and expansion of the Wardrobe as an administrative organ, and the ' household machine, which thus arose, became an efficient instrument ', even though perhaps there is little reason to add to this statement the words ' a too efficient instrument from the baronial point of view '.[1] Nor can any sharp distinction be drawn between the two periods on the basis of the accountability at the Exchequer of the successive keepers of the Wardrobe. It is difficult to see what Tout meant by his remark that ' accountability was a natural consequence of constitutional policy '.[2] The Exchequer at this time was not in any sense a baronial stronghold ; it was just as much the king's organization as the Wardrobe itself, and the normal practice whereby the latter rendered accounts to the former was merely a matter of bureaucratic routine, not a matter of constitutional policy. In any case, as Tout shows, such accounts were rendered not only between 17 May 1234 and 3 February 1240, but also between 28 October 1241 and 27 October 1252, and 10 January 1255 and 28 April 1257, and the omissions for the remaining years can hardly be attributed to any sinister ' unconstitutional ' motives.

We may therefore briefly survey wardrobe history in the years 1234-58 as a unity, and the general conclusion to be drawn can hardly be better stated than in the following words : ' Most important of all was the extremely rapid development of the Wardrobe, which, with its almost infinite adaptability and capacity for expansion, enabled the king to meet the ever-growing expenses of government and the emergencies of foreign campaigns with far less difficulty than that which the use of Exchequer or the Chamber would have entailed. It mobilised

[1] *Ibid.*, p. 242.   [2] *Ibid.*, p. 244.

the king's credit and paid his expenses with a speed possible
only to a supple and adaptable organisation; its capacity for
sub-division and expansion enabled it to meet new needs without
confusion or disorder; its methods already foreshadowed the
great development of the use of debentures and tallies by which
Edward I financed his government. In short, the Wardrobe
was by far the most important and useful addition to the machinery of government during these years, and Henry III found it
indispensable.'[1]

The early years of the period were marked by the beginnings
of the office within the Wardrobe which in the time of Edward I
was to be called the controllership. The official head of the
Wardrobe was by now often called the keeper or treasurer,
instead of simply clerk. But a second clerk appears, charged
with the duty of presenting at the Exchequer a counter-roll as a
check upon the official roll tendered by the keeper. This practice
was of course only a bureaucratic precaution in the king's interest,
and clearly shows that there was no intention of avoiding
accountability at the Exchequer. The income of the Wardrobe
in the first six years of this period is estimated to have been
about £9000 per annum.[2] The figure was very steady in these
years, but a notable feature is the fact that the proportion of the
income derived from the Exchequer declined considerably, from
about 7-9ths in the first two years to about 1-5th in the last two
years. It is probable that the Exchequer's dealings with the
Wardrobe had by then become largely a matter of book-keeping.[3]
Income and expenditure in the wardrobe balanced fairly well in
these years.

The capacity of the Wardrobe for expansion to meet administrative requirements is well shown in the beginnings of the organization which eventually was to give rise to the Great Wardrobe,
distinct from the Wardrobe itself. From the earliest days of
wardrobe accounts, it is clear that special commissions were
sometimes given to wardrobe clerks to buy on the king's behalf
such storable commodities as cloth, wax, spices, furs, and the
like; the technical considerations involved led to the association

---

[1] Treharne, *op. cit.*, pp. 38–39.
[2] Tout, *op. cit.*, pp. 248–249.   [3] *Ibid.*, p. 249, n. 1.

with the clerks of merchants and tailors from outside, and the delicate questions arising from the application of the royal rights of prisage and pre-emption inevitably drew attention to this aspect of wardrobe activity. As a result, the purchase, warehousing, and distribution of such stores were separated from the other main items in the accounts, and a distinct organization gradually developed, still part of the Wardrobe until the end of the thirteenth century at least, but growing towards independence, and later to be called the Great Wardrobe.[1]

The later years of this period of wardrobe history[2] were chiefly remarkable for the great expansion of the financial resources and expenses of the department, especially during the keepership of Peter Chaceporc between October 1241 and December 1254. The expensive military operations of Henry III in Gascony, May 1242 to September 1243, were financed by the Wardrobe, and between October 1241 and midsummer 1245, the receipt rose to an average of about £22,000 a year. Whilst the normal expenses met by the Wardrobe remained more or less stationary, the exigencies of the campaign magnified the financial requirements and administrative tasks of the department, and a similar situation arose in consequence of the king's second expedition 1253–54. Indeed, on those occasions the Wardrobe accompanied the king himself. During the whole of these royal absences, there is no trace of any wardrobe clerk or organization in England. The whole establishment went overseas with the rest of the court. The Exchequer on these occasions was left to deal almost exclusively with the financial business of the realm, raising and distributing the revenues as best it could. The Wardrobe was the sole treasury at court, and dealt with the military and general expenses incurred abroad. ' The only duty which the exchequer now had to the wardrobe was to provide it with the funds for which the king was always clamouring.'[3]

---

[1] *Ibid.*, pp. 258–259, and IV, ch. xiv. This period is also one which saw the establishment of separate Wardrobes for the queen, and later for the king's children *Ibid.*, I, pp. 252–257. It should also be remembered that the greater baronial families constantly imitated the king's methods in the administration of their territories (*v.* especially the illuminating study by N. Denholm-Young, *Seignorial Administration in England* (1937). A number of baronial wardrobe organizations existed in this period.

[2] For details, *v.* Tout, *op. cit.*, pp. 269–283.　　　[3] *Ibid.*, p. 267.

We may perhaps doubt whether the Exchequer had any other duty than this toward the Wardrobe when both were in England (apart from checking over its accounts), but it seems that the Exchequer did not, or could not, fully rise to the occasion, and failed to provide the Wardrobe with all the funds it required, with the result that the Wardrobe itself was obliged to pledge the king's credit and to procure loans. On the other hand, circumstances sometimes made it necessary for the Exchequer to purchase stores that normally would have been obtained by the Wardrobe. This kind of activity hardly justifies the supposition that ' Henry III's policy now tended to confuse exchequer and wardrobe ';[1] it was rather a question of necessity's being the mother of administrative expediency. After the king's return in December 1254, the regular administrative practice was resumed.

We have noted above[2] that Henry III acquired a privy seal of his own from December 1230, and that its custody came to be with the Wardrobe at least from the time of Peter de Rivaux's dominance in the Household.[3] Potentially, therefore, the king had the means available for developing a household secretariat additional to the Chancery, but it can hardly be said that in fact he made much use of this possibility. Apart from the special circumstances arising in consequence of the king's absences abroad, there is singularly little evidence that the privy seal was used at all as a regular instrument for administrative purposes in the period 1234–58. There are only two references to it on the Patent Rolls of these twenty-five years, and none on the Close Rolls.[4] It is true that at this time references to the privy seal on these rolls would only be accidental, and that there is some other evidence of its occasional use, but it seems to be clear that in this period, the privy seal was of little importance except in connexion with the royal absences. During the expedition of 1242–3, the great seal accompanied the king, whilst the exchequer seal was to be used for great seal purposes at home, and the privy seal for exchequer writs.[5] At the time of the longer absence, August 1253 to December 1254, the arrangements were rather different.

[1] *Ibid.*, p. 276.
[2] *V. supra.* p. 84.
[3] *V. supra*, p. 103.
[4] Tout, *op. cit.*, p. 289.
[5] *Ibid.*, p. 291.

On this occasion, the great seal was left at home in the care of the queen but sealed up under the privy seal and the seals of some of the counsellors and put out of use until the king should return ; the exchequer seal was to be used for working purposes at home, whilst the king took with him what appears to have been a special seal made for the occasion. This special seal, called the *sigillum paruum* or *minus* was certainly different in design from the privy seal of the time, and was used abroad as equivalent to the great seal. We have no information as to what happened to the privy seal during this absence.[1]

It is thus clear that the privy seal did not in this period have any important role in the administrative system, and the principal reason for this insignificance is also clear enough. The Chancery was still sufficiently close to the king, and the great seal sufficiently within the purview of the Household, to render any extensive use of a privy seal unnecessary. Indeed, the ' great ' seal was still normally called simply ' *sigillum regis* ', and the time had not yet come when the ' privy ' or ' small ' seal was so prominent as to encourage the attribution of the adjective ' great ' to the larger seal. If the ' great ' seal was readily available to the king himself, there was no need to make much use of a privy seal. The position of Chancery, chancellor, and the great seal thus requires our attention.

As we have noticed above,[2] at the time of Hubert de Burgh's fall, and during the Poitevin régime of 1232–34, and after, the Chancellorship was held by Ralph Neville, bishop of Chichester. A good deal of theorizing has been based on the notion that Neville was in some sense a ' magnate ' chancellor, and on conceptions of his relations with Henry III after 1232 that are not fully justified.

Ralph Neville[3] climbed to eminence essentially through service to the Crown, and mainly by service in the Chancery. For

---

[1] *Ibid.*, p. 293. [2] *V. supra*, p. 92.

[3] I am indebted to Mrs. E. L. G. Stones (*neé* Fradin) for an opportunity to consult her unpublished Oxford B. Litt. dissertation ' Ralph Neville, Bishop of Chichester and Chancellor of Henry III ' (1942), which corrects some currently held views on Neville's career on a number of points, and which I largely follow here. Tout seems to have over-emphasized the ' magnate ' character of Neville's chancellorship, and to have under-estimated the extent to which he acquiesced in the arrangements after 1232. *V. op. cit.*, pp. 146 n. 3, 185–6, 207–8, 223–4, 235–6.

some ten years before his appointment to the Chancellorship
on the death of Richard Marsh, in May, 1226, Neville, as
vice-Chancellor, had been virtually master of the Chancery ;
Marsh had some years before his death retired to his diocese of
Durham, and the main responsibility for carrying on the work of
Chancery had fallen to Neville, who had already received the
substantial reward of the bishopric of Chichester in 1222. So far,
Neville's career had been that of a successful king's clerk, and it
can hardly be supposed that he could have regarded himself as
under any particular 'baronial' influence up to this point. It is
true that his episcopal position at the time of his elevation to the
chancellorship—an unusual but not unprecedented circumstance
—gave him a large measure of personal independence, influence,
and wealth, and brought him among the ecclesiastical magnates ;
true also that in 1226 he purchased the office of chancellor for
life, and was granted the issues of the great seal accordingly.
True, again, that he was appointed in effect by the great council,
for at the time Henry III was not deemed to be of age for government, and there was no other way of formally authorizing the
appointment save by the great council. No doubt Neville liked
to think that all these circumstances gave him an unassailable
position, and perhaps to delude himself for a time into thinking
that he was in some sense a 'baronial' chancellor answerable
only to the great council. But the unreality of such a supposition
—if it were actually held—was soon manifested by events after
de Burgh's fall and still more after the king began to assert his
own will. It was no doubt easy enough for the chancellor to feel
independent when the king had no administrative Household to
co-ordinate and to execute business, but when he had, the state of
affairs was different, and the Chancery must again become primarily a household secretariat, whether the chancellor liked it or
not.

Only an accommodating spirit could have saved Neville
from retirement or even perhaps virtual dismissal after the fall
of de Burgh in 1232. We may doubt whether the royal life-grant
made to him just before de Burgh's dismissal would have been
given at all if des Roches had not known his man, and in any
case would not in itself have saved him, for de Burgh also at the

same time had been granted various offices for life just before his dismissal.

The only explanation for Neville's retention in 1232 and the following years is that he was willing enough to 'play ball' with the new régime; in short, to forget whatever baronial pretensions he may have entertained, and to remember that he was a king's clerk. Nor did he withdraw completely from the court; routine business of the Chancery continued as usual; the chancellor still followed the court in much the same way as he had since 1226, though it is true he did not maintain a daily attendance, and that some decisions were taken in his absence. He seems indeed to have been on friendly terms with the two Peters. There are no signs of any rivalry or friction between the revived household offices and the Chancery at this time. 'A struggle between household and chancery, between domestic officers and officers of State may have been implicit in much that was going on, but it is doubtful whether the people concerned were very consciously aware of it.'[1]

There are no signs of a plot to deprive Neville of his position in the years 1232–38, even though the king in April 1236 made a short-lived, impulsive gesture at depriving him of the custody of the great seal. The quarrel that eventually had that result arose from an issue which had nothing to do with administration. The issue was the succession to the see of Winchester on the death of Peter des Roches in June 1238. Henry III was set on procuring the election of his worthless protégé William of Valence, and his fury was great when the Chapter proceeded to elect first William Ralegh, who was not accepted, and secondly, Ralph Neville himself. This was too much for Henry III, who determined to produce the result he desired. The fact that the king's writs regarding the election were sealed with the great seal in the Wardrobe has no particular administrative significance, for there is no evidence that the seal was retained there for more than a few hours; naturally in the circumstances the Chancellor was not consulted nor expected to issue the writs himself.[2] But as a result of this quarrel, it seems, Neville was deprived of the

---

[1] Mrs. E. L. G. Stones, *op. cit.*, pp. 136–7. Cf. Tout, *op. cit.*, p. 241.
[2] Tout, *op. cit.*, p. 287, exaggerated the significance of this episode,

custody of the great seal in August 1238, but he remained chancellor,[1] and the custody of the seal was restored to him in early 1242[2] and remained with him until his death on 1 February 1244. During the years when the Chancellor was deprived of the custody of the seal, the seal was apparently committed to the charge of a succession of keepers, most of whom held some office within the Household, and the place of custody was probably the Wardrobe.[3]

The death of Neville left the chancellorship vacant, and this event marks in some measure a stage in the history of the Chancery, and it is as well to pause at this point to consider its position. The most important consideration to bear in mind is that up to 1244, no matter what the case may have been thereafter, the character of Chancery was more that of a household department than that of a ' department of State '. No doubt the circumstances of the minority, with its abnormally stunted household organization, had tended to throw the Chancery into greater relief and independence than had been the case previously, and to magnify the personal position of the chancellor. But the revival of household administrative organizations, especially of the Wardrobe, inevitably resulted in Chancery's becoming absorbed into the general scheme and resuming its old intimate relations with the Household. The personal position of Neville as chancellor could not have remained the same after 1232 as it had been before. It is true that, as Miss Dibben observed, during these years of Neville's tenure of the office, ' the Chancellor is still a powerful ecclesiastic, who is allowed to make what he can out of the issues of the king's seal ', and might appoint a deputy to keep the seal ; but in other ways, Chancery was still very much in the same ' primitive ' condition as it was under John ; its staff were still clerks and serjeants of the king's

---

[1] There seems to be no evidence for the allegation that Neville was deprived of the seal ' by force and trickery ' as Tout says, *op. cit.*, p. 284. Mrs. Stones finds, *op. cit.*, 147, that he surrendered the seal ' without fuss '. Nor does it seem appropriate to speak of Neville's ' disgrace ' in 1238, as Miss Dibben did (*E.H.R.* xxvii (1912), p. 40.

[2] Opinions differ as to the date of Neville's restoration. Wilkinson, *The Chancery under Edward III* (1929), p. 194, citing Miss Dibben, *loc. cit.*, pp. 39–51, put it at September, 1243, but Tout, *op. cit.*, p. 284 and VI, p. 4 put it in 1242, if not earlier.

[3] Dibben, *op. cit.*, pp. 42–3 ; Tout, *op. cit.*, VI, p. 4.

chapel; the chancellor and staff still made an irregular income from the profits and fees of the seal without accounting for them.[1]

In Henry III's reign only exceptionally was the authority to Chancery to issue instruments under the great seal given in writing; it was still normally given by word of mouth, and the warranty '*per ipsum regem*' still implied that the instruction had been transmitted by a person rather than a document; the absence of any authority in many entries on the chancery rolls still implies that the chancellor himself knew personally what the authority was.[2] Neville himself continued the customary regular, almost daily attendance at court, even though it seems the time had passed when the chancellor regularly resided at court as a member of the Household.[3]

In general, then, we may conclude that in these years, Chancery was still primarily a household department, as it had been before the accession of Henry III. But certain factors were at work before 1244 (and more potently thereafter), which had the effect, on the one hand, of promoting the departmentalism of the Chancery and its further differentiation from the Household itself, whilst on the other hand depressing the status of the chancellorship.

The principal factor of at any rate potential effect before 1244 in carrying further the separation of Chancery and Household was the revival of the privy seal. It is perhaps an exaggeration to say that the appearance of the privy seal in 1230 marks the beginning of the separation of Chancery and court,[4] but we may agree that the use of a small seal close to the king was a necessary preliminary to the 'going out of court' of Chancery, for verbal or personal authorizations could not indefinitely be relied upon if court and Chancery were differentiated. But, as we have seen,[5] verbal warrants were still normal in this period, and in fact there is little evidence of much use of the privy seal in the years 1234–58.[6] It was not the existence of a privy seal in itself that

[1] *Op. cit.*, I, pp. 40–41.
[2] A. E. Stamp, 'Some Notes on the Court and Chancery of Henry III' in *Historical Essays in Honour of James Tait* (1937), pp. 305–7.
[3] Mrs. E. L. G. Stones, *op. cit.*, pp. 104–6.
[4] E. F. Jacob, *C.M.H.*, VI, p. 260.
[5] *V. supra.*
[6] *V. supra*, p. 108.

I

promoted the separation of Chancery and court, but the growing separation resulting from other influences that encouraged greater use of the privy seal,[1] giving to it more scope and utility for administrative purposes than it would otherwise have readily obtained. As the king's seal became less personal to the king, *i.e.*, became the ' great seal ', the seal of England, so the privy seal became more useful as a means of authenticating warrants to Chancery, as well as for other purposes.

What these factors were which tended to carry further the separation of Chancery and Household we must examine shortly ; first, however, the position of the chancellorship after the death of Neville in 1244 needs consideration.

Opinions have differed widely on this matter. Stubbs thought that after Neville's death Henry III ' appointed no successor for many years '.[2] Miss Dibben's researches,[3] although stated in cautious terms, induced Tout to hold that ' between 1244 and 1258 there was almost an unbroken series of chancellors '.[4] This notion of Tout's, which hardly seems consistent with other views of his on the subject of Henry III's policy with regard to the Chancery, cannot be maintained. Professor Wilkinson's review of the evidence fully justifies his conclusion that ' although we have in fact the Chancellor's duties being performed, we have the Chancellorship in England being suspended between 1244 and 1258 . . . with consequences on the office of Chancery which cannot fail to have been considerable, though they have not, as yet, been fully worked out.'[5]

Whatever were the motives behind this policy, whether or not contemporary continental analogies[6] had any bearing, it seems clear enough that for some fourteen years after Neville's death, the office of chancellor was not filled, and what the ultimate consequences of this protracted vacancy were upon the office, must remain a matter for speculation. As we shall see later,[7] the

---

[1] As Tout surmised, *op. cit.*, p. 212, even though he seems to have ante-dated the process somewhat.
[2] *Constitutional History*, II, p. 51.
[3] *E.H.R.*, *loc. cit.*
[4] *Op. cit.*, I, p. 285.
[5] *The Chancery under Edward III*, App. II, pp. 197–8.
[6] Dibben, *loc. cit.*, p. 40 ; Tout, *op. cit.*, I, p. 285.
[7] *V. infra*, p. 123 f.

baronage did not approve of this vacancy, and the appointment of a chancellor was to be one among their demands for reform. There can be no doubt that by 1258 at least the baronage had come to conceive that the chancellorship was potentially a channel through which they might exert some influence upon the administration, although past experience in normal circumstances can have lent only the slenderest support to such hopes.

But so far as administration itself was concerned in the years 1244–58, there seems to be no reason to suppose that the vacancy in the chancellorship and the custody of the seal by a succession of keepers made any practical difference. It is indeed possible that the absence of a chancellor facilitated some reforms in Chancery itself.

It is hardly a coincidence that the year of Neville's death saw a break in the old system under which the profits of Chancery were the perquisites of the chancellor, and the establishment of the Hanaper Department to deal with and to account for those profits, with the result that when chancellors were once again appointed, they were to be salaried officials. A reform of this kind seems to have been eminently reasonable and desirable, and no criticism can be levelled at the royal policy in this respect. Henceforth, ' the keeper of the hanaper received the fees of the seal, paid the expenses of the Chancery organization, and presented the accounts of his administration for review.'[1] It is of interest, but not surprising, that these accounts were tendered in the Wardrobe, not in the Exchequer, and the issues of the seal regularly figure in the wardrobe accounts. Naturally the Chancery was in much closer contact with the Wardrobe than it was with the Exchequer, and since the wardrobe accounts were normally rendered to the Exchequer, no sinister motives can be attributed to the arrangement.

It may well be that the establishment of the Hanaper helped on the process of the departmentalization of Chancery. ' Chancery,' we are told, was becoming ' daily more departmentalised.'[2] The ' clerks of the chancery ' were by now clearly differentiated from ' clerks of the chapel.'[3] A Chancery with a distinct staff

---

[1] Tout, *op. cit.*, p. 286.   [2] Jacob, *op. cit.*, p. 273.
[3] Tout, *op. cit.*, p. 186, n. 1 ; Maxwell-Lyte, *The Great Seal.*, p. 4.

of its own, and in part at least with premises of its own, inevitably became more sharply differentiated from the Household. The first reference to a ' *hospicium clericorum de cancellaria* ' comes from the year of Neville's death (1244).[1] References to a *hospicium* and *hospes* of the Chancery at Hensington near Woodstock appear,[2] and when the king went to France in 1260, part at least of the Chancery organization remained *in officio cancellarie*.[3] It is possible that by then the part of the Chancery dealing with administrative writs followed the king, while that part dealing with business *de cursu* remained in a fixed Chancery office. It was eventually the use of the privy seal of authorize the great seal that enabled much of the business of the office to be transacted outside of the Household.[4] But the full fruition of this development did not come within the period of which we are now speaking.

' For a year or two, Peter de Rivaux had in effect made the exchequer an outlying department of the royal household, or, to be more precise, of its financial centre, the wardrobe. This experiment was brought to an abrupt end in 1234, but it had permanent results. The very fact that his successors in the exchequer carried on the work of reform strengthened the old traditional ties between the exchequer and the household from which it had emerged. The experience of its officials was used, in a more methodical and a better articulated way, to further the royal interests in co-operation with the whole body of the *curia regis* and with the local administration. Council, justices, sheriffs, bailiffs, escheators, and the tenants of franchises themselves, had, as they had not had before, a meeting ground in the exchequer.[5]

We have seen above[6] that reforms at the Exchequer were initiated before Peter de Rivaux's period of power, were given greater impetus by Peter, and were resumed after his fall. There seems to have been a period of ' reaction ', or at least stagnation, for two years thereafter, but by 1236 important and durable reforms were implemented. In April and May of that year Peter des Roches and Peter de Rivaux returned to England, and

---

[1] Tout, *op. cit.*, p. 286 n. 2.
[2] Stamp, *loc. cit.*, p. 308 ; Maxwell-Lyte, *op. cit.*, p. 4.
[3] Stamp, *loc. cit.*
[4] *Ibid.*, p. 309.
[5] Powicke, *op. cit.*, p. 117.
[6] *V. supra*, p. 90.

although de Rivaux remained in the background, it is difficult, as Miss Mills says,[1] to avoid the conclusion that he was the influence behind the financial reforms that were then introduced. The most important and lasting of these reforms was a change in the accountability of the sheriffs and in the farm of the counties. The result was a fundamental alteration in the sheriffs' position, and the setting up of the lines along which all later reforms in this sphere ran.

A general change of sheriffs had occurred in 1234, mostly taking the form of a recognition of the appointments previously made by de Rivaux, but a wholesale and drastic re-appointment took place in 1236–37, and on this occasion the position of the new sheriffs was changed in two major respects. The ancient desmesne lands were retained in the king's hands, and a specific allowance was fixed for the sheriffs' expenses.[2]

The ancient demesne was taken away from the sheriffs' responsibilities, and entrusted to two keepers, with a view to ascertaining its value and to making a greater profit from it ; enquiry was made into its condition, after which it was leased out directly. As a result, of the old farm of the shire, only the profits of hundred and county courts, and payments such as view of frankpledge, sheriff's aid and similar customary payments remained to the sheriff. Moreover, a strict enquiry was now made into the sheriffs' liabilities for the remaining part of the farm, and the details were entered into a series of special rolls, the *Particule Proficui*.[3] It is clear that before 1236, an enormous proportion of the revenue found its way into the pockets of the sheriffs and not into the Exchequer. Down to 1236 it was still possible to make a good thing out of a shrievalty, notwithstanding King John's demand for larger ' profits ' from the shires. But after 1236, a sheriffdom was no longer a profitable office, and an allowance for the expenses of performing the duties of the office had to be made. The result was that the sheriff

---

[1] *Trans. R.H.S.*, 4th ser. X (1927), p. 119.

[2] *Ibid.*, pp. 120 ff.

[3] Most of these are found in the Lord Treasurer's Remembrancer's Miscellaneous Rolls. Before 1232, only three of these particular rolls survive, and these are rudimentary in form ; between 1236 and 1240 well-kept rolls were made and survive, and there is no doubt that such rolls were regularly kept until far into the 14th century, *V. ibid.*, pp. 124 ff.

became ' rather a collector of debts due to the Crown than a land agent for the king's private estate.'[1]

We are not here concerned with the important enquiries that were now pursued into the values of the demesne, the survey of royal manors, the many investigations into aids, scutages, escheats, wardships, and the forests, nor the beginnings of *quo warranto* enquiries.[2] These activities, to be so conspicuous a feature of exchequer administration henceforth, may well be connected with the appearance of ' professional ' barons of the exchequer, which may be dated from 1234. But the expansion of the judicial side of exchequer work at this time must be borne in mind. The Exchequer ' co-operated with the king and his justices. It spent as much time and trouble in the investigation of grievances as it did in the maintenance of royal rights. In short, it was a court of justice, or rather a function of the judicial activity of the king's court.'[3]

From what has been said, ' it will now be clear why, in the course of the century, the sheriffs' accounts were overtaken and gave way to the "foreign" accounts in the exchequer, and the sheriff himself became merely one among a crowd of accountants. The accounts of the escheators, and of those who had the custody of castles, honours, forests, manors, and other possessions of the king, were foreign accounts ; they lay outside, or were foreign (*forinseca*) to the responsibilities of the sheriff. And so were the accounts of the royal wardrobe, of Gascony, Ireland, Wales, the customs, the custody of the temporalities of vacant bishoprics, the profits of abbeys and priories in the king's hands, and every kind of tax and aid. All of them, as they became important became the object of special arrangement, and, in due course, of special audit. All of them as they became elaborate increased the work of the exchequer. In the period of reform the necessity for a policy was understood, and the way was prepared for development in the future.'[4]

But the reform of the farm of the shire, the reduction of the sheriffs' financial responsibilities, and the multiplication of foreign

---

[1] *Ibid.*, pp. 126–27.
[2] Powicke, *op. cit.*, pp. 102–110.
[3] *Ibid.*, pp. 109–110.
[4] *Ibid.*, p. 108.

accounts, were not the only important developments in this period. The internal improvements made possible by the invention of the *tallia dividenda* in 1206 were matured fully only after 1236. Other book-keeping improvements were introduced. The evidence suggests that after 1236, debts once entered on the Estreat Rolls[1] were not again entered on the Pipe Rolls, but only the total sum collected by the sheriff for such debts. Indeed, the procedure later to be laid down in the statute of 1270, known as the *Forma Observanda in Omnia Scripturae Magni Rotuli*,[2] originated in the reforms carried out in this period, which were also the basis of the Statute of Rhuddlan of 1284.[3]

A marked improvement in the by now numerous surviving records of the Exchequer suggests improved technique and attention to method. The Pipe and Chancellor's Rolls had become regular long before 1236. ' But, in the case of the Memoranda, the *Liberate* and *Originalia*, the Receipt and Issue Rolls, the Exchequer of Pleas Plea Rolls, about this time it is possible to use them for the first time as a regular series, each telling its own share of the story of a financial transaction.'[4]

It is evident from what has been said that the Exchequer of this period was a vigorous, active and effective organ of administration. ' We should regard the exchequer ', says Sir Maurice Powicke, ' not as an independent and uncontrolled centre of mysterious activity, alone with its *secretum*, but as an open place to which all resorted as a busy clearing house. Perhaps for this very reason it was no longer so necessary to make magnates and prelates members of its board, though the barons were still far from being a closed professional body of experts . . . The exchequer became more professional just because so much was required of it. . . It had no reason for its existence except as a guardian of the king's interests and of the facts and traditions of financial obligation.' . . . ' The financial administration of the exchequer was always subject to the king,' but—and this is a crucial point—' the greatest defect of the mediaeval exchequer was that

---

[1] It was now the general practice to mark the Estreat Rolls with a symbol to show the state of the accounts—' t ', ' p ', ' d ', for total and partial payments and debts respectively. Mills, *op. cit.*, 127.
[2] *V. infra*, p. 148.   [3] *V. infra*, p. 148.
[4] Mills, *ibid.*

it had not, and could not have, any financial policy. The king lived from day to day.'[1]

Here, perhaps, we have the key to the troubles that were brewing for Henry III's administration, lack not only of financial policy, but lack of policy broad enough and attractive enough to win the support of the persons and classes who were not themselves influential in the administration. Certainly in these years Henry III succeeded with a vengeance in reviving and pressing forward the administrative conceptions of his Angevin predecessors : his efforts and the efforts of his officials in this regard ought not to be belittled, for much that was accomplished in these years was to be woven into the administrative structure for centuries thereafter, and in some respects perhaps permanently to determine the nature of English administration. For his share in this work, Henry III has hardly received his due credit. The baronial opposition, and the ' constitutional ' conflicts, and the civil wars of the later years of his reign have tended to overshadow the interpretations of the period to so great an extent that Henry III's place in administrative history has often been viewed with prejudice and lack of perspective. But in this sphere, perhaps he was not in fact an entirely unworthy successor to Henry II.

§ 4. Henry III's reign witnessed the first attempt made by the baronage to obtain a controlling influence over the executive power. The barons of Runnymede had, in the security clause of the Great Charter, sought only machinery for coercing the king in the event of his infringing the terms of the charter and for compelling him to make redress ; the barons who forced the Provisions of Oxford upon Henry III sought and for a time obtained very much more than that ; they aimed at securing and exercising the executive power themselves. They did not, indeed, contemplate the abolition of the monarchy, but they did intend to carry on the king's government themselves and to make the administration work in ways that seemed good to them, without regard to the king's personal wishes. The Council of Fifteen set up in 1258, as Sir Maurice Powicke so aptly observes, ' unlike

[1] Powicke, *op. cit.*, pp. 118, 119, 120.

any previous Council in English history, was not regarded and did not behave as an expression of the *Curia Regis* '.[1] For a time, in consequence, ' the King reigned and the Council ruled.'[2]

It is, perhaps, easy to exaggerate the constitutional significance of these arrangements ; it may be that the Council of Fifteen was not so revolutionary a body, or at least did not regard itself as so revolutionary, as we might suppose.[3] Most probably it did not regard itself as more than a temporary device to secure the execution of certain policies ; certainly it did not endure in practice for more than about eighteen months. But even if Professor Wilkinson were justified in arguing that the Council of 1258 merely gives us the ' first instance of the Council exercising undoubted executive powers ',[4] this phenomenon in itself was a sufficiently striking departure from precedent. For if an executive council were something new, the exercise of executive powers by councillors regardless of the king's personal wishes was a radical innovation indeed.

Whatever the interpretation put upon the Provisions of Oxford, there can be no doubt that the years between 1215 and 1258 had seen a remarkable advance in the ' constitutional ideas ' entertained by the baronage. It was no longer merely a notion that the king ought to be coerced by a legalized procedure if he broke the law ; it was the much more mature idea that the king's government might be carried on by others in his name, if his policies were unacceptable to those others. Stripped of its contemporary limitations, the conception seems surprisingly modern, and even if those very limitations ensured that the idea could not work for long, it would, nonetheless, be rash to deny that it had profound influences upon subsequent constitutional history.

We are, however, concerned here not with the broader constitutional bearings of the baronial plans, but with their effect upon the king's administrative system. We have already noted that the earlier manifestations of the baronial desire to

---

[1] ' Some Observations on the Baronial Council (1258–60) and the Provisions of Westminster ' in *Essays in Mediaeval History presented to T. F. Tout* (1925), p. 123.
[2] Treharne, *op. cit.*, p. 344.
[3] Cf. Wilkinson, *Studies in the Constitutional History of the 13th and 14th Centuries*, p. 187. [4] *Ibid.*

influence royal policy by securing greater weight among the *consilarii regis* had not had appreciable effect on the administrative arrangements, apart from certain changes in personnel. This broadly was the upshot of the political crisis of 1233–34,[1] and the same may be said of the crisis of 1236–38. The precedent set on this latter occasion of trying to force ' provisions ' upon the king, whereby he would be committed to ruling with the advice of a chosen body of counsellors, was doubtless one of great importance both in itself and as an anticipation of the methods of 1258, but the attempt was frustrated at the time, and had no effect upon the administrative machinery.[2] The same conclusion would have to be drawn whether the ' paper constitution ' preserved by Matthew Paris is attributed to 1238 or 1244. The extensive controversy upon the date to be assigned to this document—the weight of the argument seems decidedly in favour of continuing to attribute it to 1244[3]—does not add anything to the intrinsically somewhat slight value of the document itself. We do not know by whom, by what person or persons, this draft of ' provisions ' was drawn up, or even by whom it was so much as seen, let alone considered. Its relevance to the course of events therefore cannot be assessed. But it remains interesting to note that some one, apparently many years before 1258, had conceived the idea that counsellors and principal officers should be chosen by the great council of barons to supervise the administration and be responsible to them.[4] Certainly the ideas of 1258 were not new to that year.

Whatever other intrepretation may be placed upon the baronial schemes of reform which are known to us from the documents commonly called the Provisions of Oxford and the Provisions of Westminster,[5] there can be no doubt that their

---

[1] *V. supra*, p. 95.

[2] *V.* Powicke, *Henry III and the Lord Edward*, p. 292.

[3] The arguments of Professor C. R. Cheney in ' The Paper Constitution preserved by Matthew Paris ' (*E.H.R.*, LXV (1950), pp. 213–221) seem to dispose of the views put forward by Mr. Denholm-Young in ' The Paper Constitution attributed to 1244 ' (*ibid.*, LVIII (1943), pp. 401 ff.). Cf. Powicke, op. cit. pp. 291–2 ; Wilkinson, *Constitutional History*, I, pp. 117–130.

[4] Treharne, *op. cit.*, pp. 53–55.

[5] The real nature of these documents was not made clear in Stubbs's *Select Charters*. It has to be remembered that none of the administrative, but only the legislative portions of the Provisions were recorded in official texts. ' The so-called Provisions

result was for a time to give the baronial party complete control of the king's administration—or at least that part of it which was not wholly contained within the royal Household. We are not here concerned to examine the uses to which the baronage put their administrative power[1] when they had acquired it, but we are concerned with the ways and means by which they acquired it.

The parliament of barons that met at Oxford in June, 1258, following up the proposals of the Committee of Twenty-Four which had been at work since early May, demanded that in all State affairs the king should be directed by the advice of a nominated council responsible to the baronage, and that he should accept a justiciar, chancellor, and treasurer nominated by the parliament and answerable to the council. This council was to confer three times a year ' in parliament ' with twelve others chosen by the baronial community ' to view the state of the realm and to treat of the needs of the land and of the king '.[2]

The Council of Fifteen was nominated by four electors, and entered into its duties by 6 July, if not earlier ; it consisted of seven earls, five greater barons, two bishops, and John Mansel, an experienced royal official, and included the justiciar and chancellor. Its duties were ' to give the King counsel in good faith for the government of the realm, and in all things pertaining to the King and the realm ; and to amend and redress all things which they find in need of redress and amendment, to exercise

of Oxford are a bundle of lists, notes of administrative changes, and of regulations for future guidance. The phrase " Provisions of Oxford " thus came to be used for the whole plan of reform as it was worked out during the next eighteen months' (Powicke, *op. cit.*, p. 395). The Provisions were not all made at Oxford, and in contemporary eyes the Provisions of Oxford probably included what were subsequently called the Provisions of Westminster. *V.* Jacob, ' What were the Provisions of Oxford? ' in *History*, IX (1924), pp. 188–200 ; Denholm-Young, ' Documents of the Barons' Wars ' in *E.H.R.*, XLVIII (1933), pp. 558–575 ; H. G. Richardson and G. O. Sayles, ' The Provisions of Oxford : A Forgotten Document and Some Comments ' in *Bull. J. Ryland's Lib.*, 17 (1933), pp. 291–321 ; Treharne, *op. cit.*, pp. 81–2 ; Powicke, *op. cit.*, pp. 379 ff.

[1] *V.* Jacob, *Studies in the Period of Baronial Reform and Rebellion, 1258–67* (1925) ; Treharne, *op. cit.* ; Powicke, *op. cit.*

[2] The limitation of the baronial representatives to twelve was said to be for the sake of sparing the cost to the community. In fact, however, the parliaments were attended by the king, ministers, councillors, and many others besides the twelve. Similarly, others besides the original fifteen took the councillors' oath and might attend the council meetings. *V.* Richardson and Sayles, *op. cit.*, pp. 296–7.

power over the Justiciar and all other people.' By 4 August, Henry III proclaimed the authority of the Council, swore to accept its decisions, and ordered all men to obey its decisions.

In the meantime, provision had been made for a justiciar, a chancellor, and a treasurer. At the Oxford meetings note had been taken of the fact that the justiciarship was ' vacant ', and Hugh Bigod was appointed to fill this vacancy. At first, it seems, emphasis was put upon the judicial aspect of the office ; the justiciar was sworn to do full justice to all men, was to be appointed for one year only and to be answerable at the end of it to the king and council, and was to take no gifts or bribes. But soon the justiciar's activities exceeded those of a chief justice ; he exercised jurisdiction over all officials and private persons, supervised all courts and redressed wrongs, presided *coram rege* and over special eyres, was an important member of the Council, concerned in reforms and administrative and political work of all kinds, and acted in effect as Regent while the king was abroad in November, 1259. In short, something like the old Angevin justiciarship was revived, with the fundamental difference that the justiciar now was at all times to be the servant, not of the king, but of the Council.

The Chancery and Treasury were not vacant in June, 1258, and the existing occupants of these offices were retained. Henry de Wengham, keeper of the seal since 1255, took the oath prescribed by the Council for the chancellor, and remained in office until October, 1260. He swore to seal no writs, except writs *de cursu*, no gift of wardship, marriage, or escheat, without the order or consent of the king and council or the majority thereof, nor to seal anything by the sole order of the king, nor anything contrary to the orders of the Council ; he was to accept no gifts, to hold office for one year and to account for his term before the Council, with a fixed fee for himself and the expenses of Chancery. No vice-chancellor was appointed under the Council's arrangements, and this omission to impose conciliar authority upon the chancellor's underlings gave rise to difficulties on at least one occasion.[1]

---

[1] *V.* Treharne, 'An Unauthorised Use of the Great Seal under the Provisional Government in 1259 ', in *E.H.R.* XL (1925), pp. 403-10.

No new oath was provided for the treasurer, who, however, was to hold office for one year and to account for the issues and receipts. Lovell was retained in office until October, 1258, when he was dismissed on conviction of abusing a royal grant, and was succeeded by John of Crakehall until October, 1260.

The Council, it seems, intended to make some changes of personnel in the departments of the Household, but in fact very few such changes of any importance were made. Of great potential importance was the provision that all the revenues of the realm were to be paid into the Exchequer; this would indeed have modified considerably the administrative system, if it had become fully operative. Actually all that resulted was an increase in the proportion of the Wardrobe's income received direct from the Exchequer; in the years 1238–40 that proportion had averaged one-fifth; in 1255–57, one-sixth; in 1258–61, three-fifths.[1] The Council, in fact, found it convenient to sanction some direct payments to the Wardrobe, the income and expenditure of which did not appreciably alter during these years. So long as the Council remained in power, the Wardrobe could not, in any case, pursue rival objectives. A baronial intention to reform the Exchequer in general was also not fulfilled.

What was essentially new in these arrangements was that the Council, with or without the king, assumed the supreme direction of the government. It may be, as Sir Maurice Powicke has said, that 'in 1258, the baronial leaders had no intention of changing the machinery of government.'[2] But the government was now no longer government by the king and the *Curia Regis*. It was government by the Council of Fifteen—in the king's name, no doubt, but certainly not in accordance with the king's wishes. For the time being, the executive power, in theory vested solely in the king, was in practice exercised by others than the king.

[1] Treharne, *op. cit.*, p. 96; Tout, *Chapters*, I, p. 301. It is perhaps going too far to say that this provision ' cannot but be a faint sign of constitutional opposition to the recent development of Wardrobe independence ' (*ibid.*). What the barons wanted was as complete a control over the administration as they could get, and therefore they would not have cared to see large sums of money finding their way through devious channels into the Wardrobe. They were interested in the practical, not the theoretical implications of the matter. They wanted to control the king, and therefore also his finances.

[2] ' Some Observations on the Baronial Council ', *loc. cit.*, p. 124.

The Council kept a tight hold over daily administration for some eighteen months. The provisions of these months explicitly define the control of the Council over the chief officials, the judges, the Exchequer, and the Household ; the letters patent issued were noted by the chancery clerks as having been authorized by the Council or its members ; the Council proceeded to get a grip on local administration, to provide for the redress of many grievances, and to promote the reforms in private law which were in the long run to prove the most permanent part of all the reforming schemes.

Little else was done in the sphere of central administrative organization. The so-called Provisions of Westminster of October, 1259, included instructions for the justiciar, chancellor, and treasurer to remain in office for a further period, for the justiciar to act as vicegerent with a council during the king's forthcoming absence ; some of the Councils of Fifteen and Twelve were to accompany the king. The Exchequer was made the subject of some special commissions ; the justiciar and the treasurer were to choose suitable commissioners to enquire into the Exchequer and the Exchequer of Jews, and to report to the next parliament what reforms were needful ; the justiciar, treasurer, and three others were to control the receipt and expenditure of certain items of revenue, especially wardships and escheats, with a view to establishing a sinking fund for the repayment of the king's debts.

When the king departed overseas in November, 1259, the justiciar with a council acted as the head of the government at home. The chancellor and the great seal went with the king ; the exchequer seal was to be used at home as the great seal, but only in a prescribed manner and only on writs attested by the justiciar in one of two set forms. The justiciar attested all letters patent and close and all other writs requiring royal authority, except a few issued on direct instructions from the king himself, who also issued such letters from abroad—more indeed than the justiciar himself did.

It is probable that the Westminster Provisions contemplated a more permanent modification of the executive than had been intended at Oxford in June, 1258 ; two or three members of the

Council were to be appointed at each succeeding parliament to be with the king always, presumably to participate in his executive powers. But by the end of 1260, the baronial régime had collapsed; the last order of the Council of Fifteen was dated 28 December, and the administrative system slipped back into its traditional royal form.

Henry III's complaints against the baronial council, put forward in early 1260 (or 1261), have not been very sympathetically considered by historians,[1] but they were by no means without substance and justification. In essence they amounted to an allegation that the baronial councillors had usurped the executive authority of the king, and there can scarcely be any doubt that this had in fact occurred, and in excess of what had been at first contemplated or was necessary to correct abuses and instigate reforms. There was no real reply possible to the royal complaint that the baronage had embarked upon revolutionary courses— courses which we should call ' unconstitutional '. Moreover, ' in the nature of things, a joint administration of barons, royal servants, justices, and exchequer, under the direction of a justiciar and council who had control of the great seal, in accordance with the decrees of a parliament whose powers were delegated to it by the whole body of tenants-in-chief, could not endure.'[2]

By early 1262, the baronial council had disappeared entirely, and the king ruled once again with unrestricted personal power. When the successful de Montfortian rebellion imposed another revolutionary régime, the *Forma Regiminis* of 1263 re-established a conciliar executive with full control over the great seal, with nominated officers. We may perhaps agree that the ' whole scheme was nothing more than a veil to cover Simon's autocracy ',[3] and whatever importance de Montfort's spell of power

[1] *V.* Jacob, ' The Complaints of Henry III against the Baronial Council in 1261 ' in *E.H.R.*, XLI (1926), pp. 559–571. Mr. Denholm-Young prints a Latin version of the complaints, and attributes it to March, 1260, which seems from some points of view to be the more likely date (' Documents of the Barons ' Wars ', in *E.H.R.*, XLVIII (1933), pp. 558–575). Cf. Wilkinson, *Constitutional History*, I, pp. 152–3 ; Treharne, *Baronial Plan of Reform*, p. 344.

[2] Powicke, *op. cit.*, p. 134.

[3] Denholm Young, *op. cit.*, p. 568 ; Powicke, *Henry III and the Lord Edward*, p. 474 ; Treharne, *op. cit.*, p. 314.

may have for constitutional history, its effect upon administrative history was too short and too slight to detain us here.

The end of the Barons' Wars saw the end of the justiciarship; stripped of its powers of administrative supremacy, the office survived only in an attenuated form as the chief justiceships and later the lord chief justiceship of England. When from 1265 onwards the monarchy was free to exercise its powers again without control,[1] the old administrative scheme was restored; the executive power remained in the king alone; the administrative officers were responsible to him alone, and carried on their work through Chancery, Exchequer, and household departments in accordance with the old methods and the old loyalties.[2]

It is possible that the baronial hold over the chancellor and the great seal during the implementation of the Provisions had encouraged Henry III to look more to the privy seal than he had in the earlier years of his reign. On three of the four occasions on which he was absent from the realm in the years 1259–64, the great seal went with him; a seal of absence was first used in England in 1262–3 and again in 1264; in September and October, 1263, the king took with him a small seal which may have been the privy seal. The privy seal at any rate was used extensively on his return in October, 1263, for the documents repudiating the Provisions and the numerous mandates and summonses issued in that connection. Possibly Henry III was now aiming at using the privy seal as a substitute for the great seal, which he had learnt from experience was more exposed to outside influence than the small seal kept in the custody of the Wardrobe, and he may perhaps have anticipated the later policy of Edward II

[1] Such freedom of action, of course, was always subject to whatever restrictions and commitments had been freely entered into by the Crown, and which in effect if not in fact had become part of the law of the land. For statements of the principle of this matter, *v.* The Mise of Amiens (1264). and the Dictum of Kenilworth (1266), in Stubbs, *Select Charters*, 9th ed., pp. 396, 407–8. For a full discussion of this point *v.* Lapsley, *Crown, Community and Parliament* (1951), pp. 204–207.

[2] The effects upon the revenue of the years of trouble, the embarrassment of the exchequer machinery, and the efforts made to restore the situation in the later years of the reign, are examined by Miss Mills in 'Adventus Vicecomitum, 1258–72' (*E.H.R.*, XXXVI (1921), pp. 481–96), with which should be read the critical remarks in Treharne, *op. cit.*, pp. 370 ff. Some of the difficulties of getting the machinery to work smoothly again are illustrated in L. Ehrlich, ' Exchequer and Wardrobe in 1270 ' in *E.H.R.*, XXXVI (1921), pp. 553–4.

in this respect.[1] If so, the de Montfortians can hardly have
appreciated the possibilities involved, for at one time the custody
of the great seal itself was lodged by them in the keeper of the
wardrobe. It is doubtful indeed whether the king or his opponents were able as yet to envisage any distinction between an
office of the Household and an office of State.[2] There was,
indeed, no reason why they should have done, either then or for
many years to come.

The struggle between king and baronage had not really been
about administrative organization; it is misleading to assert
without large reservations that ' the revolt of the barons was
against the whole system of court administration which Henry
III had so long favoured '.[3] The barons may have installed a few
nominees of their own into the chief offices, but they did not in
fact upset the household system nor abolish its administrative
potentialities. What they had done for a brief spell was to
capture the whole machine and to use it for securing certain
objectives of their own; the machine itself remained intact and
unaltered.

We may therefore conclude, with Sir Maurice Powicke, that
' the issue between Henry III and the opposition of prelates and
barons was finally narrowed down to the freedom of the king to
choose his own counsellors and be master in his own household.
. . . Not logic, but hard facts, had made this issue the acid test of
royal status. In the end all constitutional theory depends upon it.
In the next three centuries strong kings kept control of their
households, and when they were wise, made criticism helpless,
while weak or unfortunate kings had to give way. Edward I
never gave way on this matter, and he so ruled that he was never
expected to give way. The issue was closed.'[4]

§ 5. The reign of Edward I may well be regarded as witness-
ing the zenith of the Angevin conception of administration
centred on the Household. ' The household with its sworn inner

---

[1] Tout, *op. cit.*, pp. 303–307.
[2] *Ibid.*, pp. 309–313.
[3] *Ibid.*, p. 295.
[4] Powicke, *op. cit.*, p. 694. Cf. Treharne, ' The Significance of the Baronial
Reform Movement, 1258–1267 ' in *Trans.R.H.S.* 4th ser. XXV (1943), pp. 35–72.

K

council of high officials and intimate advisers, its wardrobe organization capable of indefinite expansion for the handling of finances or the raising of armies, and its intricate and regulated domestic life, was accepted as the centre of business, and had to face no criticism until the end of the king's reign. Chancery, exchequer, and the courts of law looked to it and were bound to it by their higher personnel; their separate life was functional rather than political. We hear no more of the demand for justiciars, chancellors, and treasurers with independent status and fixity of tenure.'[1] ' During Edward I's reign there was little friction between these departments, and few signs that outside critics thought any one of them less suitable than any other for dealing with matters of public importance.'[2]

The absence abroad of the heir to the throne at the time of Henry III's death in November, 1272, gave rise to an awkward situation in the government at home.[3] The possibility of such a situation's arising had, however, been foreseen, and before his departure, Edward had appointed a small commission to act for him should he succeed to the throne *in absentia*, consisting of trusted advisers, among whom Walter Giffard, archbishop of York, Roger Mortimer of Wigmore, and Robert Burnell, household clerk of Edward, were the most effective members. The commission now assumed responsibility as vicegerents in the name of the king. The great seal was surrendered into the hands of Walter Giffard; Burnell used a special seal of absence to authenticate the acts issued in the king's name, and a ' caretaker government ' carried on business until the king returned. On the break-up of Henry III's Household, no such organization existed in England, and the work that was normally done by the Wardrobe had to be done by Burnell and the Exchequer between them, with the assistance of loans from the Italian bankers.

Such arrangements could be only temporary pending the king's return. Edward I was back in time to be crowned on 19 August, 1274. Before that date, ' for the first time in our history, the organized Household of the heir-apparent became the

[1] Powicke, *Henry III and the Lord Edward*, p. 695.
[2] H. Johnstone in *Cambridge Mediaeval History*, VII (1932), p. 396.
[3] Tout, *Chapters*, II, pp. 1–9.

Household of the monarch without the least breach of continuity.[1] Burnell, promoted to be bishop of Bath and Wells, and soon appointed chancellor, was destined to be the king's most trusted official until his death in 1292 ; most of the household officials of the heir-apparent became equivalent officials in the royal Household, and took their places accordingly in the administration of the realm.

Edward I brought to bear upon the problems of administration not only a far more powerful and abler personality than his father's, but also the lessons that had been learnt during the troublesome times of the middle of the century. It is broadly true to say that Edward's administrative machinery did not greatly differ from that used by his father, and that little that was new appeared in the administrative system during his reign. What was fresh was the far higher degree of confidence that was felt in the king himself, and the far greater degree of vigour that was instilled into the administration. ' The future was indeed to show that Edward's well balanced administration was maintained by the confidence which he inspired in his servants, both clerks and laymen.'[2]

Edward, like his father before him, could not keep his administration working effectively and coherently without the assistance of that ' sworn inner council of high officials and intimate advisers' referred to by Sir Maurice Powicke in the passage quoted at the beginning of this section.

We have seen above[3] that the *consiliarii* of Henry III were essentially advisory and not executive in their functions—at any rate, so far as these can be ascertained ; nor, although they attained an identity as sworn counsellors, had they become institutionalized to any appreciable degree. Instances of executive action ' by the council ', although extant, are too few and too doubtful in significance to make any other generalization justifiable. But we must always remember that the reaching of administrative decision necessarily precedes executive action, and that such decision may often have been reached among the councillors, whilst the executive action was taken elsewhere. The matter was necessarily a question of how much responsibility

[1] *Ibid.*, p. 6.   [2] Powicke, *op. cit.*, p. 695.   [3] *V. supra*, pp. 98-100.

the councillors were prepared to take without consulting the king himself, and this is a matter that cannot be clearly illustrated in the reign of Henry III. In Edward I's reign, however, some considerable development in the character of the Council took place. 'The executive council is essentially the outcome of the developments, political, military, administrative, and judicial, of the reign of Edward I'.[1]

Some changes in the formulas of the chancery records of this period indicate the growing place of the Council in administrative decision. The common phrases of the later years of Henry III, such as ' according as the king by his council should think fit to provide ', or ' the king by his council has commanded ' give way to other phrases of different emphasis, such as ' be before the king to do and receive what shall be provided by the king's council ', or ' so that there may then be done what the king shall cause to be ordained by the council '. As Professor Wilkinson observes, ' the theory behind all the formulae alike is that the king acts ; the council may temporarily take his place. But we seem to see a greater independence attributed to the council in the later than in the early phrases '.[2] From 1297, authorizations for the issue of chancery writs ' by Council ' begin to be recorded ; the exact significance of these notes is not clear, but ' we may connect it provisionally with the increasing emergence of the Council as an executive body.'[3] More definite and concrete than these evidences of executive decision by the Council, is the substantial indication of the development of its judicial work. It is true that this function was still essentially advisory in character, but it may reasonably be assumed that the development of this side of the Council's activity helped to give coherence and a clearer identity to the Council itself. This, however, is not the place to consider judicial functions in detail.[4]

We may well believe that Edward I's reign saw some transformation in the work of the Council, and that the Council was on the way to becoming an executive organ of a kind. It was a place where administrative decisions could be taken, sometimes, for one reason or another, without the king's personal

[1] Wilkinson, *Studies*, p. 121.
[2] *Ibid.*
[3] *Ibid.*, p. 122.
[4] *V. ibid.*, pp. 122–126.

participation, and sometimes no doubt without the king's knowledge. But in form, the decision was the king's alone, and any subsequent executive acts came, not from the king in council, but from the ordinary administrative organs. Such an act might be embodied in a writ of great seal, and so become an act of Chancery. It might be translated into a writ of privy seal, and thus become in effect an act of the Wardrobe. If it mainly concerned finance, it was likely to to result directly or indirectly in a writ under the exchequer seal, and the Exchequer would accordingly be the ultimate executive agent. But in no case did the Council as such act, though of course it figures often enough in the marginal annotations of the chancery rolls as the sole source of warranty for an executive act embodied in a chancery writ.[1]

No evidence survives as to whether the terms of the councillor's oath were modified or even used in the years between 1257 and 1307. But the text of the oath of 1307, preserved in official documents, differs little from the chronicler's version of that of 1257, and it is reasonable to suppose that this text represents substantially the oath taken by councillors during the reign of Edward I.[2] It is still not possible to identify all those who were as councillors, but it is evident that the composition of the Council was very similar to what it had been under Henry III before 1258; a few prelates and barons, the chief officers, including the chancellor, treasurer, principal household officials and clerks were to be found among the members. Possibly magnates were rather more prominent among the councillors than before, but ' Edward I's council remains essentially ministerial '.[3] Normally its meetings would be composed entirely of men engaged in one capacity or another in the service of the king. There were no fixed sessions or regular meetings. Meetings and the composition of meetings would depend wholly on circumstances and the nature of the business to be dealt with, and upon the availability and also suitability of the councillors in relation to the occasion and the matter in hand. The composition commonly would be simply the chancellor, treasurer, and other administrative officers; individual councillors might

---

[1] Tout, *op. cit.*, p. 147.
[2] For the text, *v.* Baldwin, *King's Council*, pp. 346–8.
[3] Wilkinson, *op. cit.*, pp. 146–8.

well give their advice without any formal meeting at all. In short, we may conclude, in Sir Maurice Powicke's words, that ' like his father, Edward had his group of household clerks, available for all sorts of business, and sometimes sworn members of his Council, but his closest advisers or secretaries were usually two or three officials who held office as keeper or controller or the newly created cofferer of the Wardrobe.'[1] The councillors were useful for discussion and advice, for reaching conclusions, but it was elsewhere that administrative decisions were carried into effect.

The great place of the Household, especially of the Wardrobe, in Edward I's system of government, is amply illustrated by the fact that nearly all the most important administrators of his reign began their careers as clerks in the Wardrobe ; of these, some were rewarded with the highest posts in Chancery or Exchequer, whilst others rose by promotion from clerkships to the charge of their departments. Of the six chancellors of the reign, only the last, Ralph Baldock, did not serve a long apprenticeship in the Household. The two chancellors who between them held office for twenty-eight consecutive years, Robert Burnell (1274–1292), and John Langton (1292–1302), had both served for many years, the former in Edward's Household, the latter in the Chancery. The treasurers of the reign varied in origin rather more ; the first three in office until 1283 were not of curialist origins, but the following three were chancery or wardrobe clerks by training, and of these, the last, Walter Langton (1295–1307), succeeded to the chief place in the king's confidence vacated by Burnell at his death in 1292, and was the first treasurer to attain to the position of virtually principal minister.

Not only was the Wardrobe the chief school of Edward I's administrators, but the heads of it were officers of high importance in the government. As Tout says, ' as chiefs among the wardrobe clerks, they had authority that rivalled the authority of the greatest ministers of the State, and from the wardrobe promotion to the most dignified and lucrative offices constantly followed.'[2]

[1] *Op. cit.*, p. 696.   [2] *Op. cit.*, p. 14 and generally, pp. 10–26.

The internal organization of the Wardrobe is revealed in part in the Household Ordinance of 12 November, 1279, the first document of the kind surviving since the *Constitutio Domus Regis*.[1] How far the regulations and scales of remuneration set out in this Ordinance were innovatory and how far merely declaratory is not clear, but it contains useful evidence of the arrangements intended in 1279, even though possibly not all of them were carried out in practice. The most significant revelation is perhaps the great place in the Household as a whole attained by the keeper or treasurer of the wardrobe. The keeper, together with the stewards of the Household, was required to meet nightly the heads of the various spending departments and to receive and check their accounts, and also periodically to check over the accounts of the Great Wardrobe, and of the chamberlain of wines, and annually the accounts of the whole Household.[2] The position of the stewards, although they were still the lay heads of the Household, seems to have deteriorated somewhat in comparison with the clerical keepers of the wardrobe (who were sometimes called the treasurers of the household), whose position in general administration and politics was far greater. The stewardships of the Household, differentiated from the hereditary stewardship in Henry III's reign, were not destined to become much more than domestic offices (to which some judicial functions within the verge appertained) ; the duality of the office ceased after 1293. Usually a layman of some rank, the steward was always a councillor and was generally summoned to parliament, but it was only his jurisdiction over members of the Household and all offences committed within the verge that attracted much public attention to him—attention which tended to become hostile as the verge tended to expand.

The second officer in the Wardrobe was now often called the controller, and was becoming an officer of high importance. His primary function was to keep the counter-roll of accounts as a

---

[1] The text is printed in Tout, *op. cit.*, pp. 158–163, with commentary, pp. 27–31. Cf. Wilkinson, ' The Household Ordinance of 1279 ' in *History*, n.s. XII (1927), pp. 46–7, wherein it is pointed out that Miss Bateson in *Mediaeval England* (1903) confused the keeper or treasurer of the Wardrobe in this document with the treasurer of the Exchequer.

[2] These duties of the keeper received attention in *Fleta, seu Commentarius Juris Anglicani* (ed. Selden (1685), p. 78).

check upon his chief, the keeper ; he was also responsible for the custody of the archives entrusted to the Wardrobe, which often included not merely wardrobe documents, but state papers emanating from Chancery or Exchequer, which, for one reason or another, were deposited in the Wardrobe. Moreover, the controller was the head of the secretarial organization of the Wardrobe, and as such acted as the keeper of the privy seal. Edward I's reign was to see an important advance in the use of the privy seal in administration, and it seems to be certain that there was a keeper of it from early in the reign, even if the Ordinance of 1279 makes no mention of it, and no mention is as yet made of any specific person as the keeper of it. Its custody as yet was merely part of the controller's duties, who, as Fleta observed, was the only keeper of a seal independent of the chancellor ; the controller was also in effect a private secretary of the king, and as such, a person of influence and consequence in the administration.

The officer third in rank in the Wardrobe was the cofferer ; originating probably as the personal clerk of the keeper, he became entrusted with the details of book-keeping and accounts, but, with the keeper and the controller often engaged in weighty affairs outside the Wardrobe, the cofferer frequently found himself in effective charge of the office.[1] With the subordinate staff, the clerks, ushers, sub-ushers, and the dependent Wardrobes of the Queen and the king's sons, we need not detain ourselves here.[2]

Inevitably, the Wardrobe, or the essential part of it, accompanied the king on his travels, both at home and overseas ; the account books of the Wardrobe, indeed, afford the most reliable evidence of the royal intinerary. But the Wardrobe was far more than a domestic office ; it was essentially ' the brain and hand of the court '. ' It was becoming, as we shall see, the office which gave unity of policy and direction to all the departments of state. It was in practice as much a wheel in the national machine of government as the chancery and exchequer themselves '.[3] The

---

[1] The cofferer's clerks became in a later age the 'board of green cloth', which is still the accounting office of the royal Household, although the cofferer and his clerks were abolished in 1782.

[2] *V.* Tout, *op. cit.*, pp. 42-3, and generally, pp. 27-59.   [3] *Ibid.*, p. 48.

Wardrobe could never ' go out of court ', but none the less needed some kind of establishment in London or Westminster, where archives and accounts could be stored and where business could be transacted, whether the king were there or not. The accounts show frequent reference to the payment of expenses for wardrobe clerks journeying *extra curiam* to London or elsewhere. Normally clerks of the Wardrobe dined in the king's hall,[1] and some were allowed to sleep in the department ; in 1300 the keeper received an annual allowance for the maintenance of himself and the clerks and esquires of his department, and presumably this arrangement tended to promote the self-sufficiency of the office. The need for permanent depositories gave rise to the establishment of various treasuries or storehouses of the Wardrobe, in the Tower of London, in the crypt of the abbey of Westminster, and elsewhere ;[2] the ' king's Wardrobe ' in the Tower of London was for a time used especially for the stores of the Great Wardrobe, particularly for arms and armour, until later the Great Wardrobe set up its main storehouse in the city of London.

The wardrobe organization was the pivot of Edward I's administration, the principal, or at least the most elastic, but not of course the sole, instrument of the royal executive power. There was not as yet any question of rivalry or friction between the chief administrative departments, the Wardrobe, the Chancery, and the Exchequer. Each of these organizations, and others as well, had its functions, in some respects overlapping, and which organization was used for this or that purpose at various times was largely a matter of convenience, or even caprice, though also at times a matter of tradition or established routine. Some business was clearly the proper business of Chancery or Exchequer, and only those departments could effectively dispose of such business ; some affairs could be cleared only by the great

---

[1] The text of the Ordinance of St. Albans, *de aula non tenenda in hospicio regis* of 13 April, 1300, does not survive, but this ordinance was designed to regulate and restrict the practice of eating in the king's hall. *V.* Tout, *op. cit.*, p. 49.

[2] For the burglary here in 1303, *v.* Tout, 'A Mediaeval Burglary', in *Collected Papers*. For the use of the Temple as a treasury and financial office by the Wardrobe and by the Exchequer, and as a record office by Chancery in the thirteenth century, *v.* A. Sandys, 'The Financial and Administrative Importance of the London Temple in the Thirteenth Century' in *Essays to Tout* (1925), pp. 147–162.

seal, and therefore fell to Chancery; other affairs required the methods of the Exchequer and could conveniently only be dealt with there. But there was not very much business that could not be dealt with in one way or another in the Wardrobe. The scope of wardrobe business was as wide almost as the king's executive discretion; it was very close to the supreme initiative in administration; not being in any way bound by precedent or routine, it was flexible and resourceful in the highest degree, very sensitive and responsive to the king's will. It could and did direct and impel the executive action of the king's government, with the whole strength of the king and his Household behind it. For government was still essentially administration by and through the Household. ' The truth is . . . that the whole state and realm of England were the appurtenances of the king's household. The army was the household in arms; parliaments and councils were the household afforced to give the king advice; the financing and administration of the whole realm belonged to the household because the whole realm was but the household considered in its widest aspect.'[1]

Exchequer and Chancery were but offshoots of the Household; Chancery was not as yet entirely distinct from the Household, but the place of unlimited administrative discretion was where the king himself was,[2] and the Wardrobe was always with the king, ready to take all necessary action to implement his policies and decisions. It was inevitable, therefore, that the Wardrobe's activities should expand and contract, according to the multifarious and varying requirements of the king's government, both in peace and in war. It must have its secretariat and its seal; it must have its finances and financial organization; it must have its methods of military and naval mobilization; it must, to the limits of practicality, be able to turn its hands to any activity necessary to ensure that the king's government is carried out.

---

[1] Tout, *Chapters*, II, p. 59.
[2] It deserves to be remembered that the Chamber was still the department of the Household in the most intimate relationship with the king; its officers were his confidential agents, and as such could be utilized for almost any executive business. Because of this latent potentiality, it was possible for the *camera regis* to assume a greater importance in the next reign.

As a secretariat, the Wardrobe, especially during the chancellorship of Robert Burnell (1274–1292), a promoted household clerk of the lord Edward, was in close relations with the Chancery, and at times the two organizations seem to have been interchangeable. On occasions of the absence of the chancellor from court, the great seal was left in the custody of the Wardrobe and was used there for sealing documents, the keeper of the Wardrobe acting as if he were the chancellor for the time being.[1] When the king was abroad in the years 1286–89, the chancellor and the whole Wardrobe accompanied the king, but a section of the Chancery remained at home and carried on necessary business with writs attested by the regent and sealed with a seal of absence. Later, after the king's return, the wardrobe officer who kept the privy seal could be described in a chancery writ as ' the private chancellor of the king '.[2] The administrative scandals, especially in the Exchequer, which materialized during the years of the king's absence, partly due perhaps to the long absence of the Wardrobe from England, were cleared up by the joint action of Wardrobe and Chancery.[3] Close co-operation between the two departments continued for most of the reign. The political events of the reign, the long succession of wars, and the consequential increasing and eventually extreme pressure on the king's finances, tended to bring the adaptable Wardrobe into the foreground of the administration, and if not actually to depress the Chancery, at least to diminish the distinctions between them. John Benstead, controller of the Wardrobe and ex-officio keeper of the privy seal, was frequently also keeper of the great seal ; the Wardrobe, groaning under pressure of work, borrowed the services of chancery clerks, and, for some purposes, especially in diplomatic business, the clerks of the Wardrobe and Chancery co-operated to such a degree that it is hard to say which of them played the greater part.

The privy seal[4] itself began to play a very prominent and growing part in administration after the early years of the reign.

---

[1] Tout, *op. cit.*, p. 61.

[2] *Ibid.*, p. 64.   [3] *Ibid.*, p. 68.

[4] The privy seal of Edward I was one inch in diameter, bearing a plain shield charged with the arms of England—three lions passant, and the legend ' *secretum Regis Edwardi* '. *V.* Maxwell-Lyte, *The Great Seal*, p. 41.

Writs of privy seal were used for warranty of chancery writs in ever increasing numbers from 1292 onwards, and large numbers of original writs of privy seal, as chancery warrants, exchequer warrants, and as used for other purposes, survive. In these years the privy seal became established, not only as the seal for the king's multifarious personal and diplomatic[1] correspondence, but also as a regular part of the administrative machinery, especially when, as often happened, the chancellor was separated from the court.[2] Nor, as yet, was there any friction between privy seal and great seal ; during Burnell's chancellorship relations between the two offices were so intimate and personal that no bureaucratic rivalry was likely to arise. ' Considerations of immediate convenience determined in each case whether the chancellor's clerks or the wardrobe clerks were to act. The only thing which limited the freedom of the latter was the tradition that matters of high state policy, writs that set the judicial machinery in motion, grants of rights, estates, and high dignities, must ultimately be authenticated by the great seal, so that the clerks of the chancery were called upon constantly to reissue in more solemn form the drafts sent to them by the clerks of the wardrobe.'[3]

The activities of the Wardrobe as a secretariat are revealed mainly in the surviving warrants or notes on chancery records of warranties by privy seal, and in evidence of its relations with the chancellor's office, revelations which are sufficient to give some picture of the Wardrobe as the personal chancery of the king ; its activities as a financial office are far more fully revealed in its many surviving accounts, which were preserved in the

---

[1] On the subject of diplomatic organization generally in this period, *v.* G. P. Cuttino, *English Diplomatic Administration*, 1259–1339, (1940). 'Chancery', observes Dr. Cuttino (p. 139), ' ceased to do more than to issue the formalized foreign correspondence, having abdicated many of its secretarial functions to the wardrobe. . . . The wardrobe came out as the department most flexible and satisfactory for diplomatic affairs, being both a mobile exchequer and a secretariat. When the privy seal left the wardrobe, it took with it the functions that the wardrobe had built up or acquired in foreign affairs, and the methods and experience of the *Custos* ; these it combined and shared with the signet '. The emergence of the office of *custos processum*, specially charged with the care of diplomatic business and archives, during the years 1306–1339, is noteworthy. Further developments in the use of the privy and other seals in diplomatic affairs are brought out in E. Perroy, *The Diplomatic Correspondence of Richard II* (Camden Soc., 3rd ser. XLVIII (1933)).

[2] Tout, *op. cit.*, p. 76. Before the reign was over, it had become worth-while for a forger to counterfeit the privy seal.

[3] *Ibid.*, p. 73.

Exchequer, and in the records of the Exchequer itself. The enormous practical importance of the Wardrobe in the financial sphere is amply displayed in these sources.

The financial receipts of the Wardrobe steadily increased all through Edward I's reign,[1] and of these a very considerable proportion never passed through the Exchequer at all. The proportion of the receipts which did pass through the Exchequer varied a good deal, but did not materially increase as the years went by.[2] The other, or 'foreign' receipt was derived from a variety of sources, from direct collection of revenue, from loans negotiated directly with foreign bankers and merchants (often for large amounts), from gifts, and a host of sundry sources. The great strain of the military expenditure involved over many years encouraged frequent recourse to loans from Italian bankers, and also an extensive elaboration of credit devices. The constant need for anticipating revenue, and the application of prospective income to immediate requirements caused the Wardrobe to play a principal part in the development of credit facilities and negotiable instruments. An ingenious adaptation by the Exchequer of the tally system provided a ready means of 'assigning' or anticipating revenue, and thus of assisting the Wardrobe in its financial difficulties. Dated tallies were prepared in advance for creditors, who could exchange such a tally for cash from the sheriff, who could then produce the tally at his next account at the Exchequer and be duly credited with the amount recorded on the tally. This simple device became greatly extended within a few years, and payments by 'assignments' became as common as payments in cash.[3]

In the years of acute crisis, it was a pressing necessity for wardrobe officers in Scotland, Flanders, Gascony, Wales and England, to secure the earliest possible possession of revenue for financing military and naval expenditure. In the earlier years

---

[1] The total receipt during the twenty-seven years for which evidence survives was over one and a third million pounds, varying from £24,000 to £70,000 a year, the average being £49,000. *V.* Tout, *op. cit.*, p. 88. For the subject generally, *ib.*, pp. 85–130.

[2] *V.* the valuable paper by C. Johnson, 'The system of Account in the Wardrobe of Edward I' in *Trans. R.H.S.*, 4th ser. VI (1923), p. 58, correcting Tout, *op. cit.*, p. 89.

[3] Tout, *op. cit.*, and references therein contained, pp. 99–102.

wardrobe officers themselves often collected revenue, but for political reasons this method was later largely abandoned.[1] Other devices for short-circuiting the slow procedure of exchequer collection and distribution by writs of *liberate* were resorted to. The extension of the tally-credit system in effect brought the Wardrobe into direct contact with the collectors of revenue whilst preserving the traditional rights of the Exchequer; large block-grants in favour of the Wardrobe were made by the Exchequer, but transmitted in dated tallies, not in cash. ' The substantial result was that the work of collection was, through this fiction, transferred from the exchequer to the wardrobe, whose agents scoured the country, and urged on the tax-collectors the need of speedily ministering to the royal necessities. The sheriff, or other minister, did his best to cash the tallies presented to him, knowing that the exchequer at its next accounting session would acquit him of the sums thus advanced on the authority of the tallies which the wardrobe surrendered to him on receipt of his cash. The result was that the Exchequer ceased to have much importance as a ' treasury ', or hoard of money, and now had its main function as an office of accounts '.[2] A large proportion of the revenues now only formally passed through the Exchequer, and much of the cash that did so pass, found its way into the Wardrobe. 'A study of the issue and receipt rolls of the exchequer for this period between 1295 and 1307 ', says Tout, ' suggests that the exchequer gradually abdicated the administration and distribution of the national revenue in favour of the wardrobe '.[3]

Other devices were used in the ever-growing difficulty of making ends meet. Repeated wardrobe deficits led to more recourse to the money-lenders. Smaller creditors were staved off with ' wardrobe debentures '—acknowledgements of debt written on strips of parchment sealed with the personal seal of a wardrobe clerk, which, if we may judge from the hundreds of these still preserved in exchequer accounts, were eventually honoured ; these debentures were commonly used to pay mercenary soldiers, and recipients of them could raise money on them by pawning them to foreign bankers.[4]

[1] *V. infra*, p. 149.
[3] *Ibid.*, p. 96.

[2] Tout, *op. cit.*, p. 103.
[4] *Ibid.*, pp. 125–6.

Thus, ' as both the spending and collecting office, the wardrobe dominated the finances of the later years of Edward I's reign, as it never dominated them earlier or later '.[1] But, notwithstanding all its resourcefulness and ingenuity, the Wardrobe could not square accounts. The king was habitually overspending his income and postponing the day of settlement. The wardrobe officers manfully drew up an account each year ; the calculation of receipts was not difficult, but so few of the payments were actually made in full or in cash, that exact calculation of expenditure became well-nigh impossible. Few of the wardrobe accounts were disposed of during Edward I's reign ; many were not cleared until a generation after his death, some not until after the fall of Mortimer in 1330, and some only by means of the most perfunctory audit.

Between 27 and 35 Edward I, the debts of the Wardrobe, including those of the prince of Wales, amounted to £60,000, all of which remained unpaid at the end of the reign. The king owed money to all manner of creditors, his tradesmen, courtiers, clerks of the Wardrobe itself, magnates, ministers, mercenaries, and menials.[2] Confusion and chaos reigned over the royal finances.

' Thus tamely and ingloriously the great king's reign came to an end with broken-down finances. The very officers of a precise and orderly king dared no longer deal in a business-like fashion with his debts and expenses, and all the checks which prudence and jealousy suggested were disregarded. One result of this confusion was, however, favourable to the wardrobe, for it was now frankly uncontrolled by any other service of the State.'[3] The consequences of this state of affairs were to be more fully revealed in the reign of Edward II.

The Wardrobe of Edward I acted not only as a secretariat and a financial office ; it acted also as a war-office, an admiralty, and a ministry of munitions. ' Though no exclusive claims can be made for it, it is not too much to say that the wardrobe supplied the machinery through which it was made possible to

---

[1] *Ibid.*, p. 104.
[2] *Ibid.*, p. 125.
[3] *Ibid.*, p. 129. We may well doubt whether control of the Wardrobe by any other department was at any time more than formal and by way of audit.

administer the wars of Edward I.'[1] The long and arduous campaigns in Wales, Scotland, and on the Continent, involved an unprecedented strain on the administration, most of which was imposed upon the Wardrobe.

With the feudal levies the Wardrobe had little or nothing to do, but it had much to do with the mobilization of household forces, the hire of military tenants and other mercenaries, the issue of indentures, and something to do with the militia of the shires. ' With the bringing up of the household of the Crown to a war level, the wardrobe had almost everything to do.'[2] The expansion of the household cadres to a war-footing, the provision of pay and all needful supplies of arms, armour, horses, and munitions of all kinds, including clothing and stores, the financial operations necessary to achieve these purposes, were all tasks that fell to the Wardrobe, or its offshoots the Great Wardrobe, or the ' Wardrobe of Arms ', soon to become the ' King's Privy Wardrobe '.

' Thus in war-time the wardrobe was to a large extent both war-office and admiralty, as well as the body ruling the household and the state. It was even more specifically the army pay-office, the central ministry of recruiting and national service, the clothing and stores department, the ministry of munitions, the board of ordnance, and the controller of such engineering, mechanical, and technical services as then existed, the army service corps, and the ministry of information. Moreover, all that it did for the army, it also did for the navy, though for wars waged within Britain against enemies who had little or no sea power the navy was little more than a means of transport and supply. . . . It was in war that the wardrobe received and distributed the greatest proportion of the national revenue, that it became the body most nearly corresponding to the foreign office and the diplomatic service; that it was in a fashion a sort of " war cabinet ". It was then that the wardrobe most fully undertook the work that the treasury and Bank of England now perform for the issue of floating loans and the maintenance of the national credit . . . Edward ruled his realm as well as his household from his quarters

---

[1] Tout, *op. cit.*, p. 145, and generally, pp. 131–145.
[2] *Ibid.*, p. 134.

in the field. He could not have done all that he did, but for this free, elastic, and energetic instrument for his supreme will.'[1]

With such wide responsibilities as these, even if few or even perhaps none of them were exclusively the business of the Wardrobe, inevitably the department expanded greatly in war-time ; the overburdened clerks could not cope with all the work needing to be done ; they borrowed staff from other departments and helpers from outside government service (the proto-types of more modern ' war-time civil servants '). Chancery clerks were brought in ; wardrobe letters and writs were supplemented with streams of chancery writs and writs under the exchequer seal ; all existing administrative organs had their part to play and their share in mobilizing resources to meet the king's needs. But the unifying and connecting link was the Wardrobe.

As we have seen above,[2] the relations between the Wardrobe and the Chancery at this time were markedly harmonious and well co-ordinated. The greater prominence given by war conditions to the Wardrobe's elastic administrative capacity tends to push Chancery a little into the background, but developments therein require some attention, even if mainly because of their importance as foundations for subsequent fourteenth-century developments.

Edward I's confidence in Robert Burnell, chancellor 1274–92, was great enough to produce a suspension of the system of a fixed chancellor's fee and the rendering of accounts to and by the Hanaper. Burnell received, as chancellors did in the old days, the issues of the great seal, and maintained his clerks out of the proceeds. This revival of grandeur, however, did not continue after Burnell's death. His successor, John Langton, an simple clerk of Chancery, was accorded a fixed fee of £500, payable not from the Exchequer, but out of the issues of the seal and of the Wardrobe.

The restoration of the fixed fee, and the removal of the *hospicium* of the Chancery *extra curiam* inevitably promoted the separation of the Chancery from the Household, to which other circumstances were tending. The process is exemplified by a marked increase in the use of the privy seal to warrant chancery

---

[1] *Ibid.*, p. 143. [2] *V. supra*, p. 140.

L

action. The use of the privy seal for this purpose seems to have been uncommon before Burnell's death, but became frequent after Langton's appointment,[1] and this circumstance argues a greater degree of separation of Chancery from the court.

The ever-increasing demand for judicial writs, the constant stream of petitions for grace and favour, the growing mass of records and rolls, and the general convenience of having a fixed headquarters for at least part of its business, all tended to encourage the location of a chancery office at Westminster. The chancellor and the great seal, however, frequently itinerated with the king, not only for administrative convenience, but also, no doubt, in response to the current opinion that Chancery and King's Bench ought to follow the king, a view imposed on Edward I by the barons in the *Articuli super Cartas* of 1300. In 1306, however, during his last expedition to Scotland, Edward expressly ordered Chancery and Exchequer to remain at Westminster.

No finally decisive step seems to have been taken as yet in separating Chancery and Household, and further developments of this kind belong to the next two reigns. Such a step would no doubt, as Professor Wilkinson suggests,[2] mean some decrease in the practical importance of the Chancery as a secretarial office and an increase in its importance as an administrative office— even though perhaps no sharp distinction can be drawn between the two functions. The administrative as distinct from the secretarial duties of Chancery were partly due to the increasing complexity of administration rather than to the physical separation from the Household. Even so, the principal example of such administrative functions is the issue of original writs, and the issue of these writs *de cursu* was limited and defined in Edward I's reign, and became largely a matter of routine. The growth of demand for them no doubt encouraged the fixation of a place for the handling of this class of business. But it is perhaps an exaggeration to say that ' with the reign of Edward I a new period in the history of the chancery may be said definitely to begin '.[3] Doubtless the practice of noting on chancery records the source of warranty was an important step, but as yet this

---

[1] Tout, *op. cit.*, p. 78.
[2] *Chancery under Edward III*, p. 9.   [3] *Ibid.*

was not uniform nor consistent, and can hardly be said to have established 'a system of controls'.[1] Substantial chancery development belongs to a later generation.[2]

We have seen above[3] how during many years of Edward I's reign, the Wardrobe loomed larger than the Exchequer in the mobilization of the financial resources of the realm. But the Exchequer itself was by no means without its history in this period. Its inheritance at the accession and in the early years of the reign was not a happy one. The troublous years of Henry III had left it a heavy burden of debt and confusion in financial business, which required strenuous efforts by the exchequer officials for their remedy. The added strain, within a few years, of Edward I's war-finance compelled some changes in exchequer procedure which conditioned the department's activities for generations thereafter.

The last years of Henry III's reign showed some recovery at the Exchequer after the difficult years of the civil wars. ' Both at the receipt and at the exchequer board,' says Miss Mills,[4] ' the sheriffs were showing great reluctance to perform their duties between 1258 and 1272. These were critical years at the exchequer, years during which the whole financial machinery appears to have been on the verge of collapse. This collapse actually took place during the period 1263–68. The subsequent recovery was a difficult process, only rendered possible by the energetic reforms undertaken by the barons of the exchequer in the next seventeen years. Even in spite of their efforts, the customary revenue of the Crown never entirely recovered from the blow which it received at this date.'

The decline in the receipt during the troubled years is not explicable by any marked increase in local assignments, although between 1258 and 1261 some payments were certainly being made direct to the Wardrobe. Some of the debts contracted in this period were not finally cleared until some years after the

---

[1] *Ibid.*   [2] *V. infra*, p. 208.
[3] *V. supra*, p. 141.
[4] In 'Adventus Vicecomitum, 1258–72 ' in *E.H.R.* XXXVI (1921), p. 493. Professor Treharne in *Baronial Plan of Reform*, pp. 370 ff., gives some reason for supposing that Miss Mills's picture of the financial plight of the trouble years is perhaps over-coloured.

accession of Edward II. Recovery was by no means complete by 7 Edward I, in which year receipt was still below the average for the years 1253–57, and the Pipe Rolls were still heavily burdened with desperate debts.

Reforms in the early years of Edward I were aimed at relieving the congestion on the Pipe Rolls and the consequential delays in routine. The problem was to keep track of debts without becoming overwhelmed by them. The Pipe Roll was becoming like a roll of Crown debtors instead of accountants. Earlier attempts at reforming this state of affairs bore fruit in 7 Edward I, when a large number of desperate debts were transferred to a separate roll (the *rotulus pullorum*).[1] Later, in 12 Edward I, further revisions of the accounting system were made, and formed the substance of the so-called Statute of Rhuddlan.[2] A *Rotulus de Corporibus Comitatuum* was now to be kept, on which were to be entered the old ferm of the different counties and subsequent gifts of land by the king, so that in future only the remnant of the ferm, for which the sheriffs actually accounted, was entered on the Pipe Rolls.[3] After the *Corpus Comitatus* were set down the desperate debts for each county, and when these lists became too full, a fresh roll (the exannual roll) was begun.

After 1273 there was a substantial improvement in sheriffs' attendances for profer at the exchequer board, and these soon became normal.[4] But from 1298 onwards, a heavy fall in cash payments manifested itself. Thus the total payments on profer were as high as £32,775 in the years 1293–1297, but fell to £7,235 in the following five-year period.[5] ' The inference,' says Miss Mills, ' must inevitably be drawn that either the sheriffs were again failing to collect, and pay in, the customary revenue, or

---

[1] Mills, *op. cit.*, p. 496. The *rotulus pullorum* was probably begun at the end of Henry III's reign.

[2] *Statutes of the Realm*, I, pp. 69–70. For a note of agenda for discussion by exchequer officials on the machinery required to give effect to this statute, *v.* Mills, ' Exchequer Agenda and an Estimate of Revenue, Easter, 1284 ' in *E.H.R.*, XL (1925), pp. 229–234.

[3] Mills, *op. cit.*, p. 496. For the best discussion of the financial organization of the counties at this time, *v.* Miss Mills's Introduction to the *Pipe Roll for 1295, Surrey Membrane* (Surrey Record Society, VII, 1924).

[4] Mills, 'Adventus Vicecomitum, 1272–1307 ' in *E.H.R.*, XXXVIII (1923), p. 336.

[5] *Ibid.*, p. 340.

that some fundamental change had been made in the method of payment '.[1]

The receipt rolls show that there was no breakdown in the collections of revenue, and sheriffs' attendances were very regular.[2]

The explanation of this heavy fall in cash receipts at the Exchequer is to be found in the evidence of the large allowances made to the sheriffs because of their local purchases and payments either to individuals or direct to the Wardrobe. Time, labour and money were saved by these arrangements, which together amounted to a drastic measure of decentralization in financial administration. The sheriffs remained responsible for the collection of much of the customary revenue, but became in effect also spending officers. The system had obvious advantages to a government which was hard-pressed to meet its war-time financial needs. Money became available for use as soon as it was collected ; the delays,[3] risks, and expense of transporting it to the Exchequer at Westminster were avoided. The arrangement ' brought in its train an important development in the relations between the Wardrobe and the local administration which in its turn had a close connection with the growth of the system of assignments. The date at which these developments took place (1298) leaves little doubt that they had a close connection with the growth of the wardrobe as a spending department, which was a direct result of the Scottish and Gascon wars at the end of the reign.'[4]

Thus it will be seen that although Edward I's Exchequer struggled and in the main succeeded in restoring the course of the Exchequer which had been gravely undermined by the chaos of the civil wars of his father's reign, and in the process reformed and in some respects simplified its accounting methods, in the later years of the reign it was forced to adjust itself to the exigencies of war-time finance and to acquiesce in measures of decentralization to meet the demands of the Wardrobe. This materially

---

[1] *Ibid.*, p. 341.

[2] *Ibid.*, pp. 342–3.

[3] For six-and-a-half years, from May, 1298 to Christmas, 1304–5, the Exchequer was located at York, and was again to migrate there twice under Edward II, twice under Edward III, and once under Richard II. *V.* D. M. Broome, ' Exchequer Migrations to York in the 13th and 14th Centuries ' in *Essays to Tout*, pp. 291–300.

[4] *Ibid.*, p. 351.

reduced the funds in the Exchequer's custody, and consequently circumscribed its importance as the custodian of the royal finances.[1]

The coherence and co-ordination of Edward I's administrative system were maintained to the end of his reign. The driving force of the masterful and energetic king was sufficient to impel the administration along the lines set out for it, to cause it to serve his imperious will, and to achieve many of his objectives. With so dominating a personality as the supreme executive, there was no possibility of disharmony or friction between the several parts of the administration. No distinction was as yet drawn between household and other officials; all were equally the king's *ministri*; all equally ministered to the king's will; Council, Wardrobe, Chancery, and Exchequer each played their part; their functions overlapped in many respects, and were not logically differentiated, but without perceptible friction arising among them. For each had a sphere of activity for which it was best attuned, and each in the long run had one and the same master—the king himself.

The opposition[2] that came to Edward I's government from outside the administration, from baronial opponents, in the late years of the reign, was singularly little directed towards the administrative system as such, and what opposition of this kind arose met with no success.

Edward's government was in a very strong position to defend itself against political attack. The chief officers, clerical and lay, of the Crown, household officers or others, took their places in the enlarged council, the parliament. A large part of the discussion and initiative in all parliaments at this time lay with them, and only a combination of magnates could withstand their lead and influence. Edward I never abandoned the view that he could take counsel from whomsoever he wished, and that therefore the choice of ' sworn councillors' was entirely his own. The baronial view that the earls and barons and prelates were the king's ' natural counsellors ', and that their policies carried more weight than those of curialists, had its influence upon

---

[1] Cf. Tout, *Place of Edward II in English History*. 2nd ed. (1936), pp. 40, 48.
[2] V. Tout, *Chapters*, II, pp. 146–156.

Edward's choice from time to time, but never in his reign dominated the political arena, nor provoked any modification of the
administrative system.

The failure of the great king's military enterprises in the
last years of his reign, the heavy burden of his financial demands,
and the ruthless pressure of his administrative agents, produced
a more virulent magnate opposition which wrested some reluctant
concessions from him. But the confirmation of the Charters, of
1297, except in the scope of its fiscal discretion left the executive
where it had been before, and if anything more firmly wedded to
curialist methods. The king relied more than ever on the devices
of the Wardrobe and its clerks, and on a primarily bureaucratic
council.

It is to these years after 1297 that belong perhaps the beginnings of an opposition consciously directed towards certain
features of the administration, with specific reference to some
wardrobe activities. There was not as yet any theory of administrative policy behind this opposition ; it is very doubtful whether
even this opposition to Edward I's government drew any distinction between household and other officials, or regarded
administration by the one as ' more constitutional ' than by the
other ; very doubtful, too, whether Tout was justified in saying
of this period that ' routine which in an earlier age had been
worked out to give effect to the will of an autocrat, was already
beginning to be regarded as a safeguard against the personal
caprice of king and courtiers '.[1] Tout was doubtless right in
believing that the bureaucratic routine of Chancery and Exchequer was to find favour among opponents of the monarchy
as a means of checking and limiting royal arbitrariness in administration, so that procedure in these departments came to be
regarded as ' more constitutional ' than other procedures, and
so that the heads of these departments came to look more like
' ministers of State ' and less like the purely royal servants that
they had been in origin and remained in legal theory. But ideas
of this kind, though they may have had their faint beginnings in
Edward I's time, were not translated into any practical effect
until later generations.

[1] *Ibid.*, p. 153.

Complaints made in Edward I's time against purveyance by wardrobe officers were complaints against purveyance rather than against the Wardrobe, and the lengthy provisions against purveyance in the *Articuli super Cartas* of 1300 were aimed at securing proper authorization for purveyance, whether under great or small seal, and in no wise modified the Wardrobe's position in regard to this always unpopular prerogative right. As Tout says,[1] the desire of the barons at this time to place some restrictions upon the use of the small or privy seal is more significant. But it was the use of the privy seal to interfere with the course of the common law, not its use in the general administration that attracted the hostility of the opposition. The baronial objection seems to have been met for the time being by the sixth clause of the *Articuli*, which decreed ' under the small seal let no writ issue henceforth which touches the common law '.[2] Even if the *Articuli* had been actually carried out, which they were not, it can hardly be said that this resolution would have made much material difference to the administrative system, except perhaps to slow down the wheels of the common law machinery in some instances. The important point is, as Tout remarked, that ' the *Articuli* recognised the legitimacy of the privy seal within its own sphere.'[3]

The explanation given by Tout for the other relevant provision of the *Articuli*, that the Chancery and justices of his bench should follow the king, is one hardly justified by the evidence, nor wholly consistent with Tout's general view of the objectives of the baronial opposition. His explanation that this provision set up ' the chancellor and his clerks as a continual check upon the clerks of the household,[4] does not square with the explanation given in the clause itself, which is to the effect that the king should have with him always *ascuns sages de la lei* who know what is needful to dispose of the business coming to the court.[5] This is not at all the same thing as placing a check upon the clerks of the household ; nor can this provision as

---

[1] *Ibid.*, pp. 153–4.
[2] *Stat. R.I.*, p. 139; Bémont, *Chartes des Libertés Anglaises* (1892), p. 104 ; Tout, *loc. cit.*
[3] *Op. cit.*, p. 154.
[4] *Ibid.*   [5] Cited, *ibid.*, p. 75.

interpreted by Tout be readily squared with his view that baronial policy was to weaken, not strengthen the curialist entourage of the king. For the continual presence of the chancellor and justices of the bench could hardly have weakened the king's position. But it was inconvenient to have them there as fixtures, and in 1306 the king, during his last expedition to Scotland, ordered them to remain at Westminster; later the chancellor and some of his clerks followed the king north as convenience determined. The baronial sense of what was administratively practicable and desirable was seldom very strong, and the magnates always underestimated the immense resilience and strength of the royal executive.

CHAPTER V

POLITICAL REPERCUSSIONS AND ADMINISTRATIVE REFORMS IN THE REIGN OF EDWARD II

§. 1. The reign of Edward II has attracted a great deal of attention from the administrative as well as the constitutional standpoint, and possibly more has been written on the administrative history of this comparatively short period of twenty years than about any other reign. Certainly we have a more detailed and comprehensive analysis of the administrative system of this reign than for any other;[1] the period has occupied a large place in the writings of the greatest administrative historian;[2] aspects of the reign have received consideration by several highly competent scholars.[3]

But it can hardly be said that any substantial measure of agreement has been reached as yet upon the broad interpretation to be put upon the very large mass of information that has been made available for this reign, nor even upon the fundamental place of the period in the course of administrative history. Views of the reign vary all the way from a belief that it witnessed a baronial movement which was ' aimed to break down the system of government which has been called the household or personal system ',[4] down to a denial that it saw any such attempt.[5] The four principal investigators of the period, Mr. J. Conway Davies, the late Professor Tout, Professor Wilkinson, and the late Dr. Lapsley, adopt views that can scarcely be deemed compatible with each other, and where experts are disagreed, it is difficult for amateurs to formulate conclusions.

Nevertheless, some attempt to reach conclusions, even if only tentative, cannot be avoided. Enough evidence has been collected

---

[1] J. Conway Davies, *The Baronial Opposition to Edward II* (1918).
[2] Tout, *The Place of Edward II in English History*, 2nd revised ed. 1936 ; *Chapters*, II (1920), reprinted with corrections 1937, pp. 165–360.
[3] B. Wilkinson, *Studies in the Constitutional History of the Thirteenth and Fourteenth Centuries* (1937), c. ix, The Ordinances of 1311 ; G. T. Lapsley, *Crown, Community and Parliament in the later Middle Ages* (1951).
[4] Davies, *op. cit.*, p. 350.
[5] Wilkinson, *op. cit.*, pp. 227–246.

to make clear that the reign of Edward II was something of a watershed in administrative history; what happened in these twenty years looks very much like the culmination of forces and tendencies that had been at work in the preceding century, and also went far to determine the nature of the administrative system for most of the rest of the mediaeval period. There was not, it seems, to be another period of comparable importance in this sphere until the mediaeval administrative system began to undergo transformation in the Tudor age. Whether or not the Lords Ordainers and their successors launched an all-out attack upon the 'household' system; whatever the effects of their Ordinances upon that system, large or small, permanent or impermanent, it seems certain that the administrative reforms set on foot in the later years of the reign went far to establish the basic administrative system as it was largely to subsist for many generations thereafter. Of course, there were to be important changes in some respects during the succeeding years of the fourteenth and fifteenth centuries, but we should probably not be far wrong if we were to say that the last great formative period before the Tudors in the administrative sphere ended with Edward II's reign—except perhaps in one important respect, namely in the development of the executive council. As we shall see later, there were to be developments in the later fourteenth and fifteenth centuries in the position of the Council, which by making the executive less personal to the king himself, were to modify considerably the fundamental nature of the government.[1]

It is therefore important for our purpose to try to obtain a clear picture of the administrative system of Edward II before the advent of the Lords Ordainers, to estimate the effect, if any, of their activities upon the administration, and to appraise the administrative reforms of the later years of the reign. Thereafter, it will probably not be practicable, in the present state of knowledge, to obtain an equally comprehensive and coherent picture of the administrative system as a whole at any later mediaeval period—scarcely indeed of any modern period except the very recent. All that we are likely to be able to attempt here is to point to apparent changes of importance in the system as it was

[1] *V. infra*, pp. 222 ff.

at the end of Edward II's reign,[1] and to examine the growth of the administrative council, and so link up with the Tudor period, which in many ways marked a new era in the administrative sphere.

'The system of government which prevailed in England during the middle ages', says Mr. Davies, 'may fairly be described as personal. The king with his court was not merely the centre of the government; he was the government.'[2]

If for the moment we do not press this assertion beyond the early fourteenth century, and bear in mind that much work of government had come to be disposed of by bureaucratic methods and at official levels, in which the king himself did not normally interfere, we may rightly take this as the starting-point in any analysis of the administrative system of Edward II. All executive power is vested in the king; all executive power is exercised by him or by his delegates and agents; usage and convenience have determined that certain kinds of administrative action are better undertaken in or by one or other of the organizations that have come into existence, in the Chamber, Wardrobe, Chancery, or Exchequer, or elsewhere. This being so, we may cordially agree with Mr. Davies when he says that 'it must not be thought that the king saw or drew any distinction between his household and the administration. In practice there was none; in theory there was none'. We may well wish that mediaevalists had held firmly to this point, which seems to be unassailable, and the neglect of which has led to much confusion in the interpretation of administrative, and indeed, also of constitutional history.

We need perhaps to go further and to remind ourselves that conceptions and phrases such as 'household government', 'household officers', 'ministers of state', and the like are, in regard to the mediaeval period, only historians' conceptions and phrases. No mediaeval observers used such terms, nor drew distinctions between household officers and 'ministers of state'. They could scarcely do so, for although some officers might be *intra curiam* and others *extra curiam*, all were equally *ministri regis*. True, the fact that some were *extra curiam* and some not, meant

---

[1] The system of the early years of Edward III was essentially in most respects that inherited from Edward II, and much of what appears in Willard and Morris, *The English Government at Work*, 1327–37 (on which *v. infra* p. 189 n. 3) is applicable to the later years of Edward II's reign.   [2] *Op. cit.*, p. 61.

that some *ministri* were more exposed to influences other than purely royal influences than others were, but this difference did not amount to a difference in kind. We may, therefore, be sure that contemporaries never conceived of the king's government as being 'household government' at all.[1] There seems to be no evidence whatever that they did ; the *hospicium regis* was simply and literally the king's household, and reforms in the Household meant primarily to those who sought them, curtailment of costs and waste, and restrictions on purveyance and prisage, not reform of the system of government. No one supposed that the king could carry on the government of the realm without using his Household, any more than any magnate could manage his domains without recourse to his *familia*.

When the authors of the Provisions of Oxford made a note ' a remembrer fet del hostel le rei et la regine amender ', we may be sure that they were thinking of domestic retrenchment rather than the reform of ' household government '. *Le Ordenement del hostel le rei* of 1279 was wholly concerned with the wages and supervision of the domestic officers and reveals no consciousness of a ' household system of government '. The *Articuli super cartas* of 1300 had nothing to say about the Household as such. The Lords Ordainers of 1311 were to ordain ' the estate of our household and of our realm ', but the Ordinances of 1311 scarcely mention the Household as such, and the Household Ordinance of 1318 follows the lines of that of 1279.

It is thus reasonable to conclude that no one in the early fourteenth century (or later indeed) conceived of the system of government under which they lived as being a system of ' household government '. What they knew and well understood was that government was the king's government, and that in carrying on his government, the king used agents, all of whom (at the centre) had originally been primarily domestic officers of his Household, some of whom were still essentially in that position, others of whom were not any longer primarily members of his Household and who therefore did not have any domestic duties, but who were nonetheless the king's *ministri* ; all of whom were agents of the royal executive power.

[1] Professor Wilkinson has some highly suggestive remarks in this connection, *loc.cit.*

If we will hold fast to these points, we can safely agree that the government of the early fourteenth century was essentially personal government by the king, and that this government was carried on partly through channels and agents that had no existence except as parts of the Household, and partly through channels and agents that did have an existence apart from the Household. We may be very sure that the king saw no difference in principle between these various instruments, and we may doubt very much whether any one else at the time saw any difference of principle either.

So long as government remained primarily personal government by the sovereign, in fact as well as in theory, inevitably household officials played their part among the *ministri* of the Crown, but in the long run, when government became less purely personal in fact, whatever the theory, these domestic officers eventually were either dropped from government or assumed a character as ' officers of state '.[1]

Granted that the executive was the king's executive and leaving aside as far as possible questions that more properly come under the heading of legislative, judicial, or consultative activity, let us try to picture the ways and means of exercising that executive power which were available to and utilized by the Crown in the early years of Edward II's reign.

The king's principal instruments for executive purposes at the centre were his Council, the Chamber (sooner or later with the secret seal), the Wardrobe with the privy seal, the Chancery with the great seal, and the Exchequer with the exchequer seal. Broadly speaking, everything that is done by the king's command will be done either because of his oral command or because of the expression of his will or favour through one or more of these instruments, or because of action taken by one or more of these instruments in the king's name.

' The king's position in the administrative machinery is fundamental and concentric.'[2] Inevitably the extent to which the king's oral command set the machinery in motion is very

---

[1] It should be remembered that officers of the king's Household were normally included in Cabinets until the nineteenth century, and that one or two posts in the Household are still political appointments and change hands with the ministry.

[2] Davies, *op. cit.*, p. 177.

difficult to estimate. In theory we can assume that there was no limit to the potency of his personal instructions ; no officer at this time could well refuse to give effect to the royal command expressly conveyed by the king himself or by his personal messenger. Naturally oral instructions figured much more largely in the relations between the king and his household departments of Chamber and Wardrobe than between him and Chancery or Exchequer ; indeed oral commands in great numbers must have initiated the bulk of the writs under privy seal that emanated from the Wardrobe, and later in the reign under secret seal emanating from the Chamber, and which issued to Chancery or Exchequer or elsewhere for further action and implementation. The comparative separation between Household and Chancery, and the pretty well complete separation between the former and the Exchequer necessitated the use, in most matters, of written instructions to move these latter departments to action, but the conveyance to them of oral instructions had by no means disappeared. Chancellors might be given oral orders by the king himself, or verbal orders might be conveyed by messengers to chancellor or Chancery ; on occasions writs might be sealed with the great seal in the king's presence or in the presence of messengers specially instructed for the purpose. Many writs on the chancery rolls were noted as being warranted ' by the king himself '. Oral orders direct to the Exchequer to make payments or grants under its seal were also frequently made.[1] It may be that sometimes written ' cover ' under privy seal for these oral instructions was sought, but we cannot doubt that ' the potency of the verbal order was as great in the routine of administration and in emergency measures as in the issue of writs and the payment of money '.[2]

Whenever the use of oral instructions was for any reason inexpedient or impracticable, the privy seal in the custody of the Wardrobe was available to authenticate a written order to any part of the administration, and later, when the privy seal became less personal to the king, the secret seal was to meet the same purpose. The great bulk of the writs of privy seal that issued to move Chancery or Exchequer or other administrative

[1] *Ibid.*, pp. 125–9, 166–9.   [2] *Ibid.*, p. 169.

agencies, central or local, must have been initiated by the king himself or by officers of his Household who were near the king, and who knew his wishes or took responsibility for initiating action. Included among such writs were not only warrants for the great seal, for Exchequer, the justices, local officials, but all the other missives and personal and diplomatic correspondence, except perhaps purely ' departmental ' writs issued by the wardrobe or other household officers on their own responsibility or in response to requests for privy seal letters from other departments.[1] For the king to exert his will fully in the administration, a personal seal was a necessity ; hence as the privy seal became more formalized, the secret seal began to take its place for this purpose, and later still (after Edward II's time), the signet. But for the time being, the privy seal in the custody of the Wardrobe fulfilled the king's needs in this respect, and we must consider both in more detail shortly.

Before, however, we turn to the administrative organs that were integral parts of the Household, we must pause to examine a governmental instrument that was very close to the king and might act with or for him, but which was not itself part of the Household nor co-terminous with it—namely, the king's Council.

The Council, says Mr. Davies, ' had no recognised head, no organised system, no specialised clerks, no great rolls or records. Its ever changing composition, due to royal policy or caprice, was a factor which acted against the growth of such formalism and officialism as the great departments had. This also tended to make it more dependent upon the will of the king.'[2] Its personnel varied according to circumstances and the business to be dealt with. ' In one aspect,' Mr. Davies observes, ' the Council was a household body, in another governmental.'[3] These expressions are not perhaps wholly fortunate, for there was no real contrast between ' household ' and ' government '. The Council's *raison d'être* was obviously governmental, whatever the proportion of household officials in its composition at any time.

The Council, however, never consisted wholly of household or curial members, even though many of its meetings might

[1] *Ibid.*, pp. 133–156.
[2] *Ibid.*, p. 286.   [3] *Ibid.*, p. 249.

consist entirely of such ; some prelates and lay barons normally figured somewhere among the councillors. The contrast between the royal and the baronial elements was real and important. The king's desire to keep the Council predominantly royal and official in character was the principal provocation of baronial opposition from the days of Henry III onwards ; the chief objective of baronial opposition and politics in the fourteenth and fifteenth centuries was to increase and retain their share of personnel and influence in the king's continual Council, and this naturally became a matter of still greater significance as the Council acquired executive functions. The most important point in the administrative history of the fourteenth century—the point at which it impinged most potently on constitutional history—was reached when, in the later years of Edward III's reign, the baronial element began to predominate over the official element in the Council, not in consequence of some temporary revolutionary pressure upon a reluctant but coerced king, but with the king's acquiescence and because of political circumstances.[1]

In the years of which we are now speaking, however, it was the curial not the baronial element that mattered in the Council. The participants in its work were drawn from a group consisting of the chancellor, treasurer, the principal officers and clerks of the Household, the barons of the exchequer, the justices, sergeants-at-law, other royal officials, and a few men of prelatical or baronial status who were not otherwise in the king's service. Just who participated on any particular occasion seems to have been entirely a matter of expediency and convenience ; whether few or many participated made no practical difference ; counsel is counsel whether tendered by many or few councillors, and it was counsel not conciliar formalities that the king or the king's service required. The forms and guises which ' counsel ' may assume are capable of infinite variation, and this variegated presentation of counsel is the real feature in this sphere of government at this time, not varied forms or phases of the council.[2] Probably ' the Council ' *i.e.*, all persons who might act

---

[1] *V. infra*, pp. 222 ff.

[2] Mr. Davies's distinction between ' phases ' of the Council, the privy or secret council, the special council, and the administrative council (*ib.* p. 244) is too artificial to be acceptable.

M

as councillors, never met together all at once on any occasion ; only those whose counsel was desired or available for the matters in hand would be summoned on any given occasion.

Doubtless much counsel was tendered by such councillors as happened to be available, without recourse to formal or written summons at all. On more formal occasions, it might fall to the chancellor or treasurer, or possibly some other councillor, to get together councillors for deliberation, with or without express royal instructions, and meeting with or without the royal presence. Letters of privy seal might be sent out of the Wardrobe addressed to the chancellor or treasurer or some other person, official or otherwise, instructing the recipient to assemble councillors—sometimes but not often specifying whom ; letters of great seal might be used for implementing such instructions ; summonses by informal warrants or by verbal orders through Chancery, Exchequer, or individuals might be utilized. Extreme elasticity of method and form prevailed—which is what we should expect, if we bear in mind that it was sufficiency of counsel for the matter in hand that was wanted, not the Council as an institution. For most purposes, however, the chancellor would be the appropriate officer to summon the councillors ; in the administration as a whole he was the key-man ; his department (and the Exchequer also) stood more in need of counsel than any others ; to his department fell more than to others the task of implementing conciliar decisions. The Chancellor therefore in this period stood out as the principal councillor and as something like the *de facto* head of it ; much of his importance was derived from these circumstances, for much of the work of the department of which he was the official head was routine in character. But as a frequent and influential participant in conciliar action and decisions, the chancellor was in a strong position, and chiefly from that position the ultimate political importance and potentiality of the chancellor's office was to derive.

The functions of the councillors in this period were very miscellaneous, and were still primarily advisory in character. Its authority was wholly derived from the king, and the business it might deal with was as varied as the business falling to the king in his executive capacity. Doubtless much business might be disposed of without reference to the king personally, but difficult points, especially points touching the king's interests, would not be disposed of without consulting the king ; the king could of course interfere at any stage, and either accept or reject the council's advice as he thought fit. Many petitions were considered by councillors in a judicial capacity, or were relegated to some other part of the administration, particularly the chancellor himself ; the king sought the council's advice upon letters received, especially from abroad, and on the administration of Gascony, or Scotland. The king with the advice of the Council might make ordinances, or indeed obtain its advice upon any matter of State. Its relations with Wardrobe, Chancery, and Exchequer were very close, and it might meet to deliberate with special reference to the departmental problems of Chancery or Exchequer, or meet sometimes in or with the latter.[1]

Much has been made of the question whether the Council's activities in the early fourteenth century were advisory or executive in character. Tout was disposed to argue that the Council was not an executive body until the fifteenth century,[2] but his argument seems too much based upon the subsidiary question of whether the Council could use a seal—the privy seal—and so directly translate its advice into administrative action. We may well agree that as yet there was no close association of a seal with the Council, and that direct executive action by the Council was not as yet apparent. But this is a subsidiary question, not the main question. The main question is whether the Council (without the king's personal intervention) was or was not the source of administrative decisions which the executive departments would and did put into effect because they were council decisions. The answer to this question for this period is undoubtedly in the affirmative.

Instances occur of the Chancery's issuing writs under great seal warranted by the Council.[3] There is no reason to doubt that the chancellor himself, usually the leading official member of the Council, would and did give effect to council decisions—in

[1] Cf. C. Johnson, ' The Exchequer Chamber under Edward II ' in *E.H.R.*, XXI (1906), pp. 726–7.

[2] *Chapters*, II, pp. 146–155 ; cf. Baldwin, *The King's Council*, ch. iv.

[3] Davies, *op. cit.*, p. 126.

matters of limited importance for which the king's personal authority was not deemed necessary. The Council might make a decision or ordinance (often acting in accordance with some specific instruction from the king) which would be implemented by Chancery.[1] Many decisions of Council were translated into writs of great seal.[2] Numerous payments were made at the Exchequer by the grant, assent, agreement, ordinance, or assignment of the Council.[3] No instance appears to be known of the refusal to issue a writ under seal on the ground that the Council's authority for the matter was insufficient. It is true that most known instances of Council decisions given without the king's personal participation are of a somewhat minor character in this period, but it is as impossible to doubt that such decisions were taken and acted upon as it is to believe that the king himself could possibly participate personally in every piece, however small, of council business. If the king could not leave his own councillors to reach some administrative decisions, and rely upon the departments to implement them, his Council must indeed have been a poor aid and comfort in the business of government. Of course there are no more means of drawing hard and fast lines between what could and what could not be settled by Council without reference to the sovereign then, than there are now between what can be settled by bureaucrats, minister, or Cabinet to-day ; it all depended and depends upon who is prepared to be responsible for what. From this very lack of definition, indeed impossibility of definition, of the precise degree of responsibility, sprang the great potentiality and ultimate destiny of the king's Council, both in administration and eventually in politics. In time the Council was to assume or acquire a much higher degree of responsibility, to attain a greater share in administrative decision, and to exercise a direct executive authority—on the king's behalf or in the king's name.

Of the permanent organs of administration available to the king, those in the Household were naturally the closest to him and the most immediately responsive to his wishes ; of these the Chamber was always the most intimate and personal. As *Fleta*

---

[1] *Ibid.*, pp. 258 ff.
[2] *Ibid.*
[3] *Ibid.*, pp. 261 ff.

said, the Chamber was the most dignified of all the offices because of its intimate association with the king himself.[1] In Edward I's reign the Chamber's activities remained largely domestic in character, though its chamberlains might be used for administrative purposes, especially confidential business, by the king. The same is true of the early years of Edward II, but there is evidence of increased potentialities from his accession. Substantially increased sums of money were paid into the Chamber early in the reign : partly from loans, partly from lands forfeited to the Crown. A considerable additional ' privy purse ' was thus built up, and an additional seal, the secret seal, in its cutsody, became available, and the Chamber, before the reign was over, began to figure again among the administrative organizations, as we shall see later.[2] But in the earlier years of the reign, the Wardrobe with the privy seal was by far the most important administrative organ within the Household.

The great utility of the Wardrobe to the king in these years rested upon the fact that it provided machinery of very wide scope and adaptability whilst remaining close at hand and highly responsive to the king's personal initiative and wishes. The Wardrobe was not in any way opposed to or set off against the more formalized organizations of the Chancery and Exchequer ; all were equally part of the system, and which part was used for what, was a matter of convenience, expediency, or usage.

The Wardrobe was related to other administrative organs in many complex ways.[3] The great seal was often deposited there for one reason or another ; many documents and secret records were placed in its custody, no doubt mainly for convenience of reference as required. Its connection with the Exchequer remained close; it received from thence—at least nominally—much of its financial supply and rendered account to it. The *liberate* writs issued in favour of the Wardrobe averaged three a year (to substantial amounts) and were issued by ' bill of Wardrobe ', or bill or writ under privy seal. The devices of collection and pay-

---

[1] Tout, *op. cit.*, pp. 43-4.
[2] *V. infra* p. 184.
[3] Davies, *op. cit.*, p. 178, Cf. J. H. Johnston, ' The System of Account in the Wardrobe of Edward II in *Trans. R.H.S.*, 4th ser. XII (1929), pp. 75-104.

ment of wardrobe finances in vogue under Edward I continued in use. Many sources of ' foreign ' receipt remained available, and as Mr. Davies remarks, ' the king in securing the payment of these foreign receipts into his wardrobe did not do so without the knowledge of the exchequer. So complete was his control over that department that he could order them to grant land and order the receipts to be paid to the wardrobe.'[1] The Wardrobe might raise substantial loans which were repayable in the Exchequer. The issues of the great seal were paid by the Hanaper into the Wardrobe, into which the Chamber might transfer funds. The considerable financial resources of the Wardrobe gave to the king funds immediately accessible and applicable without delay to any purpose which he thought fit, for meeting expenses of the Household, for making gifts, for remunerating embassies and envoys, for hiring soldiers, and for meeting the contingent expenses arising out of abnormal circumstances, military operations, rebellions, and the like.[2]

The custody of the privy seal was still a function of the controller of the Wardrobe, and by means of writs of privy seal all parts of the administration could be activated or restrained. By means of it the king or officers of the Household could initiate almost any administrative action, either directly or through the channels of the Chancery or Exchequer. ' The issue of chancery warrants under the privy seal was a normal means of communicating the king's consent or desire for the issue of letters under the great seal.'[3] Writs authorizing payments, assignments, and the like, or forbidding such, were frequently issued to the Exchequer. As we have seen above,[4] in addition, missives, letters, diplomatic and personal correspondence under privy seal gave expression to the king's own wishes in a great variety of business. Inevitably the greater the degree of personal separation between the king and the Chancery, the greater the need for the use of a personal seal to convey the royal instructions, and as we shall see later, when for one reason or another the privy seal and its procedure became more formalized and less readily adaptable to the needs of the king himself, a more personal

[1] Davies *op. cit.*, pp. 184 ff.
[2] *Ibid.*, pp. 189 ff.
[3] *Ibid.*, p. 126.   [4] *V. supra*, p. 159.

substitute for it, the secret seal, was resorted to. How far this was the consequence of the policy of the Lords Ordainers and how far the result of inherent administrative necessities, is a matter we shall have to consider later.[1] For the present, it is sufficient to say that in the early years of Edward II, the privy seal was an instrument of prime efficacy to the executive, closely and immediately responsive to the king's will, whether activated by the king himself, or on the order of the Council, or departmentally by the Wardrobe.

Of the two great administrative departments, the Chancery in this period remained much closer to the Household, from which both had originally sprung, than the Exchequer. We have seen the intimate relations subsisting between the Wardrobe and the Chancery,[2] and something of the close connection between the centre of executive power and the latter, as revealed in the king's oral orders or in writs of privy seal. In general administration, the Chancery was the official mouthpiece of the king, and the ultimate or at least penultimate source of all formal administrative processes. The great bulk of administration in all its branches was still implemented with a chancery writ under great seal.[3] But Chancery was essentially the most formal—and perhaps we may say, the most formidable—of the administrative instruments available to the king's executive ; the degree of departmental independence to which it had attained was very limited, if indeed, it had attained to any real independence of function. ' The preeminent position which the chancery occupied among the administrative departments and its functions as the source of formal executive power to the other departments suggest an amount of final authority which it had not. Though there was a growing tendency towards independence on the part of the officials of chancery, the king had well maintained his position as the source of executive authority. The powers of chancery were still very limited. The great seal itself could be completely regulated by the king; and by the use of privy and secret seals, informal warrants and verbal orders the normal and formalised use of the great seal was dictated or checked.'[4]

[1] *V. infra*, p. 187. [2] *V. supra*, p. 165.
[3] Davies, *op. cit.*, p. 119. [4] *Ibid.*, p. 238.

It is safe to say that there was no activity of the Chancery which the king could not interfere with if he liked, even if some parts of its business had become matters of departmental routine —or even become ' common law ', such as the issue of writs *de cursu,* and were not interfered with. The growing practice of referring petitions to the chancellor opened up a judicial sphere in which some measure of discretion was inevitable, but even the chancellor's judicial decisions were subject to the king's approval or acquiescence.[1]

The fact is, as Mr. Davies points out, the chancellor had not developed into an independent official with control over the whole administration.[2] He was not in any sense the successor to the old justiciarship with viceregal authority. The development of his office had perhaps been hampered by its origins in the royal Household, and by the strength which the personal system of government had maintained even after some vital departments of administration had become separated from the Household.[3]

Certainly the chancellors themselves were in no position to feel themselves independent of the king. Many of them were promoted household officers, and not even their episcopal rewards were very likely to give them delusions as to the funda- mental nature of the king's government. ' The king could exert all-powerful influence on chancellor and department whenever he so desired.'[4] The king alone appointed the chancellor, and could deprive him of the custody of the great seal or dismiss him at any time. The king retained an over-riding authority with regard to the use of the great seal—the only instrument with which the chancellor's department could give effect to administrative action of any kind. Direct verbal orders, orders by messengers, writs of privy seal or later, secret seal, orders through the Council, the sealing of writs with the great seal in the king's presence or in the presence of special commissioners,[5] by these means the king could and did control the use of the great seal and so subordinate the chancellor.

Clearly, no chancellor was going to climb to high political

---

[1] *Ibid.,* p. 239.
[2] *Ibid.,* p. 241.   [3] *Ib.*
[4] *Ibid.,* p. 242.   [5] *Ibid.,* pp. 125–9.

eminence merely by virtue of being the head of such a department as the Chancery, much of the work of which was done on the direct instructions of the king's executive, and the bulk of the rest of which was routine. Not even the judicial activity, nor the eventual equitable jurisdiction of the chancellor would have given more than judicial status. The political importance, and eventual eminence, of the chancellors rather sprang from their position in the king's Council, wherein they could influence royal policy and affairs of State. We may well take it for granted that the baronial opposition to the monarchy would never have developed much interest in the chancellor's office, if he had been no more than the custodian of the great seal and the head of Chancery, important though these functions of course were in the administration. But the chancellor was a key-man in the king's Council, and to get a baronial nominee into this position was an objective worth struggling for.

The king's control over the Exchequer was no less complete than it was over the Chancery, and evidence of his frequent intervention in its business by direct instructions under privy seal is even more abundant. ' It was almost as important for the king to retain influence over the exchequer as it was that he should remain in absolute control of the chancery. The financial department was nearly as important as the formal executive department of the administration. There was little tendency to independence of action in the chancery ; but there appears still less in the exchequer : often, on what appear to be formal and routine matters, the exchequer would not proceed without consultation with or orders from the king.'[1]

Much business could be transacted through the administrative machinery of the Exchequer which had little or nothing to do with its financial or accounting functions, and there is no apparent reason why some of such business should have been done in or by the Exchequer instead of by Chancery ; overlapping between these departments was in some respects very considerable. Sometimes the exchequer seal was used when the great seal would seem to have been more appropriate ;[2] administrative ordinances might be made by the treasurer and barons of the exchequer ;[3] the

[1] *Ibid.*, p. 246.　　　　[2] *Ibid.*, p. 245.　　　　[3] *Ib.*

judicial activities of those barons were by no means confined to pleas arising out of its financial business, and this wider jurisdiction seems to have been encouraged by the king ;[1] petitions of various kinds were often referred to the Exchequer by the king himself.[2] Doubtless, as Mr. Davies remarks, ' the extension of the judicial business of the exchequer, while it tended to increase its administrative importance, also acted as an additional source of strength to the king, as it prevented the judicial courts obtaining a monopoly of justice.'[3]

The principal means whereby the king made his wishes known to the Exchequer was by writ of privy seal.[4] Such writs were both enrolled on the memoranda rolls of the king's and treasurer's remembrancers and filed. Letters and writs of privy seal were used as direct warrants to the treasurer for a great variety of purposes ; either to give instructions to act, or, in some instances, to order him not to act in a certain matter without the king's special command ;[5] commonly to warrant payments out of the Exchequer, or grants of offices or lands to be made under the exchequer seal.[6] Writs of privy seal similarly influenced the pleas side of exchequer work, whether by way of referring a plea, interfering with it, or stopping it.[7]

The Exchequer's function of procuring revenue might be stimulated or affected in some way by writ of privy seal. The Exchequer had to provide a considerable proportion of the Wardrobe's income, and if it slackened in this task, it might hear of it by writ of privy seal from the Wardrobe itself. Thus in March 1308, the chancellor was ordered to go each day to the Exchequer to arrange with the treasurer, chancellor, and barons of the exchequer, and others of the Council, how sufficient money could be provided for the expenses of the Household, and other matters.[8]

Thus, the Wardrobe, Chancery, and Exchequer were all equally administrative departments available for the use of the king's executive, whether the initiative was taken by the king himself, by his officials, or by the Council. 'The different ways in

---

[1] *Ibid.*, pp. 243-4.
[3] *Ibid.*, p. 245.
[5] *Ibid.*, p. 140.
[7] *Ibid.*, pp. 144-5.

[2] *Ibid.*, pp. 244-5.
[4] *Ibid.*, pp. 138.
[6] *Ibid.*, p. 143.
[8] *Ibid.*, p. 145.

which the king, notwithstanding the increased bulk and intricacy of business, could exercise almost complete control of the administration, were but varied forms of one central fact, that the executive was still entirely in the hands of the king and the household. The instruments of the executive, the privy seal, the secret seal, informal warrants and verbal orders, entered into every phase of the administration, and exerted their powerful influence.'[1] ' The king had retained in his own hand complete executive power. Besides the executive reserve of the king there were other sources of great strength to him in the administrative tendency of the departments to exercise competing and over-lapping jurisdiction, processes, and instruments.'[2]

It is not, however, to be imagined that there was any divergence between the household and other organs of administration. The administration remained essentially a unity ; household departments, Chancery, and Exchequer were each and all but parts of the king's administrative machinery ; all were equally under the king's actual or formal authority ; none could expect to move the other except by use of one or other of the king's seals ; if the Wardrobe seems to have had perhaps more initiative than the others, this is because it was still very close to the king himself, and writs issuing thence under privy seal might be presumed actually or vicariously to represent the king's wishes, and the expression of the king's wishes could not be ignored by any branch of his administration ; on the contrary the king's wishes were commands, and must be obeyed. Similarly the decisions of his councillors needed to be implemented, for it could not be supposed that they would decide anything contrary to the king's wishes.

The administration was the king's alone, and he could exert his authority over any and every part of it, if he wished, whether within the Household or outside of it. But it was quite another question whether such a king as Edward II could motivate his administration effectively or pursue policies acceptable to his greater subjects. This was a question answered in the negative by the Lords Ordainers and others, and the problem whether or not the opposition to Edward II sought to modify the royal

[1] *Ibid.*, p. 175.   [2] *Ibid.*, p. 247.

administrative system is one to which we must now address ourselves.

§ 2. We have seen above the confusion in the royal finance and the heavy load of debt left behind by Edward I, and may well believe that the consequential strains and stresses in the administration and in the relations between the government and the governed were a root cause of the friction arising between the monarchy and the baronage soon after Edward II's accession. The accession itself made little change in the administration, apart from the changes in personnel in the chief offices, in the Household and outside of it.[1] The biggest change of all was, of course, in the personality of the king himself. Edward II's apparent reluctance to apply himself regularly to business and his tendency to rely upon ' favourites ' to do his work for him, and his unaristocratic habits and interests,[2] all combined to foster and focus baronial opposition to an intensity unknown in the time of his father.

No doubt the dislike of the baronage for Peter Gaveston was more a symptom than a cause of the rising tide of opposition to the monarchy's government. In any case, Gaveston's two exiles can hardly be said to have made much difference to the actual conduct of the administration ; nor did the king's purchase of his return by conceding the Stamford Articles of 1309.[3] These were no more in substance than the *Articuli super Cartas*, and received formal royal responses varying in quality from article to article, were irrelevant to any major administrative question, and were not carried out in practice.

Even if the Stamford Articles had been implemented, very likely further opposition could not have been avoided. As it was, the continuance of Gaveston's activities and the absence of reforms brought opposition to a head early in 1310, and Edward II was obliged to agree to the appointment of a committee of prelates and barons to instigate reforms. Letters patent dated 16 March, 1310, were issued by the king ' of his own free will '

---

[1] Tout, *Chapters*, II, pp. 165–187, 192.
[2] Davies, *op. cit.*, ch. iii. Cf. H. Johnstone, *Edward of Carnarvon* (1947).
[3] *Rot. Parl.* I, pp. 443–5 ; cf. Tout, *op. cit.*, p. 194, *Place of Edward II*, p. 76.

to the prelates, earls, and barons and others to appoint persons with power until Michaelmas, 1311, ' de ordener lestat de nostre hostel et de nostre roiaume . . . solonc droit et reson et le serment que nous feismes a nostre corounement . . .'[1]

The 'Lords Ordainers' accordingly chosen issued seven interim Ordinances which were not confirmed by the king until early August, when they were embodied in the so-called 'new' Ordinances promulgated in the Parliament of that month, sealed with the great seal in October and sent to all the counties. Even so, ' instead of being the ordinances of the executive with the whole force of the executive machinery behind them, they were ordinances imposed upon an unwilling executive.'[2] By this time, the authority of the Ordainers under the letters patent of March, 1311, had expired, and was never renewed.

It may be said at once that these 'new' Ordinances of 1311,[3] had nothing explicitly to say about 'household government', and having regard to the considerations mentioned above, we should not, of course, expect them to have done so. Many of the Ordinances, although concerned to correct what were regarded as abuses in Edward II's government, have little or nothing to do with modifying the administrative system itself. No contrast between 'household officers' and 'officers of state' appears, and indeed the Household in an administrative sense is not mentioned at all. By far the most important article[4] is that which relates to the future appointment of the principal officers by the counsel and assent of the baronage in parliament ; the list of such officers lumps together the officials, whether of the Household or not, and clearly included those who played a considerable part in 'national' administration. They were the chancellor, the chief justices of each bench, the treasurer, chancellor, and chief baron of the exchequer, the steward of the household, the keeper and controller of the wardrobe, a clerk suitable to keep the privy seal, the two chief keepers of the forests, the two escheators, and the chief clerk of the common bench.

The intention in this article to secure baronial assent to the

[1] Cited Davies, *op. cit.*, p. 360.
[2] *Ibid.*, p. 368.
[3] *Stat. R.*, I, pp. 157–167 ; *Rot. Parl.*, I, pp. 281–6.
[4] Cl. 14.

appointment of the chief ministers is of course important as a constitutional precedent, but so far from attacking the Household as part of the administrative organization, it accepts the fact that certain household officers are key-men in the administration, and in no way different in kind from the officers who are outside the Household. It clearly recognized that if the baronage was to influence the executive, it must influence appointments not only to Chancery and Exchequer, but also to Wardrobe and privy seal.

Another Ordinance of significance but vague import laid down that ' evil ' counsellors were to be removed and others to be substituted ; similar action was to be taken with unsuitable servants (*menengs*) and officers of the Household.

Two other Ordinances referred to administrative procedure. Ordinance 32 repeated substantially what had been said in the *Articuli super Cartas* about the use of the privy seal in legal administration ; letters of privy seal are not to delay or disturb the law of the land or common right. Ordinance 8 reiterates the point made in the Provisions of Oxford that all the issues of the realm are to go to the Exchequer and not elsewhere.

Of these two Ordinances,[1] the first said nothing againt the use of the privy seal for general administrative purposes, and the inclusion of a clerk suitable to keep the privy seal among the officers to be appointed with assent seems to recognize that the keeper of the seal had important administrative duties. The second of the two Ordinances, although clearly seeking to magnify the importance of the Exchequer as the clearing-house of royal revenues, and to simplify and perhaps to check the financial system by centralizing collection in the one department, said nothing about the disbursement of the revenues when collected. There was no question but that the Exchequer must pay out money in accordance with the king's instructions, whether into the Chamber, Wardrobe, or elsewhere ; the Ordinance would therefore have had no chance of success if it had been intended to undermine the use of household departments for executive purposes. No other Ordinance is relevant to the issue under consideration.

[1] On these and cognate points see the arguments in Wilkinson, *Studies*, pp. 236–243.

It is thus very difficult to base on the Ordinances of 1311 any theory that the Lords Ordainers sought a fundamental revision of the existing structure of administration. It is indeed hard to see why Tout, in this connection, should have asserted that ' even the household departments were allowed their natural sphere, but they were strictly limited to household affairs and sternly warned off usurping the authority of the constituted offices of state '.[1] There appears to be nothing in the Ordinances to warrant such an assertion ; in any case there was not then any department that can be regarded as a ' constituted office of state ' in the sense of this context ; the very conception is incompatible with a preceding sentence in the same work, which states, truly enough, that ' the Ordainers, like Edward I, regarded the administrative machinery as a unity '. There is nothing whatever in the Ordinances of 1311 which suggests that the Ordainers were launching an attack on ' household government '. We have seen above that there is no reason to suppose that they even conceived of such a thing. They were concerned to procure a greater influence on the general direction of the government, and to reform specific abuses. Professor Wilkinson seems to be well justified in saying that ' the real aim of the reforming movement in 1309–11 was the establishment of certain measures of reform, which aimed at the removal of certain specific grievances, but which made no attack on the system of government as a whole.'[2] It is, as he goes on to say (a stronger assertion would be quite justified) ' on the whole probable that no radical change in the system of the king's administration was contemplated in the agreement for reform of 1311.'[3]

The baronial aim of ' reforming the estate of our household ' was deferred and eventually exemplified in the second set of Ordinances of 1311–12. These do not survive in any official text ; the king was under no obligation to accept them, since the Ordainers' commission had expired, and there is no evidence that they were in fact accepted or in any way implemented.[4] In any event, these so-called Ordinances, in so far as they included

---

[1] *Chapters*, II, p. 194.   [2] *Studies*, p. 227.
[3] *Ibid.*, p. 228.
[4] *Ibid.*, pp. 234 ff.   Cf. Tout, *op. cit.*, p. 198.

fresh points, did not attack 'household government' in any
sense ; they merely aimed at purging the Household, removing
specific officers and filling their places with other persons more
acceptable to the opposition. There would, of course, have been
little object in seeking such a purge unless it were assumed that
many of these officers would participate in the work of government ; the only other interest which the baronial opposition had
in the affairs of the Household was to try to keep down its cost.

With the struggles of Edward II to free himself from the
trammels of the Ordainers and the hostility of Thomas of Lancaster we are not here concerned. The complications arising from
the murder of Gaveston, the battle of Bannockburn, the subsequent fortunes of Lancaster, and the events at the Parliament
of Lincoln in 1316, are matters outside our scope, except in so far
as they temporarily weakened the king's political position and
modified the balance of political forces at work. The rise of the
' middle party ' headed by Aymer of Valence, earl of Pembroke,
and joined or supported by a number of influential magnates and
also by some of the royal officials[1] tended to stabilize the situation,
and made possible the Treaty of Leake of August, 1318, and soon
also the initiation of real reforms by the new personalities in the
government, acting under and with, not in opposition to, the
king's authority.

The Parliament of York in 1318 ratified the Ordinances of
1311—but only those 'contained under the great seal '—the first
but not the second set.[2] The question of the reform of the Household therefore had to be taken up again, and this was now done
by a commission, some of whom were nominated by the king,
and others by the magnates, and among them were included the
principal officers of the Household itself—the steward, chamberlain, keeper, and controller of the wardrobe. A reform of the
Household drafted in this way was not likely to be radical in any
sense, and the resulting Household Ordinance of York of 1318
did no more than regulate the domestic arrangements, prescribe
the wages and perquisites of the numerous officers, and so on,

---

[1] *V.* Tout, *op. cit.*, pp. 204 ff ; *Place of Edward II*, pp. 106 ff ; Davies, *op. cit.*,
pp. 425 ff.
[2] Wilkinson, *op. cit.*, p. 244.

after the style of the previous Household Ordinance of 1279.[1]
As Tout says, ' the ordinance of York was no drastic attempt to
embody a new policy of household administration. . . . It was
in substance little more than a detailed codification of the sounder
customs of the previous generation with such additions and
improvements as the working of the machine through many
troublous years had suggested. . . .'[2]

It is indeed wholly concerned with the definition of the
duties of the household officers, their remuneration, and the
system of household finance (but not its income). It is essentially
a regulation of the domestic organization of the king, and has
nothing to say about the Household as part of the administration
of the realm. It seeks to make the king's Household more
efficient, economical, and better-ordered, but is not a reform of
the ' household system of government.'

The principal revelation of interest for our subject in this
Ordinance is that the keepership of the privy seal is no longer
assumed to be identical with the controllership of the wardrobe.
The clerk or keeper of the privy seal has provision made for him
equal in value to that of the controller and has under him clerks
' who write for the privy seal '. But the wages of these subordin-
ates are fixed by the steward and the keeper of the wardrobe,
and at best the ' office of privy seal ' was by now a sub-depart-
ment of the Household, and its functions remain the same as
before.

Part of the Treaty of Leake had provided for the establishment of a standing Council, with the assent of which Edward II
was to carry on the government in such matters as could right-
fully be done without the co-operation of Parliament.[3] From the
point of view of administration, we may well believe that this
was the most important of the arrangements ratified at the
Parliament of York in 1318. It was an expedient reviving the
shades of 1258, but now promoted by the ' middle party ' and
brought into operation and carried on at least with the acquiescence of the king, and partly as a means of side-tracking the

---

[1] The text is printed in Tout, *Place of Edward II*, App. I; for comment *v. Chapters*,
II, pp. 245 ff.
[2] *Ibid.*, p. 246.
[3] Tout, *Place of Edward II*, p. 110 ; *Chapters*, II, p. 205 ; Davies, *op. cit.*, p. 448.

N

unwelcome attentions of Thomas of Lancaster, whose influence
on the Council was to be very slight. The other main work of
this Parliament, the review of the king's officers, high and low,
resulted in the confirmation in office of most of them, and such
changes of personnel as were made did not affect the structure of
the administration.[1]

We may well agree that the scheme ratified in the York
Parliament of 1318 was 'the most workable which had yet
been devised to control the king ',[2] but it is essential to remember
that it ' depended entirely upon the good will of the king.'[3]
The dominance in administration of Pembroke, the Despensers,
and Baldock (who at one time combined the keepership of the
privy seal with the controllership of the Wardrobe, notwithstanding the implications of the Household Ordinance of 1318)[4]
could not have lasted as it did unless the king himself had
acquiesced. The great influence in the conduct of the administration of Pembroke or the younger Despenser did not depend on
any office that they held (even though the latter's tenure of the
chamberlainship had its importance and consequences),[5] but
upon the king's willingness to allow them to direct much of the
administration on his behalf.[6]

On the whole, the most surprising thing about the Ordinances
of 1311–18 is the slight degree to which they modified the existing
administrative system ; they did not materially alter the balance
between the Household and other organs of administration. On
the contrary, the ' middle party ' succeeded for a time mainly
because, with the king's goodwill, they carried with them the
key officials in the Household and outside of it, and were able,
with the standing Council, to control the administration as a
whole.[7] They were thus in a position to promote some reforms
from within the administration. These reforms were to be
important and in some ways largely permanent, but the system
as a whole still remained substantially the same after their period
of personal dominance.

[1] Davies, *op. cit.*, p. 453.
[2] *Ibid.*, p. 464.
[3] *Ibid.*, p. 465.
[4] Tout, *Place of Edward II*, p. 122.
[5] *V. infra*, p. 186.
[6] *V.* Davies, *op. cit.*, ch. iii.
[7] *Ibid.*, pp. 492 ff.

This being so, it is not surprising that after the alliance of Lancaster and the marcher lords, the fall of the Despensers, and the battle of Boroughbridge, when the time came for the revocation of the Ordinances in the Parliament at York in 1322, the king and the court party were not concerned with administrative questions, but rather with what we should call matters of constitutional principle. Then, however, they took for granted the existing administrative system, and in effect confirmed it as it was. The Ordinances were revoked, though ' good points ' were to be put in a statute. The famous Statute of York of 1322 thus has here only a very indirect interest, and into the modern controversies as to its interpretation we need not enter.

The Lords Ordainers and their immediate successors, we must conclude, failed to make any substantial permanent change in the structure of the government, and we may well doubt whether they had even intended to make any. No coercion could alter the fundamental fact that the executive power was vested in the king alone ; in the long run the royal executive power, when and if exerted, could and did triumph over attempts to control its exercise. For administrative reforms to be substantial and lasting, they needed the full force of the king's authority behind them. This, indeed, is the reason why the administrative reforms carried out in the years after the revocation of the Ordinances proved to be more efficacious and durable than anything attempted by the Lords Ordainers.

§ 3. It is a striking even if not very surprising circumstance that the most permanent and substantial administrative reforms of Edward II's reign should have been those voluntarily undertaken and carried through by the king and his officials. Doubtless the pressure of the preceding opposition encouraged, perhaps well-nigh compelled, an overhauling of the system and a consideration of ways of removing sources of criticism, and of making the machinery work better. In any case, as Mr. Davies observed, for reform of the administration to be effective, it had to come from within and be adopted by the Crown with good will ; only the administrators themselves knew and understood the intricacies of the system well enough to be able to pick on the points needing and capable of worth-while reform, and to fit these modifications into a workable machinery.

The reforms of these later years of the reign centred upon the Exchequer and mainly upon the accounting system, but were of such a nature as to affect the administrative system as a whole. The principal reforms were made during the two terms of office as treasurer of Walter Stapledon, bishop of Exeter, but the question of exchequer reform had received attention some years before his first term.

Endeavours to improve the enrolment of accounts and to speed up collection of debts were made on several occasions, in 1312, 1318 and 1319, and some of these foreshadowed the measures to be taken in Stapledon's time.[1] But his terms of office as treasurer, February 1320 to August 1321, and May 1322 to July 1325, saw the culmination of this process, by the promulgation of a series of Ordinances by king and Council. These Ordinances taken together constituted a large measure of administrative reform, and in so far as they were carried into effect, went far to determine certain features of the system for the rest of the mediaeval period, and probably beyond it ; no reforms of similar magnitude were to be made before the Tudor régime. There were, of course, to be important changes in the course of the ensuing two centuries, especially in the continual Council and its place in government, and also at least formally in the methods of royal control of the administration, but the general framework of the system was not, so far as we know, to be radically modified in that period ; on the contrary, the framework remained essentially that which Edward II left behind him.

Stapledon prepared the ground by initiating—under the authority of a writ of privy seal—an extensive examination and partial inventory of the exchequer and certain other archives, some of which were now calendared. The plan of making an inventory of all the principal archives of the Crown was not carried out in full, but the work done was important and valuable,

[1] *V.* Davies, *op. cit.*, p. 528.

not only to the contemporary administrators, but also to later historians.[1]

The substantive reforms were embodied in the Cowick Ordinance of June, 1323, the second York Ordinance of the same year, and the Ordinances of Westminster of 1324 and 1326.[2]

The Cowick Ordinance was largely addressed to the improvement of the book-keeping methods of the Exchequer, on the assumption, as Tout said,[3] that the incredible confusion of accounts was due not only to embarrassed finances, but also to old-fashioned book-keeping. The primary object in this sphere was to relieve the Pipe Rolls of all extraneous matter; these Rolls themselves were to be carefully kept and checked, but all foreign accounts and records of debt were to be omitted from them and consigned to their own rolls. The foreign accounts, including among many others, the accounts of the Wardrobe, of Gascony, Ireland, Wales, and of the customs, were to have their own rolls. The debts to the king, which, having been deemed recoverable, were still being entered on the Pipe Roll, were to be transferred to the ' exannual roll ' once and for all, and were not to be entered afresh each year. To cope with the work, additional clerks were to be provided ; the functions of the two remembrancers were defined ; a fifth baron of the exchequer and four auditors were to be appointed ;[4] the barons were to make the hearing of accounts, not pleas, their primary task, and were not to hear pleas at all without the king's special mandate or unless the plea concerned the king's financial interest or that of the exchequer officials.

The York Ordinance of 1323, made by king and Council under exchequer inspiration, was in some sense a supplementation of the Household Ordinance of 1318 ;[5] its principal object

---

[1] For details, *v.* Davies, *op. cit.*, p. 530 ; Tout, *Place of Edward II*, pp. 170–3 ; V. H. Galbraith, ' The Tower as an Exchequer Record Office in the reign of Edward II ' in *Essays to Tout* (1925), pp. 231–248. One of the products of these endeavours, *The Gascon Calendar*, has recently been edited by G. P. Cuttino (Camden Soc., 3rd ser. LXX (1949)).

[2] Tout, *Place of Edward II*, pp. 168–180 ; *Chapters*, II, pp. 259 ff ; Davies, pp. 531–44.

[3] Tout, *Place of Edward II*, p. 174.

[4] In this connection *v.* D. M. Broome, ' The Auditors of Foreign Accounts of the Exchequer, 1310–1327', in *E.H.R.*, XXXVIII (1923), pp. 63–71.

[5] Text in Tout, *op. cit.*, App. I B ; cf. *Chapters*, II, pp. 260 ff.

was to revise the system of account in the Wardrobe. The Ordinance of 1318 seems to have failed to produce a satisfactory accounting system in the Household, and now more detailed, and perhaps more practical because less rigid, arrangements were introduced. The ' daily account ' was relaxed to the extent that an account every other day was permitted whilst the Wardrobe was stationary, but the sanction behind this rule was made more severe by making the steward and keeper liable to pay the expenses out of their own resources if more than three days elapsed without an account being taken ; lesser officers were similarly to be penalized if they shared the responsibility for delay. A general tightening up was intended by the provision that the ' foreign ' accounts, such as those of the chief butler and purveyor of the Great Wardrobe were also to view their accounts three or four times a year, under a similar personal liability, and the clerks of the various offices were also to account regularly. The object was to ensure that the general wardrobe accounts should be made up quarterly, and a final yearly account rendered to the Exchequer promptly. Officials in arrears with their accounts were to be severely penalized and removed from office ; the cofferer was made specifically responsible for the due presentment of accounts, and a second cofferer was to be appointed to watch the course already determined for prospective wardrobe expenses.

The Ordinance of Westminster of May, 1324[1] was also made by king and council under exchequer prompting, and was also directed towards accounting reform, mainly in the Wardrobe. It sought to enforce the rule that all issues of the land should go to the Exchequer, by prohibiting the keeper from receiving any money from any source other than the treasurer and chamberlains, and by warrant addressed to them, except for amercements imposed by the steward and marshal, gifts to the king, and the fines and amercements of towns ; similar restrictions were placed upon the clerk of the Great Wardrobe.

Furthermore, ' foreign ' accounts were removed from the cognizance of the keeper of the Wardrobe and transferred direct to the Exchequer. The Great Wardrobe, the butler, purveyors

[1] *Ibid.*, pp. 263 ff.

and receivers of victuals for garrisons and castles, the keeper of the king's horses and studs, the clerk of the Hanaper, and envoys sent overseas, all were to account at the Exchequer.

The Westminster Ordinance of 1326, apparently inspired by Stapledon, was promulgated during the treasurership of his successor, William Melton, archbishop of York.[1] It was largely taken up with the re-statement of the Ordinances of 1323 and 1324, supplemented by a number of new points, such as that the chancellor and the keeper of the privy seal should enrol all writs issued for payments out of the Exchequer.

These Ordinances, together with the minor provisions made about this time, form an important chapter in exchequer history, and they fixed the main lines of accounting procedure for a long time thereafter. They also materially affected the relations between the Exchequer and the Wardrobe and also those between the Wardrobe and other parts of the Household.

But we must not be led into exaggerations of the effect of these reforms upon the general administrative system, nor into an excessive emphasis upon the modification of the relations between Exchequer and Wardrobe. There are no real grounds for supposing that these Ordinances were inspired by political or ' constitutional ' motives, or for believing that now the Wardrobe was further subjected to exchequer control.[2] These Ordinances were intended to produce a better working of the administrative machine by improving and tightening up the system of accounting and audit ; almost their whole contents relate to this objective, and represent a manful effort to cure the financial chaos that had accrued from the last years of Edward I. They do not reflect any theory of the relations between the household offices and the offices outside the Household. The only control that the Exchequer has over the Wardrobe and other household departments is the control of an auditing authority ; the Exchequer cannot refuse to pay money into the Wardrobe as required, and, if the accounts are in due order, it can have nothing to say about its activities. True, the removal of the foreign accounts from the Wardrobe reduced the scope and responsibilities of the latter ;

[1] *Ibid.*, pp. 267 ff ; Davies, *op. cit.*, p. 532.
[2] Tout, *Chapters*, II, pp. 266 ff.

the transference of the hanaper account from it to the Exchequer marks the severence of perhaps the last formal link between the Chancery and the Household—but, no one, presumably would therefore be disposed to argue that Chancery now became ' controlled ' by the Exchequer.

It was not, indeed, the Exchequer's business to control the Wardrobe or any other organs of the administration ; its business was to keep the accounts of the revenue to the king's best advantage ; if in the pursuit of this aim it was desirable to insist on regular and properly-kept accounts from the Wardrobe and elsewhere, it was only doing its proper work more effectively than before ; any repercussions on the administration itself were incidental, even accidental.[1] The Exchequer remained just as much under the king's ultimate control as before ; the accounts it audited were his accounts and the revenue it handled (in so far as it handled revenue as distinct from the accounts thereof) were his, to be distributed as he ordered. The practical importance of the Wardrobe as the immediate channel of the king's will had already declined somewhat before these Ordinances had been promulgated, and its place had been partially taken by the revived Chamber.[2]

Furthermore, it would be a mistake to imagine that these Ordinances were carried into effect fully or speedily ; like most mediaeval enactments they reveal intentions rather than realities. How far these measures were in fact carried out has not been fully ascertained. Tout was of the opinion[3] that although a real effort was made to put them into force in some respects, in other respects implementation was, to say the least, slow, and certainly not by any means complete in Edward II's reign.

The circumstances which contributed to the revival of the Chamber in the course of Edward II's reign cannot be determined with any precision, any more than can those which had previously led to the growth of the Wardrobe at the expense of the Chamber

---

[1] It is difficult to share Tout's view (*ib.* p. 267) that special significance attaches to the use of the term ' wardrobe of the household ' at this time. The co-existence of the Great Wardrobe and the beginnings of a Privy Wardrobe are sufficient explanations for a term which is quite non-committal and exactly descriptive in character.

[2] *V. infra.*

[3] *Chapters*, II, p. 315.

in the early years of Henry III.[1] It is difficult to ascribe this revival of the Chamber, at any rate in its early phases, to any reactions by the king and court to the baronial opposition, although later such reactions may have encouraged a process already in train.

The fact is that the revival of the Chamber in some respects began before opposition to Edward II's government became considerable, and before the Lords Ordainers had come into existence. As Tout himself showed,[2] there is evidence that chamber activity was increasing from the very beginning of Edward II's reign. Foreign bankers were paying in considerable sums to the Chamber ' for certain secret expenses ', and the funds thus made available were greatly increased by putting at the disposal of the Chamber the forfeited lands of Walter of Langton and of the Templars, before 1310. Thus it is evident that an intention to revive the Chamber was held before opposition to the government had reached a climax. We can only assume that Edward II found it desirable to build up a privy purse in the Chamber because the Wardrobe was no longer wholly satisfactory for that purpose, and we may not be far wrong in supposing that this was because the Wardrobe's place in the general administrative system and its manifold duties in that sphere had come to overshadow its utility as the king's personal organization. The Wardrobe by its very nature could not, as Exchequer and Chancery had done or would do, ' go out of court ', but it could, and probably did, become less intimately connected with the king himself, and less able to cope with his personal financial and other requirements. The desirability of developing a more personal and more ' privy ' purse, and one which would not come under the scrutiny of the barons of the exchequer—chamber accounts were not rendered to the Exchequer, but audited by auditors appointed by the king for the purpose—might thus make itself felt. The basis for such a development was ready to hand in the *camera regis*, which of course had never ceased to exist and had always remained the most intimate and personal of the organizations within the Household ; its revival savoured of a return to the remoter past. From the Chamber had sprung in

[1] *V. supra*, p. 101.   [2] *Op. cit.*, p. 315.

the old days both Wardrobe and Exchequer, and it must have been difficult indeed for these offspring to have put obstacles in the way of the revival of their venerable parent, even if they had wished to do so.

We have seen above[1] that the opposition of the baronage to the Wardrobe as a unit in the administration seems to have been much less than some historians have supposed, and we need not be surprised to find that the Ordinances of 1311 made no mention at all of the Chamber, for as yet it can in any case hardly be said to have re-attained much public importance. At the York Parliament of 1318, the chamberlain was included among those officials who were to be appointed with baronial assent, and the staff of the Chamber, with allusion to their employment on all kinds of confidential business figure in the Household Ordinance of 1318. From that year onwards, especially after 1322, the Chamber's importance grew apace, not least, we may surmise, because the king's favourite, the younger Despenser, was chamberlain, and in that confidential, though not eminent position, was able to exert his great influence upon the government, and to aggrandize both himself and the Chamber in the process.

Substantial additional sources of revenue were made available to the Chamber. Manors that had formerly accounted to the Wardrobe were transferred to the Chamber ; the administration of these lands gave rise to the use of a special seal in its custody— the future ' secret seal ', traces of which appear from 1313. An enormous increase in those ' chamber manors ' occurred after Boroughbridge, and control over the forfeitures of the ' contrariants ', including the five earldoms of Thomas of Lancaster, was accorded to the Chamber—for a time.[2]

It may be that the Crown missed a great opportunity for endowing itself with a large ' private ' income by so soon ordering the great bulk of these lands to account at the Exchequer (as Tout suggested)[3]; by July 1322 the king's writ of privy seal to treasurer Stapledon relegated the contrariants' lands to the

---

[1] *V. supra*, p. 151.
[2] In addition to Tout, *Chapters*, II, ch. viii, § v, *v*. Davies, ' The First Journal of Edward II's Chamber ' in *E.H.R.*, XXX (1915), pp. 662–680.
[3] *Chapters*, II, p. 340.

Exchequer, and so moderated greatly the scope and funds of the Chamber. But there would have been no great advantage to the Crown to have maintained a vastly swollen ' privy purse ' at the Chamber, whilst being unable to meet the debts due in the Exchequer ; the reforms in the latter pending at the time would no doubt suggest the wisdom of concentrating so large an account at the Exchequer. We may be well assured that practical, not theoretical considerations were at the root of this striking decision. To speak of it as a ' renunciation '[1] is perhaps misleading ; for there was still nothing to prevent the king from ordering the Exchequer to pay into the Chamber such sums as he thought fit—and were available.

Very considerable financial resources, however, remained to the Chamber, and a substantial organization and staff were built up to receive the accounts and revenues of the lands in its charge, and to deal with the administration of them. This class of work indeed formed the main function of the revived Chamber at this time ; in Edward II's reign it can hardly be said to have been a unit of any great importance in general administration. Money paid into it was *pro secretis regis*, and no accounts of it were rendered to any outside body. Payments out of it were of course at the king's discretion, mainly to meet his personal wishes in great variety ; some went into the Wardrobe ; some but not much for governmental purposes, such as the construction and repair of ships and the wages of mariners.

The general administrative work of the Chamber at this time was thus limited and narrow. A wider administrative importance, however, attached to the secret seal associated with the Chamber from 1312–13 onwards. It was used not merely for the business of the chamber lands, but also as the king's most personal seal for many purposes. By this time the privy seal was becoming less readily available to the king himself, and the appointment of keepers of the privy seal separate from the controllers of the Wardrobe encouraged the development of an office of privy seal differentiated from the Wardrobe. The gradual ' institutionalization ' of the privy seal inevitably reduced its utility as the instrument of the king's personal initiative and will ; its

[1] *Ibid.*, p. 343.

keeper was no longer necessarily in close relations with the sovereign, and was becoming an officer of more than domestic and household status ; he was soon to become a kind of lesser chancellor on his own account, and to take a leading place among the officers prominent among the councillors. In such circumstances the invention of a new personal seal would sooner or later have become an administrative necessity to the king, and for the time being the secret seal associated with the Chamber supplied the need.

The secret seal was soon used for a variety of purposes[1]: to authenticate the king's personal correspondence : for the expression of his personal wishes in any kind of business ; it came in useful as a substitute for the privy seal itself when this underwent the ignominy of capture by the Scots at Bannockburn ; it came to be commonly used for warranty alternatively or conjointly with the privy seal ; it might move the privy seal in order to move the great seal, or might move the latter directly ; it might convey the king's will to any administrative department, official, or person.

A fresh instrument of executive power had thus come into existence, and played its part in the administration of Edward II's later years. Inevitably an organization so personal as the Chamber collapsed with the king and the chamberlain who had magnified it. Its administrative potentiality, however, was not lost upon the new king, and we shall see that in due course Edward III revived it again.[2]

---

[1] *Ibid.*, V, pp. 165–170.
[2] *V. infra*, p. 197.

CHAPTER VI

DEPARTMENTAL DEVELOPMENTS AND THE GROWTH OF THE ADMINISTRATIVE COUNCIL, 1327–1399

§ 1. THE circumstances of the deposition of Edward II and of the accession of Edward III, and the political bearings of the short-lived ascendancy of Isabella and Mortimer need not concern us here.[1] These events do not seem to have had any particular significance for administrative history. Almost the whole official class in the end deserted Edward II—otherwise the revolution would have been much harder to accomplish— and thus a high degree of administrative continuity was preserved.[2] By this time, if not indeed a good deal earlier, the administrative officials seem to have been regarded as largely permanent, and provided they were prepared to carry out the policies of new masters, were seldom disturbed in the tenure of their offices by political vicissitudes. The traditions of a politically neutral bureaucracy were already being built up, and in any event, it was, of course, very much easier to encompass a *coup d'état* without having to replace any large proportion of executive officers. Continuity of personnel made for continuity of administrative method, and in general when Edward III came in due course to exercise the royal functions and to direct the government, the administrative machinery he had to hand was in all essentials that which Edward II had left behind him.[3]

Edward III's policy of conciliation and friendly relations with the baronage, including those with Lancastrian affiliations,

---

[1] *V*. Tout, *Chapters*, III, pp. 1–30.

[2] Tout, *ibid.*, pp. 3–5.

[3] This machinery has been analysed in detail in the three volumes of *The English Government at Work*, 1327–1336, edited respectively by J. F. Willard and W. A. Morris, W. A. Morris and J. R. Strayer, and W. H. Dunham, and published in 1940, 1947, and 1950. A number of the papers contained in these volumes are of great value, but the work as a whole suffers gravely from the omission of any adequate studies of the monarchy, the privy seal, and the Exchequer. These deficiencies are only partially compensated for by Professor Morris's Introduction to the first volume, pp. 3–81. Cf. Tout, ' The English Civil Service in the Fourteenth Century ', *Collected Papers*, III, pp. 191–223.

contributed to the general key-note of continuity and quiet consolidation of administrative technique that prevailed for some years. His aim of restoring the full powers and executive discretion of the Crown was no more than a return to normal practice, and inevitably involved some rehabilitation of those household agencies of administration without which a high degree of personal government could not be maintained.

The administrative reforms of the late years of Edward II's reign were in these years brought to fruition. The Stapledon-Melton reforms in the Pipe Roll procedure at the Exchequer were operative by 1340; the ancient debts were removed from the estreat roll and enrolled separately; substantial progress was made with the auditing of the arrears of foreign accounts; until the opening of the French war, household supplies were mainly derived, at least nominally, from the Exchequer.[1] Reforming tendencies were not confined to the centre, but carried into the local sphere, with the establishment, or re-establishment, of local exchequers and eschaetries and improvements in the local administration of justice.[2]

The renewal of war with Scotland in 1332 led to the migration of the chief administrative organizations to York, which for more than five years became the administrative centre, to the grave impoverishment of Westminster.[3] The re-orientation of policy and plans involved in the commencement of hostilities with France brought the centre back to the south. ' It was the Hundred Years' War which finally secured for Westminster the permanent position of " capital " of England '[4]—not only because of its greater convenience for the tasks in hand, but also because the financial strength of the realm lay in the south rather than in the north.

No particular administrative difficulty arose from the concentration of the offices at York as the base for the Scottish war; similar arrangements had been made under Edward I and Edward II; unity of administration could more readily be

[1] Tout, *Chapters*, III, pp. 47-8.
[2] *Ibid.*, pp. 48-51.
[3] *Ibid.*, pp. 56-60.
[4] *Ibid.*, p. 64; cf. Tout, ' The Beginnings of a Modern Capital: London and Westminster in the Fourteenth Century ', *Collected Papers*, III, pp. 249-275.

preserved, and the system as a whole be carried on more or less normally. But the war with France was to present administrative problems of an altogether different calibre ; a situation involving the protracted absence of the sovereign from the realm had to be confronted ; the difficulties of maintaining a unified administration had to be wrestled with ; and, above all, the enormous financial cost of the war was destined to put so great a strain on the administrative machinery and upon the political temper of the baronage and the realm as to produce profound consequences upon the conduct of government in England, eventually perhaps to induce modification of the very character of that government.

It is not very clear whether the Ordinances of Walton of 1338 originated from an intention to provide for the government in view of the king's pending departure overseas ; they were certainly at least adjusted to meet that contingency, but they may have been drafted before this event became assured. In any case, in intention, if not in effect, they were ' perhaps the most important administrative act of the reign of Edward III '.[1] Though most of these Ordinances were not to have more than a temporary lease of life, their revelations of intention are very significant, even if perhaps they were in part at least inspired simply by pressing needs of war-finance.

The Ordinances[2] aimed at co-ordinating the several branches of the administration by maintaining in the king and his personal advisers a strict executive control over all. The nature of the provisions was such as to suggest that the king felt the need for curbing bureaucratic initiative in Chancery and Exchequer. At any rate, it was provided that specific warrant under privy seal was to be requisite for either of those departments to authorize any kind of payments, fixed fees alone excepted. Such warrants were to be made with the assent of the king and ' a wise and sufficient man ', and were to be enrolled by a clerk appointed and sworn for the purpose, and a counter-roll was to

[1] Tout, *Chapters*, III, p. 69.

[2] For text, *v. ibid*., pp. 143–150 ; for commentary, *ib.* pp. 69–80 ; cf. Dorothy Hughes, *A Study of Social and Constitutional Tendencies in the early years of Edward III* (1915), pp. 45–72, in connection with which Tout's criticisms, *op. cit*., p. 143 need to be borne in mind.

be kept by a clerk of the Chamber under supervision. To ensure the observance of these principles, the chamberlains of the exchequer, in the presence of the treasurer, were to account before a special auditing committee, who were to have the assistance of the clerk of the privy seal's roll and the counter-roll of the clerk of the Chamber, whilst the chamberlains were made personally liable for any payments not authorized by warrants of privy seal.

The discretion of Chancery and Exchequer was further limited by other provisions. Warrants of privy seal were to be necessary for nearly all matters issuing under great seal, except purely legal business and matters touching the office of chancellor, and this provision was safeguarded by a system of rolls and counter-rolls and periodical inspections. Severe restriction was imposed on exchequer practice by the annulment of all exemptions from taxation, and the prohibition on respites of debts and permits to pay by instalments; no royal debts contracted before the king's accession, such as bills of the Wardrobe and the like, were to be paid until the king was free of his own debts.

The main pre-occupation of the drafters of the Ordinances was clearly with finance, and especially with the financial requirements of the war. Hence important provisions were included for a system of war-finance, and for the setting up of special war-treasurers and methods of financial organization for war-purposes. Moreover, the need for some survey of financial resources was expressed by the requirement that the treasurer of the exchequer should estimate the king's liabilities and assets.[1]

The Wardrobe of the Household itself was in financial matters brought under the control of the privy seal. The treasurer (or keeper) was to have no allowance for ' foreign ' expenditure not authorized by warrant of privy seal, duly enrolled and counter-rolled. The counter-roll was to remain with the clerk of the Chamber ; no prests (monetary advances) to persons not of the Household were to be made without the king's oral command and a warrant of privy seal.

---

[1] On this matter, *v. infra*, p. 213. It is a little difficult to reconcile Tout's remark that ' the ultimate supremacy of the exchequer in financial administration is clearly asserted ' in this section of the Ordinances, with the other sections which appear to subordinate the Exchequer to writs of privy seal. But obviously if an estimate was to be made, the Exchequer alone could do it.

It seems possible that these provisions, and others,[1] were intended to constitute permanent rules for the general organization of the administration. If so, they may be taken as revealing the desire of the Crown to maintain a highly unified and centralized control over the administration as a whole, a control located in or near the king himself. But it is difficult indeed to assess how far some of these Ordinances represented innovation in practice, and how far they merely stated what was regarded as orthodox usage. On the whole, it is probable that they fell more into the latter category than the former, and that for the most part they were intended to do little more than preserve and stabilize existing arrangements, with some fresh clarification, definition, and tightening up of practice. In general, perhaps they represented some attempt at maintaining the personal position of the king in administration and at restraining tendencies towards the growth of bureaucratic self-sufficiency, with the practical end in view of improved finances.

The pending departure of the king with the privy seal compelled some modification in the arrangements as at first proposed. Whenever the king should take the privy seal abroad with him, and the Council should be divided between overseas and home sections, then if the Councils needed to authorize payments or to issue written authority for the execution of business, the warrants were to be issued by the ' governors and chiefs ' of the Councils in the king's name under their personal seals. Transcripts of such warrants were to be submitted to the king as soon as possible, and, after examination, by the clerk of the privy seal, the clerk of the Chamber and his supervisor, were then to be enrolled and counter-enrolled, and writs under the privy seal were to be issued to the recipients by way of indemnification. The committee of audit was to advise the king and the council of the state of the Treasury. The effect of the arrangements was, as Tout said,[2] to put both Chancery and Exchequer into leading strings.

The Ordinances were sent under writ of privy seal dated

---

[1] We are not here concerned with the provisions relating to the ' election ' of the sheriffs for one year by their shires, and other arrangements for local government.
[2] *Op. cit.*, III, p. 71.

O

12 July, 1338, to the chancellor, to be read before the Council, and to be strictly observed. Two months later a copy was sent by Chancery to the Exchequer with instructions to observe them so far as applicable to that office.

There was not, of course, anything new in principle in using writs of privy seal as the mainspring of executive action, but the restriction of chancery and exchequer issues in nearly all business to authorization by such writs seems to have been a conscious tightening up of practice. What remains mysterious is the question of who exactly was to initiate writs of privy seal for these purposes. The king himself no doubt would originate a good many, but it is impossible to suppose he could have had cognizance of all the numerous writs that would need to issue under the scheme. The Council with him would naturally relieve him of a part at least of this burden, but otherwise we are left to surmise the process whereby the issue of letters under privy seal was initiated and authorized. Nothing is said in the Ordinances about the secret seal, but the Chamber is clearly brought into a position of importance in the control of the administration. The counter-roll of the clerk of the Chamber represents the king's own ultimate check upon administrative writs, buttressed so far as financial issues were concerned, by the special committee of audit, to consist of a bishop, a banneret, and a clerk.

It is very likely that the Ordinances of Walton were inspired not so much by any conscious desire to preserve and sustain the maximum practicable degree of personal government, as by a desire to ensure and maintain the maximum financial resources available for the French war. The dominant note in them seems to be anxiety lest the finances should be frittered away on objects unconnected with the ' war-effort ', and in some sense they represent an attempt at mobilizing and concentrating resources on war-purposes. It is at least possible, even probable, that they would not have been promulgated at all but for the pending military campaign. Even so, it is not unreasonable to take them as the expression—the last expression of this sort—of the mediaeval monarchy's conception of undiluted personal control of government ; at no later date is evidence forthcoming of so

great a place for the household agencies in the general administration.

But it seems that these Ordinances themselves sought to
put the household agencies into a higher position than accorded
with practical possibilities. Probably so high a degree of personal
government as the Ordinances implied could not in reality be
maintained in the circumstances, political and administrative,
that now prevailed, or were soon to prevail. It is indeed very
doubtful whether the Ordinances became fully operative at any
time. If they had been, we should expect to find more evidence
of their operation than has yet been found. No trace survives
of the enrolment or counter-enrolment of those privy seal warrants, or of bills issued by the Council; no evidence has been
found of the person who was to advise the king on the issue of
the warrants, nor of the clerk of the Chamber and his supervisor,
nor of the committee of audit.[1] It seems therefore that the Ordinances in their most striking features either never became operative
at all, or were operative for so short a time as to make no impression upon the records.

In any event, it seems that the king soon found that the Ordinances would not produce the financial results that had been hoped
for. A Council and departments at home so restricted in authority
and discretion as the Ordinances contemplated, failed to mobilize
resources with the speed and effectiveness that was required; the
severity of the provisions about payment of debts to the Crown
did more harm than good, and added to the importance of the
opposition to the king's policy and methods which was in any
case vociferous in the person of Archbishop Stratford and the
remnant of the Lancastrian interest. Declining financial credit,
probably more than any other factor, obliged Edward III to
modify the administrative policy he had intended to apply to
England.

By the autumn of 1339, the government at home was re-
modelled; the attempt to keep it in leading-strings was largely
abandoned. Archbishop Stratford became ' governor ' of the

---

[1] *Ibid.*, p. 78. An attempt, albeit short-lived, was made to apply the provisions
regarding the election of local officers. For some evidence of the operation of
portions of the Ordinances *v. ibid.*, p. 101, n. 6.

Council and the leading figure in the government at home ; he was thus able to elevate supporters to important offices, and so to reduce the curialist element in the home administration. But the new Council was no more successful in producing the sinews of war than its predecessor ; it was this circumstance that induced the king to return in early 1340, and forced from him the fiscal concessions embodied in the famous statutes of that year, which were wrung from him by the pressure of magnates and commons in parliament.

The failure of even these concessions, and of the re-constituted administration, to produce the supplies demanded by the king, led on to the ' ministerial crisis ' of 1340–41, which involved, perhaps for the first and last time, something like an open conflict between the curialist and non-curialist elements in the administration. The king returned again suddenly in November, 1340, with few followers, including however William Kilsby, the keeper of the privy seal, as the only administrative official among them, and proceeded to make a clean sweep of the home administration. The royal right to dismiss all and any of the officers was exerted to the full. If only the scheme of the Ordinances of Walton could be made to work, unity of administration might be procured by removing antagonists from office and replacing them with lesser men—laymen if necessary—who could be relied upon to strive to administer the king's will. But it was still necessary to procure harmonious relations with the magnates and the commons in parliament, for without their co-operation in financial grants, it was not possible to prosecute the war in France. With the king's quarrel with Stratford, and the proceedings of the parliaments of 1341, we are not at present concerned.[1] The principal repercussion of these events upon administrative history was in relation to the composition of the king's council, not upon the executive organizations themselves, and to this matter we must return later.[2] Broadly speaking, it seems true to say that for the rest of the fourteenth century, and indeed for much of the fifteenth as well, political conflict between

---

[1] For the events of 1340–41, *v. ibid.*, pp. 100–142, and cf. G. T. Lapsley, *Crown, Community and Parliament*, pp. 231–272.

[2] *V. infra*, p. 224.

monarchy and opposition turned largely upon the question of the composition and functions of the king's ordinary council, and before we examine this subject, it is desirable to survey developments within the administrative departments and agencies. No doubt some of these developments were induced or at least affected by the course of political events, but administrative organization remained much the same throughout the political vicissitudes. For whosoever could control the Council could largely control the policies administered, and it was for the control of the Council, not the modification of the administrative structure, that oppositions contended with the Crown in the later middle ages.

The reigns of Edward III and Richard II saw the renewed revival and also the decline of the Chamber as an organization of importance in the administration.[1] Apart from the utility of the secret seal in the custody of the Chamber as the king's personal seal, the Chamber can scarcely be said to have attained a position of first importance in the general administrative system, even in this period, though no doubt it would have done so, if the intentions of the Ordinances of Walton of 1338 had been fully carried out. But the Chamber as such remained primarily a useful 'privy purse', capable of substantial expansion under the pressure of war-time needs, and so supplementing the efforts of Wardrobe and Exchequer in financing military requirements ; it was important also as providing an organized staff close to the king, readily adaptable to his confidential business, most important of all as providing a secretariat armed with the secret seal to give expression of the king's personal wishes, a function for which the keeper and office of privy seal were no longer so readily available.

Soon after his assumption of full powers, Edward III clearly set himself the objective of reviving the Chamber and of making it as useful to him as it had been to his father. The principal action to this end which required royal initiative was the provision of adequate funds for the Chamber, and this purpose was pursued, with varying results for some twenty years from 1333. The reservation of lands to the Chamber, without accountability

---

[1] Tout, *op. cit.*, IV, ch. xiii, pp. 227-348.

at the Exchequer, was revived from that year—a process greatly accelerated after the beginning of the French war, and a variety of sources was used for the purpose. Forfeited lands, escheats, wardships, enemy-alien priories and benefices, temporalities of vacant benefices, even rents from overseas, were diverted to the Chamber, with the result that part of the Chamber staff was engaged in estate management on a large scale, and this part tended to settle permanently in London or Westminster. The needs of this business, and no doubt the over-riding necessity of keeping the secret seal close to the king himself, gave rise to the use by the Chamber of a second seal—the 'griffin', for estate affairs. The first mention of this seal comes from 1335, and after some show of reluctance, both Exchequer and Chancery were obliged to recognize its validity for the estate business of the Chamber ; after 1346, its scope was extended to cover any chamber business, until, in 1356, it disappeared with the system of reservation of lands to the Chamber.

The opening of the French war gave an importance to the Chamber in national administration which perhaps it would not otherwise have attained. The Ordinances of Walton brought it, or intended to bring it, into the very centre of the administrative system, and though this purpose seems not to have been achieved, the financial needs of the war brought increased resources and responsibilities to it. Funds sufficient for the war needs could not, however, be obtained from the reserved lands alone, even when supplemented by loans, and large subventions from Wardrobe and Exchequer were made. This arrangement brought the Chamber once more into close relations with the Exchequer. By these means, the Chamber handled a good deal of the military, naval, and munitions[1] finance of Edward III in the 1340's.

The large degree of independence of exchequer audit enjoyed by the Chamber seems to have evoked opposition from the Exchequer, and certainly the arrangements tended to promote a rival financial organization within a certain field of activity. The administrative friction and difficulties arising were probably the main reason for the gradual decline of the self-sufficiency of the

[1] V. Tout, ' Firearms in England in the Fourteenth Century ', *Collected Papers*, II, pp. 233–276.

Chamber. Decrease in the income from the reserved lands led first to an increase in the proportion of the Chamber's subvention from the Exchequer, for which the former had to account at the latter, especially from 1348–9, and in 1356 the system of the reservation of lands to the Chamber was brought to an end. By a writ of 20 January, 1356, all lands reserved to the Chamber (with one minor exception) were to be transferred to the Exchequer, and the chamber accounts outstanding in this connection were to be audited at the Exchequer; with this termination of the Chamber's estate management, the griffin seal disappeared from use.[1]

With these arrangements, the importance of the Chamber in the national administration greatly declined, and, before long, the importance of the secret seal remaining in its custody passed under Richard II to the newer instrument and agency of the signet and signet office, and these were to have great futures before them.[2] The Chamber, however, never became negligible in the mediaeval period, and it was to be revived again with great effect under the Tudors.[3] It continued to receive a regular subvention from the Exchequer—the ' *certum* '—which varied in amount, as well as considerable casual sums from the same source—enough to furnish the king with a substantial ' privy purse ', for the disbursement of which there was no accountability except to the king himself. Politically and administratively more important than this financial resource, however, was the availability of chamber staff for the king's confidential business of every kind. Richard II especially utilized the chamberlain, underchamberlains, and knights of the Chamber, some of whom were brought into the ordinary council, for administrative business, and some were eminent enough to figure among the leaders of the curialist party, and to suffer accordingly in the final collapse of the régime in 1399.

Concomitant with the revival of the Chamber had been the re-emergence of the secret seal[4] as the instrument most personal to the king. The substitution of the signet seal for the secret

---

[1] For details of the griffin seal, *v.* Tout, *op. cit.*, V, pp. 181–192.
[2] *V. infra*, p. 214.
[3] *V. infra*, p. 264.
[4] Tout, *op. cit.*, V, pp. 171–181.

seal is a process that remains mysterious, but was completed in Edward III's reign. The secret seal, properly so called, became obsolete before Edward III's death, and the change was perhaps at first little more than a change in terminology, probably connected with the curious vicissitudes in the form and design of the secret seal itself. No fewer than five successive seals were utilized, and some of the later specimens came to be gradually designated ' our signet '—no doubt because that is what in form they actually were or resembled.

From 1337 onwards the term ' signet ' began to be used officially as a synonym for ' secret seal ', and the model of 1354 actually carried the legend ' *Signetum Regis Anglie et Francie* '. More than one secret seal was in use concurrently, and a mysterious seal called the ' *signum* '[1] makes its appearance for a time, in addition to the secret or signet and griffin seals. By the later years of the reign, however, these duplications dropped out of use, leaving the signet as the sole immediate instrument of the king's personal wishes, and this, as a new creation with a great destiny, requires, along with such devices as the royal sign-manual, separate consideration below.[2]

The history of the Wardrobe[3] in this period is for a time one of revival, and thereafter of decline, so far as its importance in national administration is concerned. By the end of the period the Wardrobe of the Household had sunk back into being mainly a domestic office—a process no doubt encouraged by the rise of the privy seal office separate from both Wardrobe and Household,[4] as well as by the growth of the Great and Privy Wardrobes,[5] and by other more general causes.

During the early years of Edward III, the Wardrobe's activity seems to have been on a very limited scale ; this at any rate is the inference drawn from the paucity of its surviving records for the first ten years of the reign. Possibly the aftermath of the administrative reforms of the late years of Edward II had the effect of depressing the Wardrobe, although little definite evidence on the

---

[1] *Ibid.*, pp. 192–194.   [2] *V. infra*, p. 214.
[3] Tout, *op. cit.*, IV, pp. 69–225 ; cf. J. H. Johnson, ' The King's Wardrobe and Household ', in Willard and Morris, *op. cit.*, I, pp. 206–249.
[4] *V. infra*, p. 204.
[5] *V.* Tout, *op. cit.*, IV, pp. 349–437, 439–484.

point is forthcoming. But the outbreak of the war brought the Wardrobe once more into prominence for a time, as the traditional organization for war-expenditure. It was, however, no longer in the same position even in this respect as it had been in the days of Edward I. It was on the whole less successful than its predecessor had been, and its burden was shared to a greater extent. The Great and Privy Wardrobes were now separate organizations and carried their own responsibilities, and now the Chamber had a share in war-mobilization. In the early years of the Scottish and French wars, the burden fell on all the departments, and all co-operated to the same end ; Chamber and Wardrobe, Exchequer and Chancery, and Office of Privy Seal all bent their energies to the task. Large sums were paid into the Wardrobe from the Exchequer, and also from ' foreign accounts ', the proportion of which enormously increased as the war dragged on.

With the king's departure overseas, the office of the Wardrobe accompanied him and remained abroad with him, located mainly at Antwerp, and became the headquarters of the army administration abroad, and indeed the king's principal channel for the control of the administration at home. The pressing necessities of the war brought larger sums than ever into the Wardrobe's receipts, including huge loans from foreign and English merchants and bankers. When these resources did not suffice, the Wardrobe exploited its credit with the issue of numerous ' bills of the Wardrobe '. The failure of the Exchequer at home to meet these bills, and its failure to supply cash to the Wardrobe in the quantities demanded, were the root cause of the crisis of 1340–41, to which reference has been made above.

There are, however, indications that the old methods of war finance and mobilization no longer sufficed for the large-scale operations engaged in by Edward III. ' The system of Household control which under Edward I had barely sufficed to finance wars on a small scale, proved altogether inadequate for the administration of the great continental campaigns of the Hundred Years' War.'[1] ' Only by increased exchequer grants, that is, by increased taxation, could the king maintain the State.'[2] The demand for greater and more frequent grants of money inevitably

[1] *Ibid.*, p. 114. [2] *Ibid.*, p. 127.

provoked a greater reliance upon the magnates and commons in parliament, accelerated the growth of the political importance of the commons in parliament, evoked a more concrete and precise interest in parliament upon administrative questions, especially in the appointments of officers and council, and, it is hardly too much to say, produced a change in the balance of power within the State.

The consequences of some of these large developments were not unfelt in the Wardrobe, which although it was of great practical importance in the field as the immediate source of war-finance and supplies, gradually became at home little more than a court office, mainly concerned with household finance. Attempts made to buttress up the Wardrobe, mostly by way of reducing its dependence upon exchequer contributions, whether inspired by policy or merely by opportunism, in the long run did not prove successful; probably they could not have done so in the general decline and increasing chaos of the royal finances in the middle and late years of the reign.[1] The efforts at reform may have done something to produce a better co-ordination of administrative agencies in the early 1360's, but by then the great days of the Wardrobe were nearly over. The emergence of a duplicate Wardrobe at home for dealing temporarily with household expenses in 1360, coupled with the invention under parliamentary pressure of special treasurers of war after the renewal of the war in 1369, undermined the position of the Wardrobe in the sphere of national administration. Its destiny now was gradually to sink into identity with the Household, and apart from a brief revival for war-purposes under Henry V, to occupy itself so exclusively with household affairs as to be absorbed therein, and eventually to lose even its distinctive name. These tendencies, not of course completed in the time of Edward III or Richard II, were doubtless encouraged by the process of concentrating the administrative machinery at Westminster, whilst centring the king's Household at Windsor, leaving the more amorphous *familia* to accompany the king's person always.

These tendencies were continued and confirmed under

---

[1] *V. infra*, pp. 211 ff.

Richard II. The military expeditions of 1377–89 were financed through special war-treasurers chosen in parliament. Richard II never tried to subsidize the Wardrobe directly from taxation, and made no extra-ordinary use of the Wardrobe except for his two Irish expeditions. It is not the officers of the Wardrobe who figure prominently in the politics and turmoils of Richard II's reign, but rather the chamberlains and stewards of the Household ; no wardrobe officer in this reign became either a ' minister' or a bishop ; the Wardrobe ceased to be the principal school for ambitious administrators, and the secrets of power behind the throne were passing elsewhere. Later on still, when the Tudors in some measure revived the personal direction of government through household agencies they looked, not to the Wardrobe of the Household, but to the Chamber and the secretaries as the likeliest instruments.

In the second half of the fourteenth century, the office of privy seal became firmly established on its course independent of the Wardrobe and the Household, and began to take its place as the third of the extra-curial departments of administration.[1] The privy seal itself largely lost its old importance as the authenticating instrument of the king's personal wishes, for which purpose the secret seal, the signet, or the royal sign-manual replaced it. But it gained greater importance still as the principal initiating instrument for administration, whether moved by the king or by the Council.

By October, 1323, the keepership of the privy seal became finally separate from the controllership of the Wardrobe and by the time of the appointment of Richard Bury to the keepership of the privy seal in September, 1329, it was considered promotion for the keeper of the wardrobe to be so appointed. The tenure of the office by Bury (' the beloved clerk without whose presence the king cannot be, both because of things pertaining to the custody of the privy seal and for other reasons')[2] raised its importance ; it was still regarded as being within the Household ; Bury

<hr/>

[1] *V*. generally, Tout, *op. cit.*, V, pp. 1–160. Singularly little information upon the privy seal is provided in Willard and Morris, *op. cit.*, but its great practical importance is well brought out in the article therein on 'The Chancery' by B. Wilkinson, pp. 162–205.
[2] Cited, Tout, *op. cit.*, V, pp. 6–7.

himself in 1333 passed on to the great bishopric of Durham, and the precedent for a keeper of the privy seal of outstanding personal prestige had been set.

We have seen above[1] the crucial place in the administrative machinery intended for the privy seal in the Ordinances of Walton of 1338, which would have made writs of privy seal the controlling instrument of the whole administration. We may well imagine that the energetic William Kilsby as keeper did all that was feasible to make this scheme work whilst it lasted, all the more when he himself was given the custody of the great seal whilst abroad with the king, and could be called ' our chancellor'. A dominant position in the administration such as this inevitably tended to bring the keepership of the privy seal on to the ministerial level, and before long put the keeper third after the chancellor and treasurer among the principal officers. From November, 1360 at latest, the Exchequer paid the wages of the keeper direct, and no longer through the Wardrobe, and the severance of this link with the parent body may be taken as marking for practical purposes the final separation of the office from the Household. The custody of the privy seal by the powerful William of Wykeham, 1363–67, further glorified the office, for at the same time he was the chief minister and confidential adviser of the king, although the custody of the privy seal was not his only or even chief function.

As always in such matters, full recognition of the evolution out of court of the keeper of the privy seal was slow. The first parliament of Richard II, when it petitioned for the nomination in parliament of the chief officers, left the keeper of the privy seal to the king's discretion, but subsequent parliaments placed him among the five principal officers, along with the chancellor, treasurer, steward, and chamberlain. The culmination of this development occurred in the parliament of 1386, and further consideration of it is better postponed for treatment in connection with the political repercussions discussed below.[2]

The importance of the office of keeper of the privy seal was greatly increased by his growing importance as a member of the

---

[1] *V. supra*, p. 191.   [2] *V. infra*, p. 232.

ordinary Council, by which both administrative and judicial authority was delegated to him. By the end of the fourteenth century, the keeper of the privy seal, like the chancellor before him, had acquired a share in the judicial discretion of the Crown, and presided over proceedings which were initiated and executed by writs of privy seal, and which perhaps in some measure foreshadowed the jurisdiction of the later Tudor Court of Requests.[1]

By the end of Richard II's reign, the keeper was definitely out of court, and the close association of the office of privy seal with the Council had become firmly established.[2] ' The immense growth of administrative machinery, and the inadequacy of a single office to act as sole secretariat of State, furthered the development of the keepership into a permanent political office.'[3]

The separation of the office of privy seal from the Household, the multiplicity of its administrative work, and the availability of the secret or signet for the king's personal needs—an availability in part at least necessitated by the ' institutionalization ' of the privy seal itself—all promoted the location of the office of privy seal in a fixed place. About 1346, the office may have been housed in new buildings next to the Exchequer of Receipt, between Westminster Hall and the palace, near to the new Council chamber (the future *camera stellata*). This process of fixation, however, was inevitably impeded by the frequency and duration of the privy seal's sojourns with the king overseas in the time of Edward III, but after 1360, if not earlier, the office became permanently located at Westminster, with the seal itself and its establishment of clerks and paraphernalia.[4]

By far the greater part of administrative action requiring the exercise of discretionary powers was initiated in this period by writs of privy seal.[5] The warranties for issue preserved in chancery

---

[1] Tout, *op. cit.*, V, p. 63, and I. S. Leadam, *Select Cases in the Court of Requests* (Selden Soc., 1888).
[2] *V. infra*, p. 206.
[3] Tout, *op. cit.*, V, p. 56.   [4] *Ibid.*, pp. 72–74.
[5] *V.* B. Wilkinson, ' The Authorisation of Chancery Writs under Edward III ' in *Bull. John Ryland's Library*, 8 (1924), pp. 107–139, and the same writer's article in Willard and Morris, *op. cit.*, pp. 162–205. On the diplomatic of the privy seal, *v.* E. Déprez, *Études de diplomatique Anglaise*, 1272–1485 (1908), and cf. Tout's remarks thereon, in *Coll. Papers*, I, pp. 185–189. Cf. also Maxwell-Lyte, *The Great Seal*, ch. ii.

and exchequer records reveal how great was the place of the privy seal in the administrative system. Letters under the secret and griffin seals, and later under the signet and royal sign-manual, played their part ; oral commands by the king, and probably by king and Council, or by the Council alone, also had a share in moving the great seal and the Exchequer, as well as ' bills ' by officers and departments within the limited spheres of their respective responsibilities. The extensive administrative activity of the ordinary Council, implemented by way of writs of privy seal, is one of the outstanding features of this period, and requires to be discussed in more detail later.[1] The privy seal was not, of course, exclusively the seal of the Council in this or any other period—the Council possessed no seal of its own until 1556[2], nor was it the only means employed to give effect to conciliar decisions —the king's signet, royal sign-manual, or even the signatures of the clerk of the Council or of Councillors might be used from time to time. But the association of the privy seal with the Council, especially when the keeper of it became an important member of the Council, was very close, and in consequence a highly effective means of executive action was developed. Council meetings themselves were sometimes summoned by letters of privy seal.

Over and above these executive uses, the privy seal was constantly employed with direct force, for communications with foreign courts, for letters to private persons and officials for administrative purposes. The privy seal was thus the key-pin in the administration, and ' whoever could become the recognised means of moving the privy seal, could also thereby direct its authoritative commands to the chancery, and through the chancery, could dispense the immense royal patronage, lay and ecclesiastical, which was one of the chief perquisites of office.'[3] When the Council could secure the implementation of its decisions through the privy seal, naturally dominance in the Council became a still more desirable objective in the eyes of magnate oppositions, in and outside of parliament, and in this field

---

[1] *V. infra*, p. 217.
[2] *V.* L. W. Labaree and R. E. Moody ' The Seal of the Privy Council ' in *E.H.R.*, XLIII (1928), pp. 190–202.
[3] Baldwin, *op. cit.*, p. 178.

important developments occurred during the later fourteenth and early fifteenth centuries.

The reign of Edward III is the latest for whi'ch we have a detailed study of Chancery as an administrative department,[1] but it may be doubted whether any substantial changes in this side of its work occurred in the later mediaeval period, or indeed for a good deal longer. As a secretariat and administrative organ, Chancery remained very static, and the great developments were in the political importance of the chancellor and in his position as a judicial officer. With the development of the judicial and equitable functions of the chancellor we are not here concerned, but the place of Chancery and chancellor in the administrative machinery of the late fourteenth century requires our consideration.

It can perhaps hardly be said that the place of Chancery differed very much in the later fourteenth century from what it had been in the earlier years of the century.[2] Chancery was still primarily and essentially the office of the great seal, and its essential function was the solemn expression of the king's will —essentially its expression to the public, and to a lesser extent to other departments and officers of the king. The department possessed no other seal, and all its acts were issued under the great seal ; it had, of course, apart from the small seals, a potential rival in the exchequer seal, which sufficed for that department's activities and was sometimes used indeed when the great seal might seem more appropriate ; after 1344 the king's bench and the common bench possessed seals of their own for judicial writs, even if the proceeds thereof found their way into the Hanaper.[3]

A great part of Chancery's work was to implement in formal letters under the great seal administrative decisions that had been reached elsewhere, and allowed of little or no discretion ; in this sphere Chancery was strictly no more than a secretariat. It depended for this work upon the instructions it received from the king or Council conveyed to it by oral commands or letters

[1] *V*. B. Wilkinson, *The Chancery under Edward III* (1929), and the article in Willard and Morris, *op. cit.* The subsequent history of Chancery on the judicial and equitable side has so far received more attention than its later history as an administrative organization.

[2] *V. supra*, p. 167.

[3] Cf. B. Wilkinson, ' The Seals of the Two Benches under Edward III ' in *E.H.R.*, XLII (1927), pp. 397–407.

of privy seal or letters under one of the other small seals, or later under the royal sign-manual or signature. Chancery had become 'the instrument not of the king so much as of the Crown.'[1] Only one instance has come to light in this period of hesitation by chancery officials to implement a writ of privy seal, and for this they were visited with a stinging rebuke from the king.[2]

Not all of chancery work depended upon the initiative of authorities outside of the department, and therefore not all letters enrolled on chancery records show a warranty for issue. An important, even if limited, field of work was within the responsibility of the chancellor himself, and in this sphere Chancery may be said to have performed administrative as distinct from secretarial functions. As Professor Wilkinson wisely observes, 'such a distinction between the two aspects of the Chancery does not clearly exist in contemporary records and was no doubt on occasions very indistinct.'[3] The work, moreover, in this sphere was very largely of a routine character, and of a sufficiently minor importance as not to give the chancellor any great position as an administrator in his own right. The absence of any mention of warranty in a number of instances on the Chancery rolls, which in the thirteenth century implied that the king himself had authorized the issue, tended, however, after 1293 to imply authorization by the chancellor himself. The most important issues of this kind were original writs *de cursu* for commencing actions in the king's courts and actions relating to freehold in any court, as well as writs of judgment until 1344; the issue of commissions in set form to various officials under the Crown ; the exercise of minor powers of patronage, especially to benefices in the gift of the Crown of under 20 marks annual value, and the issue of a variety of commissions and letters especially appertaining to financial administration, many of which were issuable by Chancery in conjunction with the Exchequer.

The organization of Chancery becomes somewhat clearer in this period, and the first Ordinances for Chancery are attributed

---

[1] Wilkinson, *The Chancery under Edward III*, p. 24.

[2] *V.* Wilkinson, 'A Letter of Edward III to his chancellor and treasurer', in *E.H.R.*, XLIII (1927), pp. 248–51. The matter in question involved ecclesiastical susceptibilities, and arose on an order to seize the temporalities of the bishop of Ely in 1355.

[3] Wilkinson, *The Chancery under Edward III*, p. 26.

to 12 Richard II.[1] By this period the main sub-departments of the Chancery were the departments of the Rolls and of the Hanaper. The recording of issues was the duty of the Office of the Rolls, so called because most of the recording was by enrolments classified according to the type of letter, the nature of the business, or the locality concerned, although bundles of writs and inquisitions returned to Chancery were also preserved, and also memoranda, especially of legal process. At least ten distinct series of Rolls were kept in the time of Edward III,[2] and still survive in the Public Record Office. The method by which these Rolls were compiled is not entirely clear, but probably they were composed mainly from drafts of the actual letters issued, or transcripts of them, copied at leisure in the clerk of the rolls department, which was probably separate and differently located from the rest of Chancery. The actual letters probably passed straight from the seal to the Hanaper department, where some remained until collected by the applicants, and others were dispatched by messengers.[3] The Hanaper was the fee-collecting department, paying its receipts, less expenses, into the Exchequer.[4] The staff of Chancery was by the late years of the century considerable; the twelve clerks of the first grade included the keeper of the Rolls, who was the chancellor's lieutenant, and the *praeceptores* of writs, all of whom were officials of substance and standing, whose ranks supplied the clerks of parliament, receivers of petitions, and assistants to the chancellor in his judicial work. Twelve clerks of the second grade and twenty-four cursitors (writers of routine writs), together with the spigurnal, chafewax, the portejoie, and others made up an establishment with an *esprit de corps* and self-sufficiency of its own, sharing in part at least the communal life of a *hospicium*.[5]

The official headquarters of Chancery—in the sense of the place where the chancellor appeared publicly to discharge his

---

[1] Text printed *ibid.*, App. VI, pp. 214–223.   [2] *V. ibid.*, p. 54.

[3] Cf. Willard, ' The Dating and Delivery of Letters Patent and Writs in the Fourteenth Century', in *Bull. Ins. Hist. Res.*, X (1932–3), pp. 1–11. Although practice varied and is sometimes obscure, the date given in letters patent and other issues was usually that of the authorizing warrant.

[4] For details of fees, *v.* Wilkinson, *op. cit.*, pp. 59 ff.

[5] For discussion of the somewhat obscure subject of the ' household of the Chancery ', *v. ibid.*, pp. 87 ff, and the references given therein.

P

office—was in Westminster Hall in 1310—'at the great bench where the chancellor is wont to sit'; here the chancellor performed the judicial duties of his office, and here in his presence the great seal might be applied to letters and documents, but doubtless much sealing was done elsewhere, and not necessarily in the presence of the chancellor himself. Early in Edward III's reign permanent headquarters for Chancery were located in Westminster, but parts of the department continued to itinerate, but no means exist for determining the itinerary.

The chancellor was thus at the head of a large, compact, well-organized department, with indispensable secretarial duties, with considerable and vital, even if mainly routine administrative functions, and with growing judicial duties falling to him by way of the petitions relegated to him by king, council, or parliament or sometimes addressed to him direct. But these functions, however important in themselves, do not explain why it was that the chancellor's office in the late fourteenth and the fifteenth centuries, was first among the offices of political importance, nor why until the time of Wolsey, the chancellor was reckoned the leading minister of the Crown, so that to this day the Lord Chancellor retains his precedence over all other ministers of the Crown. The reasons for this primacy of place and importance have to be sought not in the chancellor's position as the head of the Chancery, but rather in his position in the king's Council and in the political forces operating upon and within the Councils of the later mediaeval period. The great importance of the chancellor in this period was no longer based upon his intimate relations with the king himself, as to some extent it had been in earlier times, but grew with the political importance and administrative power of the Council, of which the chancellor was a prominent and usually the leading member. But this is a topic better postponed for consideration in the following section.[1]

No comprehensive modern study of the Exchequer exists for the later mediaeval period, but a number of investigations[2] into

---

[1] *V. infra*, p. 231.
[2] *V.* A. Steel, 'Some Aspects of English Government Finance in the Fourteenth Century', in *History*, n.s. 12 (1927–28), pp. 298–309; 'English Government Finance, 1377–1413', in *E.H.R.* LI (1936), pp. 29–51, 577–597; 'The Practice of Assignment in the later fourteenth century', in *ibid.*, XLIII (1928), pp. 172–180;

finance and exchequer practice reveal the extent to which the royal finances and exchequer procedure became embarrassed in the late fourteenth century. The financial history of the period was on the whole one of failing resources, greater resort than ever to declining credit, of attempts, not very successful, to procure a general survey of assets and liabilities, of growing deficits, and of a state of affairs in which there was a ' rapidly narrowing gap between the financial resources of the Crown and those of its greater subjects'.[1] This general condition, the full consequences of which were to be felt under the Lancastrians in the first half of the fifteenth century, was of course primarily due to the unprecedentedly heavy cost of the French war, but was aggravated by the weaknesses of the Exchequer as a revenue-collecting authority,[2] and by its disastrous and unscrupulous methods of inflating its credit. ' Fourteenth-century finance was built upon the assignment and the tally, or writs of privy seal or bills of Wardrobe or letters of great seal'.[3] A great increase in borrowing from foreign and other merchants and bankers enabled Edward III to finance his French war-policies.[4] The enormous expansion of the practice of assignment, with frequent dishonouring of such tallies, or their conversion into fictitious loans, and the consequent issue of fresh tallies of assignment, resulted in the same amount of money often doing duty as revenue twice over or more, to the grave detriment of creditors and the growing resentment of the public, not to mention the

---

' The Negotiation of Wardrobe Debentures in the fourteenth century ', in *ib*. XLIV (1929), pp. 439-443 ; ' The Marginalia of the Treasurer's Receipt Rolls, in *Bull. Inst. Hist. Res.*, VII (1929-30), pp. 67-84, 133-143, VIII (1930-31), pp. 1-13 ; ' The Distribution of Assignment in the Treasurer's Receipt Roll, 1364-5,' in *Camb. Hist. J.*, II, pp. 178-185 ; and J. F. Willard, ' The Memoranda Rolls and the Remembrancers, 1282-1350 ', in *Essays to Tout*, pp. 215-30 ; ' The Crown and its Creditors, 1327-33 ', in *E.H.R.*, XLII (1927), pp. 12-19 ; ' The Treasurer's Issue Rolls and the Clerk of the Treasurer, Edward I–Edward III ', in *Bull. Inst. Hist. Res.*, VIII (1930-31), pp. 129-135. On the whole subject *v*. Steel, *The Receipt of the Exchequer, 1377-1485* (forthcoming).
[1] Steel, in *E.H.R.*, LI (1936), p. 30.
[2] Much information on this subject is to be found in Morris and Strayer, *The English Government at Work*, vol. II (1947), Fiscal Administration. *V*. especially the Introduction by J. R. Strayer.
[3] Steel, in *History*, n.s. 12 (1927-28), p. 302.
[4] On this subject cf. E. B. Fryde, ' Materials for the study of Edward III's credit operations, 1327-38 ', in *Bull. Inst. Hist. Res.*, XXII (1949), pp. 105-138, XXIII (1950), pp. 1-30.

heavy discounting of such tallies when used as negotiable instruments. Moreover, ' whatever the means adopted, the practice of assignment meant that the Exchequer of Receipt was becoming more and more a clearing house for writs and tallies, and less and less the scene of cash transactions.'[1] Some cash of course continued to enter the Receipt, and some sort of relation between cash and credit was maintained,[2] but by the early fifteenth century, the low level of cash at the Receipt led to the virtual repudiation of exchequer obligations in the later Lancastrian period.[3]

The floating and re-floating of credits inevitably added greatly to the difficulties of reaching any balance in the royal accounts of revenue and expenditure, a process difficult enough with the prevailing methods of book-keeping and the complicated methods of collections and disbursement. As Sir Hilary Jenkinson and Miss Dorothy Broome have pointed out,[4] the head of the State, like the heads of departments who were not ecclesiastics, did little reading or writing. 'Accounting therefore ceased at the point where the official who presided over the department had sufficient record for his own purposes of his relations with his sub-accountants—could tell by reference to his rolls how much a given man had brought in at a given date, what allowances he had claimed for expenditure, and how much had still to be exacted from him. Henry VII at the end of the mediaeval period was struggling to gain a personal knowledge of, and control over, his finances—his signature in numerous accounts and the changes introduced during his reign into the auditing system bear witness to it; but it was not till the full development of parliamentary control made unavoidable the regular preparation of statements, balances, and estimates that the old machinery in which such routine work had no place was very gradually scrapped.'[5]

Nevertheless, the growing difficulty of making ends meet gave rise during the fourteenth century to attempts to present

---

[1] Steel, *op. cit.*, p. 303.
[2] Willard, in *E.H.R.*, XLII, pp. 12–19.
[3] Steel, in *Bull. Inst. Hist. Res.*, VIII, pp. 8–13.
[4] *V.* 'An Exchequer Statement of Receipts and Issues, 1339–40', in *E.H.R.* LVIII (1943), pp. 210–216.
[5] *Ibid.*, pp. 210–11.

an over-all picture of the financial position. Some partial ' views ' of daily and weekly ' states ' of the finances survive from the years 21 Edward I to 10 Edward II, and occasional attempts at a general balance were made. An ordinance of 1326 foreshadows the endeavour ; the Ordinances of Walton of 1338 specifically ordered the treasurer to enquire into the extent of debts and liabilities and to estimate the revenue needed to meet them and to enable the king ' to maintain his estate ', and such an attempt actually was made for the period 15 January, 1339 to 4 May, 1340.[1] The attempt was repeated in 1358-59, for several years together, and the first attempt at making a balance sheet for a financial year is dated 1362-63.[2] The interest of this document is that it seems to be ' the first attempt in a series of efforts to impress on parliament and public opinion the enormous sums of money which the king was compelled to disburse and the absolute impossibility of meeting such expenditure save by special grants on a scale comparable to the grants made avowedly for the conduct of the war '.[3] The revelation made by this balance sheet was sufficiently alarming—a deficit of over £55,000 —an amount exceeding one year's revenue. A somewhat better prospect was shown in the estimate made for 1363-64, but the low level of the ancient revenues of the shires, and the decline of net income induced by the practice of assignment, doubtless inspired the effort to convince parliament that the king could not ' live of his own '. No adequate solution to these problems, however, was forthcoming, and later, when Henry VII tackled them afresh, it was not to the Exchequer, but to the Chamber, that he looked for a restoration of financial order and stability.[4]

Late in the period with which we are at present concerned, new administrative instruments appeared, and require some consideration here, for the future lay very much with them. The king's secretary and the signet seal and office, the royal

---

[1] *Ib.*, pp. 210–216.
[2] T. F. Tout and D. Broome, 'A National Balance Sheet for 1362-3 ', in *E.H.R.* XXXIX (1924), pp. 404–419.
[3] *Ib.*, p. 407. For a detailed discussion of the Exchequer's method of dealing with collectors of taxes in the period 1290–1334, *v.* Willard, *Parliamentary Taxes on Personal Property* (1934), pp. 250–343, and on the collection of taxes, *v.* articles in Morris and Strayer, *op. cit.*
[4] *V. infra*, p. 264.

sign-manual and endorsed bills, did not, perhaps, attain to a place of any great importance before the middle or later part of Richard II's reign, but by that time all were in use and the foundations of their later immense development had been laid.[1]

We have seen above[2] how in the thirteenth and early four-teenth centuries, some of the king's most confidential clerks were commonly called *secretarii*. For long this term was employed as a description of certain individuals rather than as the designation of an office, and in so far as it had any precise connotation in the earlier fourteenth century, it meant the keepers of the privy seal, who, between 1307 and 1367, were habitually called *secretarii*. William of Wykeham, who gave up the keepership of the privy seal to become chancellor, was the last keeper to be called secre-tary. By Richard II's reign, the king's secretary had come to hold a recognized office, and its holder was the keeper of the signet seal.

The signet, as we have seen,[3] was not new at this time. The term 'signet' began as a synonym for the secret seal in the reign of Edward III, and it may be that French analogies[4] gradually ousted the term ' secret seal ' as the designation of the most personal seal of the king. It is perhaps not very clear how or why the secret seal in the custody of the Chamber came to be replaced by the signet seal in the custody of the secretary, but this replacement occurred, and presumably was mainly due to a need for a strictly personal seal closer to the king himself than perhaps the Chamber and its seal could by this time be. Richard II used a finger-signet ring as a substitute for the privy seal for a short time after his accession. Soon the signet came to be the king's personal seal, and as such to play a considerable part in the initiation of administrative action ; during the reign a distinct signet office emerged, with its own clerks and organization. From this time onwards an unbroken series of signet letters is

---

[1] Tout, *Chapters*, V, pp. 195–230 ; L. B. Dibben, ' Secretaries in the thirteenth and fourteenth centuries ', in *E.H.R.*, XV (1910), pp. 430–444 ; F. M. G. Evans, ' The Pre-Tudor Secretary ', in *Essays to Tout*, pp. 361–366, *The Principal Secretary of State* (1923), pp. 1–18 ; J. Otway-Ruthven, *The King's Secretary and the Signet Office in the XV century* (1939) ; Maxwell-Lyte, *The Great Seal*, pp. 113–117.

[2] *V. supra*, p. 100.

[3] *V. supra*, p. 200.

[4] Cf. Tout, *op. cit.*, pp. 197–199.

preserved among the chancery warrants ; before long similar warrants were issued to the keeper of the privy seal, and many letters of signet were sent to individual officers, including the principal officers in their capacity as councillors.

The practice of using letters *sub signeto* for the initiation of action was greatly extended in the years 1383–86, but inevitably receded during the years of the ascendancy of the Lords Appellant, when the exercise of the king's personal initiative was under restraint. At this time Archbishop Arundel went so far as to refuse to recognize the signet as a sufficient direct warrant for the great seal, and the Merciless Parliament of 1388 attacked its use, prohibiting the issue of letters of signet ' to the disturbance of the law and the danger of the realm '. But naturally it came back into use when Richard II regained his position, particularly in connection with his Irish expeditions, even though not so prominently or frequently as before ; the number of signet warrants to Chancery declined. When the time came for the Lancastrians to draw up accusations against Richard II, they included a somewhat fatuous charge that he had made the sheriffs swear to obey all mandates under the great seal, privy seal, and signet—which presumably they ought to have obeyed whether they had sworn to do so or not. But Henry IV in his turn was only too eager to display to the estates the signet which Richard II had taken off his finger and presented to him as the symbol of the transference of personal sovereignty. The greatest days of the signet were yet to come.

In this period kings were becoming literate, and consequently the royal sign-manual or signature began to play some part in administrative processes. The earliest known incursion of royal literacy into this sphere dates from 1330, with the young Edward III's superscription of the words ' *Pater Sancte* ' to give added personal significance to a letter to the Pope of that year sealed under the privy, secret, or signet seal.[1] The royal sign-manual— initials or full signature—came to be used with some frequency in the time of Richard II ;[2] in some instances to give additional

---

[1] *V.* Tout, *ibid.*, III, p. 28. For a facsimile *v.* C. G. Crump in *E.H.R.* XXVI, (1921), pp. 331-332, and Johnson and Jenkinson, *English Court Hand* (1915), pl. XXII.

[2] Tout, *ibid.*, p. 28 n. 1; V, pp. 61, 216, 224 n. 2.

authority to letters under the signet, or sometimes, the privy seal; in other instances on ' immediate warrants ' or signed bills, i.e., bills or petitions received by him and endorsed by him with initials or signature and handed on for implementation to one or other of the administrative officers. The use of the royal sign-manual did not in this period attain to any significant proportions, but the precedents for it had been set, and were to be followed on a growing scale in the fifteenth and later centuries.

§ 2. We have seen above that, as Professor Morris has said of the early part of this period, ' the exercise of prerogative power in one form or another, was almost a daily feature of government '.[1] There was much personal exercise of executive power, but in some spheres and connections, there was also much that was impersonal. A sharing of royal power with the Council was still a matter of administrative convenience, rather than of constitutional tradition.[2] As yet, personal government by the sovereign manifested itself through ' his own assertions of power, and partly through action by the Council ', whilst what we should call constitutional propriety was exemplified by ' customary action through the automatic operations of the institutions of government '.[3] For as yet the Council was essentially the king's agent. ' The Council was the mainstay of the king's government and an agent of his prerogative. It was a most effective force in administration, either in conjunction with him, or as often, when he himself did not act '.[4] ' The king did not act through, but with his Council. Standing alone, the Council was in no sense the vehicle of the unimpaired and unlimited prerogative of the Crown '.[5]

We must not suppose that as yet the Council stood or acted apart from the king, or could act independently of him. Professor Wilkinson's judicious words on this subject deserve to be quoted. ' Government ', he says,[6] ' was still in a real and effective way government by the king ; the king alone was central and essential

---

[1] Willard and Morris, *op. cit.*, p. 3.
[2] *Ib.*, p. 12.
[3] *Ib.*
[4] *Ib.*, p. 29.
[5] Wilkinson, ' The Chancery ', *ibid.*, p. 164.
[6] *Ib.* p. 162.

to the whole. All ministers carried out the king's commands however expressed, or stood in his place. Standing in place of the king, a minister exercised a power narrowly limited and defined ; the great and only universal distinction in administration was that between acts which did and acts which did not involve the prerogative of the king. Not even the Council was above this general law. It applied equally to the ministers of state and the *familia et servi* of the king ; the distinction between the theoretical and even the practical independence of these two categories is largely modern and unreal. Where the prerogative of the king was involved, all ministers steadily refused to act alone. Nothing had happened since the days of Henry II to invalidate the administrative ideals of Richard FitzNigel . . . In the last analysis the king was, from the administrative point of view, supreme ; to question his judgment beyond a certain point was to transmute administrative zeal into political opposition ; it was to go *countre lestat de la Coronne* '.

This lucid description helps to give a clear and intelligible perspective to our picture of administration in the mid-fourteenth century—a perspective which has often been sadly lacking in many canvases depicting the period. We shall, however, have to consider in due course how far this picture became modified by the course of events in the later part of the century, how far, that is to say, the practice of personal government became modified. But first, we must look more closely at the Council as an administrative body in the reigns of Edward III and Richard II.[2]

We have already noted[1] how the king's councillors developed administrative functions and reached decisions which were implemented through one or other of the seals. This process continued in the period of which we are now speaking. 'After 1332 the Council often appeared in an executive rather than an advisory capacity'.[3] The commonest form of implementation was by a writ of privy seal, although the signet was sometimes used for this purpose in the later years of the period. Many

---

[1] In addition to the above, *v.* Baldwin, ' The Council ', in *ibid.*, pp. 129–161 ; *The King's Council in England during the Middle Ages* (1913) ; Wilkinson, *Studies*, pp. 108–173.

[2] *V. supra*, p. 163.

[3] Morris, in Willard and Morris, *op. cit.*, p. 57.

chancery letters under great seal were warranted *per regem et consilium*, *per consilium*, *per petitionem de consilio*, or *per privatum sigillum*. Many petitions were now relegated by parliament to the Council, and subsequently dealt with by counciliar methods.[1] The king's councillors themselves formed an administrative core to parliaments ; some of them were individually summoned ; the chief management of affairs in parliament had been, and in part still was, in the hands of the king and his councillors, who between them often transacted business in the presence of the magnates, who might often fill the role of watchful but inactive spectators ; it all depended upon the nature of the business in hand and the extent to which it might affect baronial interests. For some kinds of business, administrative decisions might be reached in parliament, and the authority for action might be recorded as that of the king and council in parliament, or by petition in parliament, or simply by the Council without specific reference to parliament at all.[2] From the official point of view, parliament was a meeting of the king and his Council,[3] and we must beware of drawing too sharp distinctions between the ' ordinary ' council and the council in parliament. As we shall see below,[4] a baronial aspiration later on in the century was at times to make the king's ' continual ' council more like a parliament in miniature and less like a group of officials, and this objective was to be a matter with large implications, not all of which, we can be sure, were foreseen at the time.

We may not say that the privy seal had become the seal of the Council, but it seems clear that from the reign of Edward II, the privy seal was closely associated with the Council, and where we cannot prove it, we can take it for granted that a great many writs and letters under that seal were issued on the authority of the Council rather than of the king himself.[5] The keeper of the privy seal, along with the chancellor and treasurer, was among the principal official councillors. The large extent to which the office of privy seal was utilized by the Council is doubtless part

[1] Baldwin, in Willard and Morris, *op. cit.*, p. 147.
[2] Morris, *ibid.*, pp. 12–13.
[3] *Ib.*, p. 13.
[4] *V. infra*, p. 231.
[5] Wilkinson, in Willard and Morris, *op. cit.*, p. 179.

of the explanation of why the signet emerged as the king's personal seal in this period. By 1332, there was a chamber at the Exchequer ' where the king's council is commonly held ', and about 1340 a new chamber was built at Westminster—the future *camera stellata*.[1]

' The reign of the three Edwards thus witnessed the establishment of the executive powers of the Council. The independent actions of the king's ministers of an earlier period were now supplemented and in some cases superseded, by their collective action in the council. The new institutions assumed far more of the king's functions than the earlier ministers acting individually '.[2] Further development of this kind occurred in the reign of Richard II. ' The emergence of the Council with large executive powers did not grow out of, but was one of the decisive factors contributing towards, the political events of Richard II's reign '.[3] A symptom of this development is the emergence of records of the Council itself, in addition to endorsed petitions and memorials. There may have been such records kept earlier, but the earliest surviving is the journal of 1392.[4] In this journal forty-three meetings of the Council without the king's presence are recorded, at which all manner of business was transacted. The Ordinance for the Council of 1390, and the slightly later 'Advice' of the lords touching the good government of the king and of the realm[5] reveal the large place in the administration now assumed by the Council. ' It is quite evident from other sources that the independent activities of the Council now formed a large part of the government of the State.'[6]

The question of the composition of the ordinary Council cannot be considered without reference to some of the political events of the later fourteenth century. The composition of the Council is the point at which administrative, political, and constitutional history converge most conspicuously in this period. We have seen above how comparatively slight were the

---

[1] Wilkinson, *Studies*, pp. 128-9.
[2] *Ib.*, pp. 129-30.
[3] *Ib.*, p. 132.
[4] For text, *v.* Baldwin, *The King's Council*, pp. 489-504. The journal was kept by John Prophet, a clerk of privy seal, who is usually regarded as the first clerk of the Council.
[5] Wilkinson, *Studies*, p. 133.   [6] *Ibid.*

effects of political opposition upon the permanent structure of the administration in the mediaeval period. Administration was the king's business, and short of putting the king out of business, it was exceedingly difficult, if not impossible, for baronial opposition to make much impression upon the forms and methods of the administration. It can hardly be said that the monarchical principle, with its implied unlimited executive power for the monarch, was either seriously attacked or undermined in the mediaeval period ; such activities belonged to the seventeenth century rather than to any preceding period. Baronial oppositions might seek to force reform of abuses or sometimes fresh policies upon the king, as in 1215, 1258 and 1311, or to force a change in the occupancy of the throne, as in 1327, 1399 and 1461, but no faction as yet proposed to abolish the monarchy or even to strip it of its ultimate executive authority, or to change radically the administrative institutions and methods which the monarchy had created.

All mediaeval oppositions and factions aimed either at capturing the monarchy itself for one or other of their number, or at getting a larger share in the actual exercise of the monarch's executive powers, and the maintenance of the customary administrative institutions and methods was regarded as the best safeguard against arbitrary and capricious government. Critics and opponents of the king's policies tended to be very conservative in their attitudes, and to attach great importance to traditional methods of doing things. Preference was given to the carrying on of such government as had to be carried on ' in the open '— in the institutions which, because they were not too embedded in the recesses of the royal Household, could be increasingly regarded as ' public ' not ' private ' institutions, and the officers at their head as ' public ' officers not *domestici*. This attitude was to have fundamental consequences in the long run upon English history, for it meant that eventually the king's *ministri* were to become Ministers of the Crown, and the offshoots of the royal Household were to become departments ' of State ', whilst the powers vested in the king personally were to become the powers of the Crown. This transmutation, and all that went with it is, of course, the very essence of English constitutional history, and alone made possible the eventual combination of the immunity of the Crown with the legal and political responsibility of its Ministers.

The first steps towards this ultimate and very gradual transmutation were taken when, for whatever reason, the king felt obliged to admit to a share in the exercise of his executive power others than those whom he would have freely chosen for himself. In so far as any king was obliged to do this, the principle of personal government was encroached upon in practice, no matter what the theoretical position might continue to be. A reduction in the scope of the king's discretion in practice was the sole means of starting the long and slow process of development towards what we call ' constitutional monarchy '; no other starting-point could have produced that unique result. No simple enforcement of ' the rule of law ', vital though that was, could have done it; no Great Charters and committees of resistance, no coercion of the king nor any revolutionary commission could have evoked such a result. To produce it the executive powers of the king must remain intact, whilst their exercise must gradually pass in practice to others than the king himself and his freely chosen agents.

No doubt in practice the king's discretion became curtailed with the growth of routine and departmental procedure. In theory the king could of course intervene in administration at any point, dismiss all or any of his officers and start afresh in any field of executive action. But in practice the sheer bulk and scope of the administrative work of government in the thirteenth and fourteenth centuries made reliance upon conciliar or official decision inevitable over a large area of the field. There is much truth in the view that the earliest restriction upon the king's personal action was a bureaucratic check, and an indirect consequence of the monarchy's own creation of administrative agencies. Routine and customary procedure doubtless determined much that was done and how it was done; but this kind of restraint, like the delegation of authority in certain fields to the Council, was not, of course, an external check upon the king. It was merely a self-evolving restraint, emerging from administrative convenience or necessity; it could be cut across by the king at any point if he chose to assert himself, and in any case was confined to comparatively minor matters, not affecting either major affairs of policy nor the king's personal interest. Such developments certainly narrowed the normal range of personal government without affecting its exercise at the level of high policy and affairs of State.

Two ways of modifying purely personal government were possible in practice even at this level—over and above, that is, the periodical exercise of pressure through the advisory, consultative, and fiscal machinery of great councils and parliaments, the summons of which was normally entirely a matter for the king's discretion; two ways, that is, of bringing continuous influence to bear upon the actual exercise of the royal executive power. One way was to secure at least a share in the composition and therefore in the work and decisions of the king's ordinary council; the other was to exert an influence upon the king's choice of principal administrative officers. Both these methods were resorted to at various times in the reigns of Edward III and Richard II, and continued to be resorted to in the Lancastrian period. That as a consequence personal government in practice became in some measure modified cannot be denied ; in so far as success attended these efforts, by so much the royal discretion was curtailed. But no permanent results accrued from these late mediaeval endeavours. For reasons that we cannot attempt to discuss here —some of them will perhaps always remain conjectural—the partial modification of personal government that occurred in the late fourteenth and early fifteenth centuries proved to be impermanent—perhaps mainly because it was too partial to be lasting, perhaps because it was too premature in relation to the general needs and circumstances of the time. Whatever the reason, the fact is that the Yorkist régime in some degree, and the Tudor régime to a vastly greater degree, represented a revival and a triumph of personal government in the executive sphere. It was to be the events of the seventeenth century, not the fourteenth, that produced a permanent modification of the mediaeval principles of personal government by the king. But, in the long run, the methods whereby this result was achieved, were not fundamentally different from those foreshadowed in the fourteenth and early fifteenth centuries—by influencing the Council and the choice of officers ; indeed there could scarcely have been any other methods if the monarchy itself were to be preserved. The result, however, was eventually to be achieved not by magnate factions and baronial oppositions, in or outside of great councils and parliaments with or without the support of the Commons, but by the Commons in parliament, with or without the support of the Lords.

We cannot suppose that in the fourteenth-century oppositions to the monarch's policies were actuated by any theories of ' constitutional ' limitations or any philosophical doctrines. Such results as were achieved were determined by purely practical considerations and by the circumstances of the moment. Consequently they were spasmodic in character and more or less temporary in duration. Possibly, indeed, more was actually achieved by co-operation than by opposition, and more by force of circumstances than by force of any other kind. It would indeed be a grave mistake to suppose that in administrative or constitutional history the most enduring changes were produced by such simple phenomena as ' baronial ' or other oppositions to the monarchy. Straight fights of this sort were apt to produce little but deadlocks or evasions by the monarchy, which usually held the trump cards. Changes came rather from the contingency of innumerable circumstances and forces, over some at least of which neither monarchy nor baronage had any conscious control.

As we have seen already,[1] the composition of the ordinary king's council in the time of Edward II was normally official in character ; this was the model followed in the early years of Edward III, and was undoubtedly the conciliar ideal favoured by him as by his predecessors. Practice in this matter, once Edward III assumed the personal direction of government, continued to be much as it had been in the time of his predecessor. The chancellor, treasurer, and other officers continued to form the core of the Council, with the occasional assistance of other sworn members, some of whom might be ex-officers, whilst a few had not served the king in other capacities. There is no evidence that the customary form of the Council was seriously modified until the crisis of 1341. This crisis has often been

[1] *V. supra*, p. 160.

represented as a struggle between officers of the Household and the ' officers of State ', but, as Professor Wilkinson observes,[1] it was first and foremost a struggle between two sections of the Council—the one abroad and the one at home. Both of these sections were mainly official in character at the time, but the political difficulties in which Edward III found himself, the antagonism of Archbishop Stratford and the Lancastrian interest, and the necessity of securing the maximum co-operation of the baronage in the French war, induced the king to make some modification in the composition of the Council, reducing the curial element and increasing the aristocratic element. The controversy brought a direct attack upon councillors of low estate,[2] and from this time dates the tendency to omit from the personnel of the Council officials of lesser status and to include instead a proportion of men of baronial standing, with a strong preponderance of laymen. 'After 1341, there can be little doubt the barons obtained an influence on the Council greater than they had ever exercised before . . .'[3] Moreover, Edward III was induced to promise that in future his chief ministers, *i.e.*, his principal councillors, should be chosen with the advice of the magnates.

This promise was not exactly followed in the ensuing years, but it is symptomatic of the changing situation. It was not possible for Edward III to carry on the French war without a great deal of goodwill on the part of the baronage, and the modifications of 1341 were induced not by violent opposition between the king and the baronage, but by a prudent desire for conciliation and ' combined operations '. This is an important point, and is well expressed by Professor Wilkinson when he says, ' The change, when it came, was not the outcome of baronial hostility to the Crown, but rather of its opposite, of a long process of co-operation which established the barons securely in a new tradition of administrative activity and participation in the daily work of the council. It was helped by the troubles of Edward II's reign, but equally by the co-operation of Edward I and Edward III with the barons in active policies of war. It was

---

[1] *Studies*, pp. 168–9.
[2] *Ibid.*, p. 170; John Stratford complained about those ' qe ore se fount governours et conseillers pluis avount qe lour estat lour done '.
[3] *Ib.*, p. 171.

due not so much to conscious policy as to the changing needs of administration and the changing character of the barons themselves. The old council of " *domestici* " was based on an ideal of "personal" monarchy such as that of Henry II. The bureaucracy of the fourteenth century made the council, almost as much as parliament, the centre of the national life, and the old view of the Council inevitably disappeared.'[1]

Little further change in the composition of the Council occurred for thirty years, and no substantial difficulties arose in this period. But there is little doubt that most of the work of the Council continued to be done by the principal officers, whether themselves of baronial rank or not. Great lords were reluctant to take a regular and active part in the routine work of administration, and probably seldom attended meetings of the Council unless the occasion was special. The effective core for ordinary purposes continued to be the chancellor, treasurer, and keeper of the privy seal, and a few others; this practice aroused no opposition, for the chief ministers were acceptable to the baronage. ' The king, without abandoning his pretensions, had found it prudent to abate his claims in practice, and to rule through ministers whom the magnates were willing to accept.'[2]

The restoration of harmony and the absence of political difficulties in these years helped to consolidate the administrative system at the centre, perhaps also to reduce such distinctions as may have arisen between ' household ' and ' public ' ministers. Security of tenure of official posts was a marked feature of these years, which saw the further development of a homogeneous civil service ; posts in the Household came to be regarded as training grounds for politicians of a professional type, some of whom were able to combine duty to the Crown with sympathy for baronial attitudes. Laymen became more prominent in administrative posts, high and low ; already the Inns of Court were providing laymen with education and training rivalling those of the ecclesiastics.[3]

---

[1] *Ib.*, pp. 136–7. ' Insensibly too, the warriors of the early period were changing —in spite of the Hundred Years War—into the courtiers and politicians of the sixteenth century, as versed in the arts of government and as competent and as much at home in the council as any king '.

[2] Tout, *Chapters*, III, p. 163.　　　　　　[3] *Ib.* pp. 171, 201–202.

The principle that the king's ministers needed at least to be acceptable to the baronage as well as to the king, had in effect been admitted, and this admission was for the time sufficient to procure harmony within the administration and harmony between the administration and the political interests outside of it. In the process, however, it seems clear, the king's discretion in the choice of councillors and ministers had become less free than it had been before.

No serious administrative difficulties were manifested during the king's absences abroad during these years, and no doubt the large responsibilities falling to the Council at home on these occasions did much to enhance the administrative experience and capacity of the councillors.

The more the king was absent, or, as time went on, the less personal intervention by him in government, the greater the practical importance of the part played by the Council, and especially that played by the chief ministers. The growing ascendancy of William of Wykeham as the king's chief minister marked a decline in the king's own activity and a revival of curialist predominance in the Council. Wykeham's rise from obscure origins to be a king's clerk in 1357, secretary and councillor, keeper of the privy seal in 1363 (nothing was done, it was said, in any respect without his advice), and chancellor in 1367, is reminiscent of an older style of appointing ministers. This and other circumstances, especially the failure to achieve success in the French war, led to a partial breakdown of the prevailing harmony and to a renewal of opposition to the government in 1371.

Probably this episode would not have occurred but for the ambitions of John of Gaunt and his supporters, even if he himself was out of the country at the time.[1] In the upshot, a magnate party was able to sweep the whole of the king's Council out of power, and to install a Council more favourable to John of Gaunt and his policy towards France. This Council remained in the ascendant from 1371-1376, whilst the king himself counted for less and less.

---

[1] *Ib.* pp. 275-6. The mere fact of the absence of John of Gaunt abroad at this time does not disprove his connivance in these proceedings, nor mitigate the conclusion that the changes made were to his advantage.

The parliament of 1371 would not grant a subsidy until the king had agreed to replace his clerical ministers by laymen, and consequently all three chief offices, the chancellorship, treasurership, and keepership of the privy seal changed hands ; similar demands were made in respect of the barons and chamberlains of the Exchequer, the controller of the wardrobe, and ' other great officers and governors of the realm '. Not all these demands were granted, and there was not now, as there had been in 1341, any demand that these new officers should be nominated in parliament.

The episode of 1371[1], though of importance in the history of the subject with which we are concerned here, was not the result of any real conflict between the Crown and the magnates : its results and circumstances were different and less significant than those of 1341. The anti-clericalism of the parliament of 1371 may have been shared to some extent by the king and court themselves ; the new officers, though laymen, and supporters of Gaunt's war-policies, were not magnates of high standing : the immediate advantages of the new arrangements to John of Gaunt were indirect rather than direct, and most of the disadvantage was felt by William of Wykeham. The decline in the king's personal energies and faculties at this time, however, inevitably tended to transfer the real work of government to the Council. The results, in terms of efficiency and good governance, were not happy, and the consequence was the heavy attack on the Council and ministers that was launched in the Good Parliament of 1376.

This attack was remarkable for the apparent initiative taken by the Commons.[2] How far this initiative was in reality inspired by magnate opponents of John of Gaunt is a matter for specula-

[1] *Ib.*, pp. 266 ff ; Wilkinson, *Studies*, p. 171, and *The Chancery under Edward III*, pp. 127 ff.
[2] *V. Anonimalle Chronicle*, ed. V. H. Galbraith (1927). It is difficult to agree with Professor Galbraith's observation (*ib.*, p. 182) that ' the appointment of " continual councillors" was robbed of most of its practical value by the important qualification that the chancellor, treasurer, and keeper of the privy seal and other ministers should be allowed " faire et esploiter les busoignes qe touchent lour offices sanz la presence desditz counseille[r]s" '. Modern Cabinets do not attend upon and supervise departmental ministers whilst they perform the duties of their offices, and it is not likely that the continual councillors would or could have done so.

tion, but is not germane to the present discussion.[1] The attack, when it came, was directed primarily at the corruptions and inefficiencies of the Council and upon John of Gaunt's influence therein. The king himself attended only the opening of the parliament, and then retired, leaving John as his lieutenant to handle the business. The attack seems to have come as a surprise, and the activities of Peter de la Mare as the spokesman (possibly the Speaker) of the Commons, and his tactics in seeking conference with a committee of the lords, could not for the moment be resisted. No complaint of the ministers as a whole was made : the attack was not now against the Crown as such nor against the employment of clerics in the government, but was directed to removing abuses in the administration and to punishing individual ministers for corrupt practices. The latter objective was pursued by resort to the device of ' impeachment ',[2] a procedure implying some sort of responsibility of individual ministers to parliament as well as to the king.

The hope of avoiding bad administration for the future was pursued, and a change in political balance procured, by a reconstruction of the Council. It was to be ' afforced ' by three bishops, three earls, and three barons, without whom nothing important was to be done. The lords supported this proposal by the Commons, and the king assented to it. The lords, considering that the government of the realm was the king's business and not parliament's, asked the king to select the nine new councillors, which he agreed to do with their advice.

The Commons soon went further, and expressed no confidence in the ministers' capacity to wage the war ; they asked for a further strengthening of the Council by ten or twelve lords and prelates, so that no great matter should pass without the advice and assent of the whole Council, whilst lesser matters should be dealt with by the advice and assent of six or four of them, and six or four councillors should be in continual attendance. The

---

[1] *V*. Stubbs, *Constitutional History*, II, pp. 453–55 ; Tout, *op. cit.*, III, pp. 292 ff ; Wilkinson, *Studies*, pp. 171 ff ; *The Chancery*, pp. 132 ff. ; Baldwin, *op. cit.*, pp. 115 ff.

[2] T. F. T. Plucknett, ' The Origin of Impeachment ', in *Trans. R.H.S.* 4th ser. XXIV (1942), pp. 47–72, and ' The Impeachments of 1376 ', in *ibid.*, 5th ser. I (1951), 153–164, which largely supersede M. V. Clarke, ' The Origin of Impeachment ', in *Oxford Essays presented to H. E. Salter* (1934), pp. 164–189.

chancellor, treasurer, keeper of the privy seal, and other ministers, however, were to continue to perform the duties of their respective offices without the presence of the new councillors. ' This showed that the careful renunciation of executive authority, which marks this parliament, still influenced their action.'[1]

The comparative moderation of the attack, comprehensive as it was, is one of the most remarkable features of the episode, and it was perhaps all the more moderate because by now the most effective mode of attack had been discovered. The royal prerogative was untouched; the government was subjected to purge and reform by the attack on individual ministers and the demand for a reconstructed Council; particular abuses were remedied, but the administrative system was left alone. ' The administrative system came out of the storm unharmed. The commons were satisfied with the institutions of the country as they were, and had no wish to make drastic changes. They did not criticise the chancery; and they gave a handsome testimonial to the efficiency of the exchequer. The privy seal was recognised as an office of state, not denounced as drag on the wheel. Even the chamber was not assailed, though some of its officers were the prime offenders against good government. The old complaints against the courts of the household were renewed, but with little emphasis. A contrast between the great ministers and the household staff was hardly suggested. No organised office of the household was blamed, though many individual officers were criticised. In all this we can see real administrative progress.'[2]

But the king's discretion had been once more curtailed in practice, and although he himself was acquiescent, there were others at court who were not so disposed. When the parliament came to an end in July, 1376, a new court party under the leadership of John of Gaunt set itself to reverse the policy of the Good Parliament and to throw off the trammels that had been devised. John himself had not been included in the new Council, which could not be got rid of nor materially changed in composition until October. By then John and his supporters had sufficiently organized their forces as to procure the whitewashing of reaction in a great council of magnates,

[1] Tout, *op. cit.*, p. 300. [2] *Ib.*, pp. 306–7.

at the cost of making a scapegoat of William of Wykeham, who had returned to the Council in 1376 in the guise of a champion of the opposition. We are not here concerned to notice the political manoeuvring of John of Gaunt and his party in the last few months of Edward III's reign, his moves to secure a docile parliament in January, 1377, his relations with the Church, the effect upon his fortunes of the death of the Black Prince, nor the rise of the political importance of the young Richard and his followers. Suffice it to say that in these months the work of the Good Parliament was undone, and a court party secured control of the government. But it was now a court party in which the king himself counted for little or nothing personally. The administration had in effect passed into the hands of an aristocratic faction acting in the king's name, predominating in the Council and with its nominees in the principal ministerial offices.

The seventy years that had elapsed since the death of Edward I had thus culminated in a decline of personal government by the king such as would have seemed inconceivable to that monarch. ' The middle years of Edward III witnessed indeed for the baronage the triumph of their most cherished constitutional ideal. They obtained from the conciliatory policy of Edward III what they could never extort, in spite of all his weakness, from the hostility of Edward II. They obtained that place on the royal council which they never really lost until the days of Henry VII.'[1]

The increase in aristocratic elements in the Council in the later fourteenth century was accompanied by a reduction in the number of the lesser officials attending the Council, and also by a magnification of the public and ministerial character of the three principal officers. The justices ceased to be normally sworn of the Council from 15 Edward III, although some of them were summoned from time to time to advise upon legal business; clerks of the household departments tended to be dropped out; aliens, financiers, and casual helpers of the Crown, who had sometimes been sworn even if they had seldom attended, were also eliminated from the Council; lesser lay officials of the Household, knights, bannerets, or ' bachelors ', attending the

---

[1] Wilkinson, *The Chancery*, p. 144.

Council were reduced in number, though by no means eliminated in the time of Richard II.[1]

But the chancellor, treasurer, and keeper of the privy seal always figured among the councillors, and seem in 1376 to have been the only officials recognized as having an *ex officio* right to be included. As the heads of the three most important departments of administration, they were more than ever the key men, and the filling of their posts became a major political question, and the public importance of their offices became emphasized. In the process they became something more than the king's servants, though of course they remained that in theory. ' In the weakness of the monarchy the political importance of the chancellor and treasurer [and may not we add, the keeper of the privy seal ?] and their pre-eminence on the Council was assured. Their greatest power in general politics, perhaps, came with the predominance of the council under the weak Lancastrians ; it was only with the recreation of the monarchy by the Tudors that they once more began to be relegated to a secondary place.'[2]

In the minority of Richard II, no formal regency was appointed.[3] The larger ill-defined ' great ' Council of magnates continued to meet from time to time, whilst the small Council was given full authority to deal with all State business in the king's name. Two ' continual ' Councils were appointed by letters patent in 1377 ; the first of twelve members by the great Council in July; the second in parliament in October, in which it was also agreed that the chancellor, treasurer, steward, and chamberlain of the Household should be chosen. Four political elements were reflected in the composition of these Councils : the followers of John of Gaunt, the anti-' popular ' party associated with them, the personal followers of the late Black Prince, and the ' popular ' party associated with them. The first two of these were predominant in the July Council, but a more even balance was in evidence in that of October. The latter Council remained in being, possibly with some changes, until early

---

[1] Baldwin, *op. cit.*, pp. 75–87.
[2] Wilkinson, *op. cit.*, pp. 146.
[3] N. B. Lewis, ' The " Continual Council " in the early years of Richard II ', in *E.H.R.* XLI (1926), pp. 246–251 ; Tout, *op. cit.*, III, pp. 323–43.

1380, when a parliament petitioned for its discharge. In this parliament the Commons were dissatisfied with the councillors' work, asked for their discharge and for the appointment in parliament of the five principal officers. The continual Council remained in obscurity for some years, during which the principal officers presumably conferred with each other as need arose. For several years parliament gave up the idea of trying to control the course of government by securing the appointment in parliament of a continual council.

The intervening years between 1380 and 1386 saw the consolidation of a new court party. The Peasants' Revolt of 1381 had no appreciable effect upon administrative history ; for six years the course of parliamentary and administrative life went on much as before, and such efforts at administrative reform as were made were largely fruitless.[1] The growing strength of the court party, and the assertion of power by the young king himself, frustrated attempts by the frequent parliaments of these years to influence the administration. The steward and chamberlain of the Household figured more prominently in government, and the signet and signet office were more commonly employed to give effect to the king's wishes ; signet warrants were recognized by the chancellor as obligatory for the chancery. The result was the provocation of a fresh opposition party, facilitated by the departure of John of Gaunt to Spain in July, 1386, for four years. The opposition was now headed by Thomas, duke of Gloucester, and by Gaunt's son, Henry, earl of Derby, and other magnates of high rank.

This opposition reached a climax in the parliament of 1386.[2] Richard II, it seems, was not prepared for the onslaught made on his ministers when the parliament met, nor for the brutal strength of the political forces ranged against him. The demand for the nomination in parliament of ' sufficient officers ', including the chancellor, treasurer, keeper of the privy seal, the steward, and also other ' lords of his great and continual councils ', and the impeachment of Michael de la Pole, earl of Suffolk, the then

---

[1] Tout, *op. cit.*, p. 385. For the events of the reign in general *v.* Steel, *Richard II* (1941), *passim*.
[2] Tout, *ib.* pp. 408 ff ; Baldwin, *op. cit.*, pp. 127 ff.

chancellor, were at first resisted (' the king would not dismiss the humblest scullion '), but a savage reminder of the fate of Edward II soon brought him to submission. The chancellor, treasurer, and keeper of the privy seal were dismissed, and partisans of the opposition nominated in their places, though the demand for a new steward was shelved. To secure influence on the future government, the opposition sought to impose upon the king a reconstructed Council or commission with very wide powers to review and reform the administration. Richard II was obliged to agree to this arrangement for one year from November, 1386, but at the dissolution of the parliament on 28 November, the king declared that he would save the prerogatives and rights of his crown.

For the time being, however, the commission ousted the king from the actual direction of government. 'With the great and privy seals in hostile hands, with the signet pushed aside as unconstitutional, with all finance controlled by an unfriendly treasurer, and with the commission dismissing his servants at its pleasure, the king could neither give effect to his wishes nor procure supplies for his necessities.'[1]

This indeed was not merely a modification of personal government by the king; it was a suspension of it, and Richard II prepared to resist. He built up a party, established the nucleus of an alternative administration consisting mostly of household officers, the steward, the secretary, the under-chamberlains, clerks and knights of the Wardrobe and Chamber, and gathered together military forces. In the course of his perambulations he consulted the judges at Shrewsbury and at Nottingham as to the legality of the proceedings of the parliament of 1386.[2] The judge's pronouncement that some of these proceedings encroached upon the prerogative and were illegal is a pronouncement of great interest in constitutional and legal history ; there can be no doubt that the opinions of the judges on most of the points raised were inevitable in the then existing state of the law. We are not, however, concerned to discuss this matter with the detailed attention

---

[1] Tout, *ib.*, p. 418.

[2] *Ib.*, p. 422 ff ; Steel, *op. cit.*, pp. 131 ff. The best commentary at present available is that by Plucknett in his revised edition of Taswell-Langmead's *Constitutional History*, 10th edition, pp. 192-3.

which it deserves but has not yet received. Richard II in fact was not yet strong enough to throw off the trammels imposed upon him; his opponents retorted by 'appealing' his five principal supporters, and coerced him into agreeing to the summons of another parliament. The commission, although its time had expired, continued to direct the administration, issued many warrants *per concilium*, arrested royal partisans, and purged the Household and judicial bench of 'undesirable elements'. The Lords Appellant secured their triumph in the Merciless Parliament of February to June, 1388.[1]

A new Council including the five Lords Appellant was set up, and no one not appointed to it was to interfere with the government in any way, except by order of the continual Council and with the assent of the king; the purge of the Household was continued, as well as a review of the administrative offices and the law courts.

All initiative and discretion on the part of the king was thus ruled out, and his government was carried on in his name by the councillors. During the rule of the Appellants not a single warranty by the signet appears on the chancery rolls; warranties were now by the king and Council, by the Council, by the king and Council in parliament, or with the assent of the prelates, nobles, magnates, and Commons in parliament, or by petition of parliament. The Chancery as an administrative department had a prominent part to play in the administration, and Chancellor Arundel seems to have seized the opportunity to procure ordinances for the better regulation of chancery work and organization, whilst the Council sponsored some minor administrative reforms.

The undiluted régime of the Appellant Council did not, however, last very long, and it rather tamely collapsed in May, 1389,[2] when Richard II asserted his sovereignty. He was able to announce to a 'great' Council the assumption or re-assumption of his powers, to dismiss the continual Council, and to transfer the great seal to William of Wykeham, and to replace the other principal officers. As yet, however, the king walked warily, and still left the direction of the administration largely

[1] Tout, *ib.*, pp. 430 ff; Baldwin, *op. cit.*, pp. 130 ff.
[2] Tout, *ib.*, pp. 454 ff.

to a reconstituted Council, and adopted a conciliatory policy towards the Appellants, which he could well afford to do with the return of John of Gaunt in October, 1389, and the accession of the Lancastrian interest to the support of the court party. The result was undoubtedly favourable to the consolidation of what we may call the conciliar method of directing the administration, now with the king's favour and backing. The ' Ordinance for the government of the king's council ', dated 8th March, 1390— the earliest of the kind now surviving—may be taken as representing a formal recognition of the fact that much business of State would be dealt with by and in the Council. By its terms, the first business to be considered in Council as soon as the ' great men ' and the officers were present, was the affairs of the king and kingdom ; business that touched the common law was to be relegated to the justices of the two benches ; what concerned the chancellor was to go to Chancery, and financial business to the treasurer in the Exchequer. All other matters requiring the special grace and permission of the king were to be referred to him to ascertain his opinion and pleasure. In certain respects, however, the king's will was to be limited by the councillors. No gift or grant which might reduce the royal resources was to pass without the advice of the Council and the assent of the dukes of Guienne (John of Gaunt), York, and Gloucester, and of the chancellor, or any two of them. No ministerial office was to be granted without first taking the advice of the Council. No business of great importance was to be determined without the advice of the Council and the ministers, but the bills of individuals might be examined and determined by the keeper of the privy seal and other councillors present. Orderly procedure was prescribed, and John Prophet's journal[1] for the years 1392-3 is a tribute to the businesslike proceedings of the newly regulated Council. The consolidation of the Council as the apex of the general administration is perhaps the most important feature of these years. ' The Council ', says Tout, ' becoming in some ways the real source of executive authority, remained the body which, by the generality of its appeal and the width of its range, kept together the various branches of the State. . . The last word was

[1] *V. supra*, p. 219.

usually with the Council, which may therefore be regarded as the actual ruler of England.' Some examples of council in resistance to the king's wishes exist in this period.[1]

The king did not as a rule attend the meetings of this 'work a day' Council,[2] which often met several times a week, and might sit for a good many hours a day. Inevitably magnate members could not face a régime of this kind, and such meetings usually comprised five or six persons only, with the chancellor, treasurer, and keeper of the privy seal as the permanent nucleus, and other officials, such as the steward or under-chamberlain, and ' bachelors ', whose duties in the Household required residence at court, re-inforced from time to time with justices, sergeants-at-law, or a bishop or earl. For discussion of major questions, it was necessary to summon a number of magnates (never in this period exceeding twenty-nine), to make up what was usually called a ' great ' Council, which the king himself attended. These great Councils, however, were essentially consultative in character, and the translation of their deliberations into administrative action remained for the small Council and the departments. Government by the Council was a reality in these years. Few and short parliaments were the rule at this time, and so far from any attacks being launched on the prevailing system of government, in the parliament of November to December, 1391, a declaration was made, nominally at least, on a petition of the Commons, that the king should be as free in his royal dignity as any of his predecessors, notwithstanding any statute to the contrary.[3]

It looked therefore as though stability in the governmental system had been secured ; the king was in theory to be no less king, that is to say, vested with no less executive power, than his predecessors, whilst much of his power in practice was to be exercised by a Council in which magnates and parliaments should have confidence. As it turned out, however, the balance was soon to be upset, not by renewed opposition, but by the king himself, and the eventual reaction to this was indirectly to cost him his throne and his life.

[1] Tout, *ib.*, pp. 468-9.
[2] *Ib.*, pp. 470 ff.
[3] *Ib.*, p. 474.

With Richard II's building up of party strength and the precise moves he took to rid himself of the trammels of the settlement of 1388–89, we are not here concerned.[1] That at this stage he played his cards with great skill seems clear. He won over several of the magnates, lay and ecclesiastical, who had hitherto supported the opposition or had held aloof; he developed the military strength of the Household, and employed officials upon whose help he could rely ; the secretary and signet office played an important part in the royal *coup d'état*. This office of the signet became better organized, probably whilst Roger Walden was secretary, as the personal secretariat of the king ; Edmund Stafford, keeper of the privy seal from 1389, and chancellor from January, 1397, brought his administrative potentialities into the cause ; lesser officials of the Household, especially knights of the Chamber, such as Bushy, Bagot, and Green, and others, drawn mainly from the ranks of the minor aristocracy, added their zeal and energy. But, as Tout observed, ' a monarchical *coup d'état*, like an aristocratic withdrawal of all power from the crown, could only be effected through and by parliament.'[2] In the parliaments of January, 1397, September, 1397, and at Shrewsbury, January, 1398, the king was able to procure, at any rate with the use of persuasive methods, all that he wanted : his revenge on the Appellants, the revocation of the Act of 1386, of the commission, and the Acts of the Merciless Parliament of 1388.

As a consequence, the unfettered executive power of the monarchy was completely restored ; the modifications of and encroachments upon the personal power of the king to govern which had been made in the course of the previous thirty years were swept away entirely, and the only restraints on the king's own executive authority were the bureaucratic restraints of routine and procedure and departmental custom. The revival of undiluted monarchical power did not, of course, involve any substantial change in administrative machinery, which had been created by the monarchy itself. The secretary and signet office now were regarded as normal elements in the machine, and the

---

[1] *Ib.*, IV, pp. 1–36.
[2] *Ib.*, p. 14.

signet took its place among the credited instruments of administration ; all the seals were now in the charge of ministers who
were wholly dependent upon the king, and all parts of the central
government resumed their normal positions and relations with
each other, under the king and the general direction of his
councillors. ' The permanent administrative machinery had now
been stabilised by generations of use and wont. Whether the
final word belonged to the king or the aristocracy, the offices and
officials were the same. The chancery, the exchequer, the privy
seal, the two benches, and the various local authorities had each
its well-defined sphere. Each tended to acquire a more clearly
cut individuality, but each became an integral part of a single
public service. The household offices in the same way were
co-ordinated more and more with the public offices in a general
scheme. Whosoever controlled the central State controlled also
its various departments.'[1]

Notwithstanding the casting off of trammels, Richard II in
the few months (February, 1398–May, 1399) of freedom of
power that remained to him, made little show of acting upon his
own initiative, and the advice of his Council, or even the ' authority of parliament ' (meaning the parliamentary commission set
up at Shrewsbury in January, 1398,)[2] was frequently cited as the
authority for executive acts. ' The result was a strengthening
of the tendency, already clearly apparent, of reducing the king's
council to a small bureaucratic body.'[3] The Council became more
than ever ' a group of " experts ", from whose deliberations
unwanted persons were excluded, and which the king himself
seldom attended.'[4]

We cannot here enter into the circumstances of the reaction to
Richard II's policies, the successful *coup d'état* of 1399, and of
Richard II's deposition. The revolution of 1399[5] did not arise
out of an organized opposition to Richard II's administrative or
constitutional system, but out of the personal grievances of Henry
Bolingbroke and out of dissatisfaction with Richard II's govern-

[1] *Ib.*, p. 42.
[2] *V. ib.*, pp. 30–36, and Steel, *op. cit.*, pp. 246 ff.
[3] Tout, *ib.*, p. 51.
[4] *Ib.*, pp. 51–2; Baldwin, *op. cit.*, pp. 138–144.
[5] Tout, *ib.*, pp. 53 ff.; Steel, *op. cit.*, pp. 260–288.

ment. The success Henry obtained in pursuing his quarrel with
the king was far greater than he can have anticipated, and the
rapid collapse of Richard's régime must have been unexpected.
The consequential dynastic change was an incident rather than
a landmark in administrative history, and did not involve any
substantial institutional changes. ' If the fall of Richard II
proves anything at all, it is that administrative history presents a
continuity which is broken neither by reaction nor by revolution.'[1]

Henry Bolingbroke, in acquiring the Crown for himself and
his heirs, manifested no desire to acquire any less regality than
that which had been vested in Richard II and his predecessors
the kings of England,[2] and he took over and worked the same
administrative machinery. But he could not avoid being, to
some extent, hoist with his own petard of former days. He
had been a Lord Appellant, and could not altogether rid himself
of the consequences of his own and others' promotion of conciliar
government, nor in any event in practice could he rid himself of
his aristocratic associates in the revolution, who inevitably
expected to share in the spoils and fruits of success. But as now
king himself, the heir of Lancaster could hardly regard the prerogatives of the Crown in quite the same light as he had viewed
them in the days of his opposition. Thus Henry IV in his turn,
and his heirs after him, struggled to maintain the free exercise of
the executive powers of the monarchy, but only with partial
success. The first half of the fifteenth century was to witness a
series of vicissitudes in this struggle, in which the essential stake
at issue was not, indeed, parliamentary government, but the
maintenance of personal government by the king and his chosen
agents, or its diminution by aristocratic encroachments, whether
in the continual Council, great Councils, or Councils in Parliaments. In the course of this struggle, little or nothing that was
new in administrative machinery or method was invented. No
matter what political vicissitudes occurred, the administration
carried on in much the same ways. ' The point at issue was only
whether this machine of State was to be controlled by the king

[1] Tout, *ib.*, p. 65.
[2] Lapsley, *op. cit.*, p. 283, and Chrimes, *English Constitutional Ideas in the Fifteenth Century*, (1936), p. 8.

or by the nobles.'[1] The administrative system of the Plantagenets remained, to serve the turn of Lancaster, York, and Tudor successively. The difference between these régimes lay essentially, not in any very great differences of administrative machinery, but in the difference in the degree to which they were successful in making the machinery work effectively.

[1] Tout, *op. cit.*, p. 65.

EPILOGUE

THE TRANSITION FROM MEDIAEVAL TO TUDOR ADMINISTRATION

The difficulties of viewing English administrative history in in the fifteenth century still remain formidable. Singularly little work has as yet been done on the relevant record material for this period, and indeed much remains to be done to elucidate the history of the executive in every century of the modern period. Until more has been done, much will remain obscure, not only in the history of administration proper, but also in the broader domain of constitutional history. Until far more light has been thrown upon the actual working of the executive in the various periods of the modern era, much of our knowledge of the later history of English government must be regarded as provisional, and some of our commonly accepted interpretations of it may come to be revised considerably in that light when it is shed.

Nothing like the detailed studies that have been made in fourteenth-century administration as yet exist for the fifteenth century; only one of the executive instruments has received close study for this period, and that not the one of chief importance at the time,[1] and until we have more studies of the kind for the principal departments and offices in the administration,[2] generalizations about the period as a whole must be subject to large reservations. We are accustomed to many broad statements and assertions, such as ' the breakdown of administration ', ' the lack of politique reule and governaille ', ' the outrunning of administrative order by constitutional progress '. But in fact we know too little of the actual working of government in the fifteenth century to be sure whether assertions of this kind are

[1] J. Otway-Ruthven, *The King's Secretary and the Signet Office in the XV century* (1939).
[2] The researches now in hand by my former pupil and present colleague, Mr. A. L. Brown, on the privy seal in the early fifteenth century may be expected to advance knowledge materially on this subject. The recent admirable study of *The Court of Common Pleas in Fifteenth Century England* by Margaret Hastings (1947) is of great value, but naturally in the legal rather than the administrative sphere.

R

really justified or not, and we may well doubt whether quite the same statements will hold the field when the administrative history of the century has been adequately studied.

Subject, however, to the revelations of future researches, we may venture to make some provisional assumptions and to formulate some tentative generalizations on the basis of such information as we at present possess—information which is mainly confined to the Council, the signet and secretary, and to the financial difficulties of the government of the Lancastrians. Probably enough is known of these things to enable us to form a picture of the main lines of transition from fourteenth century administration to that of the early sixteenth century—which is all that we can attempt here.

It seems sufficiently clear that, notwithstanding the successive political and dynastic changes of the fifteenth century there were no fundamental modifications in the administrative system of the period. There were certainly changes of emphasis, variations in administrative practice reflecting in part at least the political vicissitudes, but little that was really new was invented or evolved in the machinery or devices of administration. The essential themes in administrative history are still those of the fourteenth century, and it is little more than variations on these themes that have to be recorded. The period of the Yorkist régime certainly shows characteristics different from those of the Lancastrian years, and the early Tudor period shows still further differences, but there seems to have been no fresh phase in administrative history until the reign of Henry VIII, when the reforms contemplated in the Ordinances of Eltham of 1525–26, and still more the activities of Thomas Cromwell as king's secretary materially modified the mediaeval character of the administrative system. These may be taken as inaugurating a new period in administrative history, which in many respects was to persist until the beginnings of a fresh series of reforms in the later years of the eighteenth century. The long course of mediaeval administrative development was in some degree interrupted when and in so far as the Ordinances of Eltham became operative, but the modified mediaevalism of later Tudor and early and restored Stuart administration sufficed until the so-called 'Economic

Reform' measures of the 1780's introduced more modern conceptions of administration in response to newer parliamentary, political, and constitutional attitudes, and eventually induced fundamental changes into the administrative system.

It must never be forgotten that the mediaeval administrative system was the creation and instrument of the monarchy, designed and fashioned to give expression to the principle of personal government by the king, in whom alone supreme executive authority was vested. It followed inevitably from this basic *raison d'être* that modification of this principle would bring about modification of the administrative system itself. The system would vary with variations in the actual degree to which the principle was realized in practice. In theory, government is, of course, still His Majesty's Government, and Cabinet Ministers are still in theory His Majesty's Servants ; but in practice, supreme executive power has come in modern times to reside elsewhere than in the sovereign himself. The fundamental differences between the modern and the mediaeval administrative systems are the product of the very gradually widening gulf between the theory and the practice in this matter.

In the period we now have to review—the period from 1399 to 1526, or for some purposes, to 1540, the vicissitudes in administrative history seem due primarily to vicissitudes in the degree to which executive authority was asserted by the kings themselves; and it was the considerable variation in this degree of royal initiative that gave to the several phases of the hundred and forty years their principal characteristics. 'The truth is', says Mr. McFarlane, 'England was a monarchy, which is to say that it depended for its healthy functioning upon the exercise of the kingship.'[1]

These words express the point precisely ; the administrative system inherited from the past could not function properly without the proper exercise of the royal authority. The decline of the kingship under Henry VI inevitably brought a decline in administration, for the mediaeval system was not designed to respond fully to a merely conciliar authority ; it was the revival,

---

[1] 'Bastard Feudalism' in *Bull. Inst. Hist. Res.*, XX (1943-5), p. 179.

partial under Edward IV and Richard III, much more complete under Henry VII and Henry VIII, of the personal direction of government by the king himself, or through his immediate agent, that brought a revival of effective administration. Inevitably also, with the revival of the king's personal power, the personal instruments of royal administration, some household agencies, above all the secretary and signet and sign-manual, revived as well, for without them the administration as a whole could not be galvanized into effective and purposeful action. The time was to come, under Henry VIII, when the revival of royal power was so great that, for all practical purposes, the sovereign could dominate the whole administration with but one important survival of the old household agencies—the secretary and the signet, and so could allow the others, the steward, the chamberlain, and controller, the Chamber, and the Wardrobe to revert largely to those merely domestic and courtly purposes which, in the remote days of origins, they had been designed to fulfil.

The nearest approach to a substantial innovation during the Lancastrian period is perhaps to be found in the ' institutionalization ' of the administrative Council. All the other administrative organs, Chancery, Exchequer, and Privy Seal, of course, retained their spheres of action, but the essential question of the degree of personal government exercised by the king, is naturally reflected most in the fortunes of the Council and in the practical importance or otherwise of the signet seal. Moreover, these two executive agencies, the Council and the secretary, were destined to be the two above all others which enabled the Tudor sovereigns to work their administrative revival and to instil new life into the government. On the basis essentially of these, continuity of administrative development was preserved, and the way from the mediaeval to the modern State was eventually bridged.

We have noticed above[1] the prevalence of two views of the king's Council in the later fourteenth century; the one seeking a ' continual council ' (a term first appearing in 1376 and forming an objective of the opposition) in which elements other than the purely official and curial should predominate—a view pressed from time to time by the aristocratic and parliamentary opposi-

[1] *V. supra*, p. 220.

tions to the king and the curialists ; the other view seeking to preserve the king's freedom of choice of councillors, among whom the principal officers should predominate, for they, in more or less degree enjoyed the king's especial confidence and shared his secrets. This difference of view, and the tendency for councils, however constituted, to sink into being *ad hoc* meetings of a few officials for the regular dispatch of business, and the somewhat nominal membership of many of those who were formally of the Council, inevitably impeded, or even perhaps prevented, its development as an institution. As Mr. Jolliffe justly remarks, ' from such a council there was absent all that sense of equal participation and responsibility which is sought in Cabinet government, and, for that reason, if for no other, it could never be used to embody the politics of the nation or of a predominant party, and to enforce them upon the king. Inevitably it was upon these defects—the need for " continuous " attendance, and equal participation—that parliamentary criticism centred when the Crown fell out of favour with the nation.'[1] On the one hand, such a Council could not be representative of ' parliamentary interests ', nor would it necessarily exclude unpopular royal ' favourites ' or self-seekers.

Fresh ideas and new attitudes had to be evolved before the king's Council could develop into an institution which should have a definite position in the State, not merely that of a ' committee ' imposed upon the king, nor merely that of a conference of administrative officials, and in the period with which we are now concerned some distinct progress was made in these directions. The newer conception regarded the Council as not only an executive agency of the Crown, nor merely as an outpost of the feudal magnates, nor only as a clearing house for the needs and jealousies of the various officers, but as ' a neutral guardian of the interests of both king and nation. Such an advance in function called less for constitutional change than for a new political type, almost for a new political morality. . . More than for a new political institution the Commons were petitioning for coun-

---

[1] *Constitutional History of Medieval England* (2nd ed., 1947), p. 458. The best general account of the late mediaeval Council is to be found in this work, pp. 461–485.

cillors who should understand the elements of their own function, loyalty to the Crown, to the parliament, and to each other, disinterestedness, diligence, freedom from factions, secrecy, and discretion. In short, solidarity in the interest of the king, the nation, and in their own—a new technique of counsel.'[1] Certainly all these objectives were not attained in the fifteenth century, but we can say that consciousness of the need for them became manifest in the course of the Lancastrian period ; awareness of the need for something like them is at the root of Sir John Fortescue's advocacy of a reformed Council[2] ; the realization of most of them in practice was indispensable to the development of the later Privy Council of the Tudors.

As we have already mentioned,[3] whatever ' Lancastrian ' views Henry Bolingbroke may have entertained in his younger days, when he came to the throne himself he had every intention of exercising to the full the prerogatives of his predecessors, and displayed no desire to have their exercise fettered by continual councils not of his own choosing. ' From the first he revealed a determination to rule as Richard II had done, by the help of servants of his own choosing, and to resist any attempt to impose upon him that aristocratic or " natural " council which was to be the principal aim of baronial policy '.[4] He had, it seems clear, gone out of his way to avoid a merely parliamentary title to the Crown,[5] and certainly accepted a parliamentary declaration to the effect that his regality was no less than that of his predecessors the kings of England.[6]

But Henry IV was not to be by any means as free in the choice of councillors as he doubtless would have wished to be, and his first public pledge was that he would be governed by the counsel of the ' sage and discreet persons of the realm '.[7] He inevitably

---

[1] *Ib.*, pp. 461–62.
[2] *The Governance of England.* ed. Plummer (1885) ;   Cf. Chrimes, *op. cit.*, ch. iv, Excursus II, Fortescue's Administrative Proposals, pp. 292–331.
[3] *V. supra*, p. 239.
[4] K. B. McFarlane, in *Cambridge Mediaeval History*, VIII (1936), p. 363.
[5] Lapsley, *Crown, Community and Parliament*, pp. 273–340.   [6] *V. supra*, p. 239.
[7] Chrimes, *op. cit.*, p. 40 ; *Rot. Parl.*, III, p. 420 ; ' qil est la volunte du Roy d'estre conseillez et governez par les honorables, sages, et discretes persones de son Roialme, et par lour commune conseil et assent faire le meulx pur la Governance de luy et de son Roialme ; nient veullant estre governez de sa volunte propre ne de son purpos voluntarie, singulere opinione, mais par commune advis, conseil et assent '.

could not ignore the political importance of the aristocratic groups by whose support he had become king. He was therefore ' kept in perpetual subjection by almost annual meetings of Great Councils,'[1] at which the more important decisions of policy were reached. Moreover, the financial position of the Crown, as we shall see later,[2] was very weak, and grew worse rapidly. ' Not only the machinery of the Exchequer, but the whole administrative system had been dislocated to pay for expensive wars. It was the first duty of a prudent usurper to restore and to maintain financial stability.'[3] But this could not be done without the assistance of parliamentary grants, and Henry IV therefore found himself obliged to pay attention to the views of parliament, and indeed of the Commons in parliament, as to how the ordinary council should be constituted. For, whilst Great Councils, Parliaments, and Commons did not at this time seek to impair the royal prerogative, they did place their hopes for better governance in a ' sad and sufficient counsel ', and were several times at pains to try to ensure that the continual council should be constituted and work according to principles that were not left to the king's discretion alone.

Henry IV's first councillors were appointed without any nomination in parliament, and a petition by the Commons as early as 1399 asking that the king would make no grant without the advice of his Council was met with a temporizing answer saving the liberty of the Crown.[4] In 1401, the Commons wanted to be informed of the names of the councillors, and wanted them to be charged in their presence to hold office until the next parliament—a request refused on the advice of the existing Council.[5] By 1404, circumstances were such that the king agreed to announce in parliament the names of his councillors, without, however, making any alterations to the existing membership.[6] In the Coventry Parliament of October, 1404, the councillors were not re-appointed in the parliament, and it was not until

---

[1] T. F. T. Plucknett, ' The Place of the Council in the Fifteenth Century ', in *Trans. R.H.S.*, 4th ser. I (1918), p. 165.
[2] *Infra.*, pp. 255 ff.
[3] McFarlane, *op. cit.*, p. 362.
[4] *Ib.*, p. 369 ; cf. Baldwin, *op. cit.*, pp. 147–8.
[5] McFarlane, *loc. cit.*
[6] *Ib.*, cf. Baldwin, *op. cit.*, pp. 153–4.

1406, in the ' long parliament ' (1 March to 22 December), that the
king was obliged to make substantial concessions as the price of a
desperately needed financial grant and to meet the rising tide of
criticism. The audit of accounts which had been promised in
1404 was now conceded and extended in range ; the councillors
and chief officers were nominated in parliament, and more
important perhaps, the king was obliged to agree to a series of
articles more closely defining the duties and procedures of the
Council than had ever been attempted before.

These articles went far to recognize and develop the continual
council as an institution ; they served as a model for the later
Articles of 1423 and 1426, when during the long minority of
Henry VI, the whole government of the realm rested in the
Council, and when the need for definition and rules of business
was greater than ever.

The Articles of 1406, which were enrolled on the records of
the parliament, and to which, by the king's command the councillors reluctantly swore obedience, give a clear indication of the
attitude of their authors towards the Council as an institution
of government, and may be taken as representing a desire to
make the executive more distinctly conciliar in form than, except
on revolutionary occasions, it had been in the past. But this was
not a moment of revolution, and what was now intended was to
be normal.[1] In general the king was expected to put more faith
in the Council, and the councillors were to be so ordered that he
might have more confidence in them. Its secrets were to be
shared by the councillors alone ; those in attendance were to
keep those absent informed of the more important council
business ; the king was to put equal trust in all the councillors,
was not to be prejudiced against any of them by charges of mis-
conduct without proof, and was to refer pleas to their advice
before reaching decisions thereon. Petitions for office in the
king's gift were to be made in their presence, and every matter
before the Council was to be fully considered by its members.
The king was to support his councillors in all things, and to

---

[1] It must however be remembered that at this time the king was in bad health,
and his acceptance of some of the articles may have been determined by this circumstance.

place all his confidence in them, and suffer no hindrance to them in the discharge of their duties.[1]

Provisions of this kind were obviously intended to promote royal and public confidence in the Council, and did not in themselves seriously interfere with the exercise of the royal prerogatives. But a further provision agreed upon seems to belong to a different category. It agreed that all bills endorsed by the chamberlain and all letters under the signet, as well as other warrants addressed to the chancellor, treasurer, and the keeper of the privy seal, except pardons and appointments to vacant benefices and offices, should either be endorsed by the Council or written by its advice. It is difficult to avoid the conclusion that this provision, if observed in practice, would have fundamentally restricted the exercise of personal executive power by the king. If all letters of signet and all other warrants to the other seals (apart from the specified exceptions) were to go through the Council, then the Council must become the sole intermediary between the king and his administrative departments ; a conciliar sieve would have been riveted over the flow of the king's personal initiative. No incurrence of expenditure without the Council's approval would have been possible, and it is not too much to say that ' this provision would leave the king practically nothing of his independent prerogative '.[2] In agreeing to this article, the king sustained a severe defeat.[3] The Council could of course, make use of the privy seal in this period as in the past, but if the king could not concurrently use the signet to move the other seals and therefore the departments, without passing the Council, he was reduced almost to a position of administrative impotence, except with the goodwill of the councillors.

[1] Jolliffe, *op. cit.*, pp. 462–3 ; Baldwin, *op. cit.*, pp. 156–9. For a detailed account of the political events of this time *v.* J. H. Wylie, *History of England under Henry IV* (1884–94).   [2] Baldwin,*op. cit.*, p. 157.
[3] Plucknett, *loc. cit.*, p. 179. Miss Otway-Ruthven's suggestion (*op. cit.*, pp. 32–3) that this provision ' seems to have been a matter of administrative convenience of no constitutional significance ' can hardly be accepted ; still less her further suggestion that the arrangement may have been to resist and limit interference by the Council. Such suggestions appear to ignore altogether the basic question of the location of executive power. Cf. Stubbs, *Constitutional History*, III, p. 57, ' The demands of the Commons and the concessions of the king amounted to a supersession of the royal authority '.

Much more detailed research needs to be done on the actual mechanism of the administration during the ensuing years before we can ascertain with confidence exactly how far this crucial article was observed in practice. But the point was **not** formally reversed until the early years of Henry VI's assumption of regal powers, as we shall see later.[1] In general, the Articles of 1406, even though they probably did not become operative in every particular, seem to have assisted the development of the Council as an institution of government. With the substantial retirement of the king from active participation in business, the burden of government inevitably fell to the Council. ' The best evidence of this increase of responsibility is found in the files of bills or warrants both of the great and the privy seals, which shows that from this time few grants or orders of any kind were made that were not written or at least endorsed by order of the Council. Only a few letters of the signet from time to time reveal the personal interposition of the king.'[2]

The vicissitudes in the personnel of the Council and the changes in the balance of political forces in the later years of Henry IV's reign need not detain us here. Nor can anything very pertinent to our purpose be said of the actual position of the Council in administration during the reign of Henry V. We may perhaps agree with Mr. McFarlane's assertion that ' in his capable hands at least the mediaeval kingship betrayed no sign that age had brought fragility ',[3] and we may well believe that his reign witnessed a substantial revival of personal monarchy acting now in general harmony with great councils and parliaments in the pursuit of aggressive policies in France. But the fact remains that very little has so far been revealed of the relations between Henry V and his administrative Council, or of the actual direction of the government at home. The king, however, was absent from the realm for rather more than half of his reign altogether, and we may assume that the main burden of administering the realm fell to the ' lords of the Council ', and since the attendance of the

---

[1] *V. infra*, p. 254.

[2] Baldwin, *op. cit.*, p. 160.

[3] ' Henry V, Bishop Beaufort, and the Red Hat, 1417–21 ', in *E.H.R.*, LX (1945), p. 316.

magnate members was now rare, mostly to the principal officials.[1] Directions under the signet were certainly sent to the Council by the king whilst he was abroad,[2] and nothing is heard of difficulties or rivalries between him and the Council over executive powers or procedures. The exigencies of war-organization had inevitably revived the Wardrobe of the Household to some extent,[3] together with the financial resources put at its disposal, but no friction seems to have been thereby engendered. Yet the enormous strain of the campaigns on financial resources and upon the administration was destined,[4] perhaps more than any other factor, to undermine the strength of the Crown, and eventually to bring the House of Lancaster to ruin.

Many of the councillors who served under Henry V were commissioned to govern during the minority of Henry VI,[5] and no doubt the experience they had gained in the absence of the king stood them in good stead when they were faced with the whole task of government in the long years of the minority, and to these years of the apogee of the mediaeval council we must now turn.

In the minority of Henry VI, the government of the realm fell, not to a regent (despite Humphrey, duke of Gloucester's attempt to obtain such a position for himself),[6] but to the lords of the Council. The fact that this should have been so undoubtedly reflects the advance that had been made in conciliar development during the preceding decades. 'There is, then,' says Mr. Jolliffe, 'a specific constitutional form which may be called the Lancastrian Council. It is not wholly the creation of either king or parliament, and, though the rise of parliament

---

[1] Baldwin, *op. cit.*, p. 166 ; usually the chancellor, treasurer, keeper of the privy seal, sometimes also the chamberlain, steward, controller, keeper of the wardrobe, and the kings' secretary, or some of them. The most extended survey of the reign, Wylie and Waugh, *The Reign of Henry V* (1914–29), has little to say on administrative questions.

[2] Baldwin, *op. cit.*, p. 168 ; Otway-Ruthven, *op. cit.*, p. 12.

[3] Tout, *Chapters*, IV, p. 225. The use of both the Wardrobe and Chamber for public administration was probably greater than Tout supposed. *V*. Eileen de L. Fagan 'Some Aspects of the King's Household in the reign of Henry V' (Summaries of Theses no. cxlviii) in *Bull. Inst. Hist. Res.* XIV (1937), pp. 194–5.

[4] *V. infra*, p. 256.

[5] Jolliffe, *op. cit.*, p. 464.

[6] Chrimes, 'The Pretensions of the duke of Gloucester in 1422' in *E.H.R.*, XLV (1930), pp. 101–103.

had made either a wholly feudal or a wholly ministerial council almost impossible to maintain, it is not the outcome of a consistent parliamentary scheme to control the State. More immediately, it comes into being in response to certain defects which characterize the age, of which the greatest is the prolonged weakness of the monarchy, which from 1370 to 1461 never gave the country a strong king resident in England for more than a few years at a time ... The crisis of 1376 and 1377 had fallen upon a Crown which lacked any conciliar system capable of carrying on the king's government without the decisive leadership of the king. The death of Henry V showed that this defect had been to a large degree remedied, and that fifty years of canvassing of the ethics of the councillor's office, and the habit of action in council formed in the nobility under Henry IV and Henry V, had provided the nation with a Council which could master the offices of State, reduce faction to manageable proportions, and conduct what was, in effect, if not in name, a regency of peers and great officers.'[1]

The minority Council appointed by the lords spiritual and temporal in the king's name continued to function with little internal change from 1422 to 1437. During these years the government was definitely conciliar in character ; no countenance had been given to any assumption of special powers by the duke of Gloucester, who was, in the absence of John, duke of Bedford, allowed only the title of Protector and Defender of the Realm and Principal Councillor. That Bedford approved of this arrangement seems clear, but Gloucester did not take kindly to the conciliar idea, and some difficulties arising from his personal ambitions were to be experienced in the years to come, but on the whole, for fifteen years the Council was able to maintain its coherence and collective responsibility. To secure itself against encroachments by the Protector, and to maintain its procedure, it promulgated Articles in 1423 and 1426, modelled in part on those of 1406.[2] Following upon the difficulties arising from Gloucester's activities, in January, 1427, the theory of the form of government was specifically formulated. During the

[1] *Op. cit.*, pp. 472–4.
[2] *Ib.*, pp. 464–5 ; *v.* generally Baldwin, *op. cit.*, pp. 169 ff,

king's minority, it was declared, the execution of his authority belonged to the lords spiritual and temporal when they were assembled in parliament or great council, or otherwise, to the lords of his continual council, which represented the king's person for the execution of the ' politique reule and governaille ' of the realm.[1]

We may well believe that the continual council attained a substantial degree of success in maintaining its unity and cohesion during these years, but the degree of success that attended its efforts to govern the realm is a matter that requires more detailed investigation than it has yet received. The probabilities are that its lack of administrative efficiency and the difficulty of repressing the personal ambitions and interests of individual councillors and lords contributed much to the ultimate ruin of the dynasty, and also invoked a reaction against government by a council of this type. The future was to rest, not upon an aristocratic council ruling in the king's name[2] but upon a king ruling with the assistance of a ' privy ' council powerful because backed with the whole strength of the revived monarchy.

Whether government could have been carried on indefinitely along the lines of the conciliar ideas of the minority we may well doubt. In any case, the beginnings of Henry VI's assumption of royal powers in 1437 soon modified the form of government. In that year the king himself began to sit in the Council, and before long the practice of government by a Council striving to maintain its unity declined. With the quarrels of Gloucester and Beaufort, the rise and fall of the duke of Suffolk as the chief minister, the rivalries for power between Somerset and York, and the vicissitudes of the parties of Lancaster and York in politics and in battle during the ensuing years, we are not here concerned. More to our purpose are the efforts of Henry VI

---

[1] Chrimes, *English Constitutional Ideas in the Fifteenth Century*, pp. 148-151 ; cf. ' John, duke of Bedford, his work and policy in England, 1389-1435 ' (Summaries of Theses no. li in *Bull. Ins. Hist. Res.* VII (1929), pp. 114-117.)

[2] Doubtless Fortescue had the Council of these years in mind when he wrote in the *Governance*, ch. xv : ' The kyng is counsell was wonned to be chosen off grete princes, and off gretteste lordes off pe lande, both spirituelles and temporellis, and also off oper men that were in grete auctorite and offices. Wich lordes and officers had nere hande also mony maters off thair owne to be treded in the counsell, as hade pe kynge.' Hence his recommendations for a differently constituted council. Cf. Chrimes, *op. cit.*, pp. 329-331.

and the court party to revive the personal authority of the monarchy, and to reduce the Council's hold over executive power.

As early as 1435-6, the king had begun to interfere in the making of grants, and to apply the royal sign-manual to bills ; in November, 1437, he formally re-appointed his Council without as yet making any changes of personnel, and in causing the Articles of 1406 to be read out to the councillors, with emphasis upon the reservation to the king himself of charters of pardon and appointments to benefices and offices, he brought sharply to mind the fact that the Council was not entirely a law unto itself ; and at the same time he forbade the Council to conclude important business without his advice, and reserved to himself the decision in cases of disagreement. Minor changes in the membership of the Council were made in the next few years, the most significant perhaps being the appointment to it of Thomas Beckington, the king's secretary, in 1439.[1] Fundamentally important was the revival of the king's power of initiative in administration by way of the royal sign-manual and letters of signet. During the years 1440-43, new articles for the Council revised those of 1406, and testified to the resurrection of the personal executive power of the king himself. The king was enabled to move the signet at his will, and by this or by sign-manual or by signature of the chamberlain, to move the privy seal, which could no longer refuse a signet bill. The keeper of the privy seal was still authorized to refer to the Council any matter ' of great charge ' if he thought fit, so that the Council might make representations to the king before the matter should pass the privy seal. Whether the keeper of privy seal ever ventured to have recourse to this provision we may doubt ; in any case the importance of the privy seal itself was much reduced by a further article in 1444. The privy seal had in the previous decades come to be more than ever the seal utilized by the Council to implement its decisions, and the Chancery had for long been inclined to insist upon a warrant of privy seal for most ordinary purposes before issuing under the great seal. The article of 1444 decreed that all grants made from the tenth year of the reign onwards by virtue of bills under sign-manual, signet of the eagle or

[1] Baldwin, *op. cit.*, p. 186.

signet of arms, or bills signed by the chamberlain or clerk of the council, were as valid as if authorized by warrant of privy seal.[1] The authority of the king's personal initiative was thus restored, and in this respect the unfortunate Henry VI paved the way for the exercise of personal government by the more robust Yorkists and Tudors alike.

The supremacy of the ' Lancastrian ' Council was thus brought to an end. Once again the re-assertion of the king's own executive power had undermined conciliar administration. With its powers curtailed, especially in the sphere of patronage, the Council lost its unity ; the magnate members dropped away, leaving the administrative officers to carry on the government as best they might. The king had done something to revive the executive power of the monarchy, but his personal inability to instil sufficient strength and purpose into the administration brought in time the collapse of the Lancastrian régime. ' If,' as Professor Plucknett says, ' Henry VIII had been King in 1450, commanding a position so firmly founded on prerogative and precedent, we might guess what would have happened, but the Crown's opportunity was lost through Henry [VI]'s own misfortunes ; his personal affliction, indeed, may have been amply counter-balanced by the disorder in the baronial ranks, but his birth was fatal. The advancement of the Yorkist title cut the ground from under his feet ; because he could not claim to be the undoubted representative of the kingship, so the ancient feud of Crown against baronage was never fought out on a straight issue. Nevertheless, the Crown won.'[2]

By what methods the Crown eventually won, we must consider shortly ;[3] one further reason why the Lancastrian Crown did not win may be mentioned here. We noted above,[4] quoting from Mr. McFarlane, that it was the first duty of a prudent usurper to restore and to maintain financial stability. But Henry IV showed himself to be anything but a prudent usurper in the financial sphere, and neither he nor his heirs succeeded in achieving financial stability. The failure of the Lancastrians either to

---

[1] Plucknett, *op. cit.*, pp. 181–3 ; Otway-Ruthven, *op. cit.*, pp. 34–7.
[2] Plucknett, *op. cit.*, p. 185.
[3] *V. infra*, pp. 259 ff.   [4] *Supra*, p. 247.

restore or to maintain their financial resources was, if not the cause, certainly the symptom of their administrative weakness. Henry IV's position, perhaps, was never strong enough to enable him to take the drastic action needed ; Henry V's French diversions not only postponed any serious treatment of the problem, but also enormously added to its gravity ; the Council of Henry VI's minority, although certainly very conscious of the urgency of the position,[1] failed to remedy it ; by the time of Henry VI's assumption of royal powers, short-lived indeed as it was, the Crown was saddled with a huge and rapidly increasing debt, from which it could not free itself.

Henry IV's average real revenue was only five-sixths of that enjoyed by Richard II ; the amount of his real loans was about the same as Richard II's, but his fictitious loans were three times greater.[2] Henry V's reign saw the peak of borrowing, and for the time the percentage of cash receipts at the Exchequer was maintained and even increased.[3] But the financial incompetence, or perhaps corruption, of the Council during the minority of Henry VI is revealed by the heavy fall in revenue during the years after Henry V's death. The ' real ' revenue declined by nearly thirty-six per cent, notwithstanding the heavy increase in loans, real or fictitious, from the magnates and gentry.[4] The Crown's debt, estimated at £168,000 in 1433, had become £372,000 by 1449 ; for the Crown sought to meet its current obligations by raising fresh loans on which it had to pay very high rates of interest,[5] rates which no doubt increased as its credit fell sharply after the outbreak of civil war. It was not a question of exacting

[1] E.g. The lord Cromwell's financial statement as treasurer in 1433 ; v. Stubbs, op. cit. III, p. 121 ; cf. Chrimes, *John, duke of Bedford, his work and policy in England,* 1389–1435 (unpublished London M.A. thesis, 1929), Appendix V. The study of this subject has been carried further by J. L. Kirby, ' The Issues of the Lancastrian Exchequer and lord Cromwell's Estimates of 1433 ', in *Bull. Inst. Hist. Res.* XXIV (1951), pp. 121–151.

[2] A. B. Steel, ' English Government Finance, 1377–1413 ', in *E.H.R.* LI (1936), pp. 29–51, 577–597. On the whole subject, v. Steel *The Receipt of the Exchequer,* 1377–1485 (forthcoming). Cf. F. C. Dietz, *English Government Finance,* 1485–1558 (1921), Ch. I.

[3] A. B. Steel, ' The Receipt of the Exchequer, 1413–1432 ' in *Camb. Hist. J.* VI (1938), pp. 33–54, and ' Receipt Roll Totals under Henry IV and Henry V ' in *E.H.R.* XLVII (1932), pp. 204–215.

[4] A. B. Steel in *Camb. Hist. J., loc. cit.* Mr. Steel's analysis of the source of the loans is an illuminating commentary on Lancastrian credit.

[5] Fortescue, *Governance,* p. 118, estimated the rate at 25 to 33⅓ per cent.

forced loans, but a question of inducing voluntary loans by paying high rates of interest.'[1] But borrowing cannot pay for itself nor for more borrowing indefinitely ; the evils of the condition were fully expounded by Sir John Fortescue after Henry VI's fall,[2] and he suggested some at least of the remedies. The application of these remedies, however, was not, and perhaps could not be, made by the Lancastrians. Perhaps nothing short of a *coup d'état* could have produced the needful action.[3]

When in due course the Yorkists were established on the throne,[4] the new régime clearly turned to some of the more obvious means of reviving the executive power of the monarchy —to the signet as the instrument of the king's personal authority, and to a re-constituted Council which should be in no position to grasp executive power for itself.

By 1461, the signet in the custody normally of the king's secretary, and the signet office, had come to be well-recognized elements in the administrative system.[5] We have seen above[6] how Henry VI established the validity of letters of signet and other expressions of the personal will of the king. The secretary-ship assumed a further importance with the appointment of Thomas Beckington in 1437. Beckington remained secretary until 1443, when he was promoted to be keeper of the privy seal and bishop of Bath and Wells. During his tenure of the

---

[1] K. B. McFarlane, ' Loans to the Lancastrian Kings : The Problem of Induce-ment ' in *Camb. Hist. J.* IX (1947), pp. 51–68. There is no reasonable doubt that Mr. McFarlane's explanation of Fortescue's account of ' chevisaunce ' as a system of evasion of formal usury by crediting the lenders at the Exchequer with a sum greater than the actual loan is correct. This explanation was first clearly suggested, without demonstration, by Sir James Ramsay in *Lancaster and York* (1892), II, p. 465. Plummer seems rather to have missed the point about the usurious nature of these loans, but the fact that Fortescue refers to the payment of interest was recorded by Stubbs, *op. cit.*, III, p. 250, and Chrimes, *op. cit.*, p. 329. Mr. Steel's forthcoming work cited n.1 above produces further evidence on this subject.

[2] *Governance*, ch. v.

[3] The fall in government credit in the later years of Henry VI was catastrophic. The analysis of the sources of loans, and the marked changes in the social groups lending to the government under the Lancastrians and Yorkists, is one of the most important parts of Mr. A. B. Steel's forthcoming work, *The Receipt of the Exchequer*, 1377–1485.

[4] For a very general sketch, *v.* C. H. Williams, ' England : The Yorkist Kings, 1461–1485 ' in *C. M. H.*, VIII, ch. xii, pp. 418–449.

[5] *V.* generally *Otway-Ruthven, op. cit.* ; Florence M. G. Evans (Mrs. C. S. S. Higham) *The Principal Secretary of State* (1923) ; ' A Note on the Pre-Tudor Secretary ' in *Essays to Tout* (1925), pp. 361–66.

[6] *Supra*, p. 254.

S

secretaryship, he was especially employed on diplomatic missions, primarily perhaps, as had been the case in the past, in his capacity as the king's confidential clerk rather than as custodian of the signet, which presumably must have been transferred to other care during his absence abroad. Beckington's successors in the office of secretary in the time of Henry VI were less important individuals, and the king's own disabilities inevitably involved a decline in the use of the signet. As yet the secretary was hardly more than a household officer, whose importance and functions depended upon the strength and activities of the king himself.

A stronger initiative by Edward IV brought the secretary and the signet into greater prominence. In this reign, the secretary began to take on the character of a public officer, and was usually also a councillor, even though until the time of Thomas Ruthal (1509), every secretary resigned on becoming a bishop. The quantity of business passing under the signet greatly increased in Edward IV's reign, and continued to be large under Richard III; about half of Edward IV's signet letters also show the sign-manual. 'No class of business was dealt with by means of the immediate signet warrant that could not be paralleled from previous reigns, but the quantity was greatly increased and the chancellor was no longer left any discretion, many grants being drawn up in the precise form in which they were to be issued under the great seal.'[1] The signet office, as yet usually called the office of the king's secretary, was still part of the Household, and although as yet it had no fixed headquarters or *hospicium* for the 'writers to the signet', it systematically maintained and stored its archives ;[2] it made no enrolments, but registered the instructions it received day by day, and preserved its warrants ; probably some collections of precedents were made at this time.

[1] Otway-Ruthven, *op. cit.*, p. 41. Cf. Plucknett, *op. cit.*, p. 186, ' There is however reason to believe that many instruments formerly under the privy seal, were now passed under the signet, which certainly executed a great amount of business and some may have been expedited by the Council, but this is doubtful '.

[2] Otway-Ruthven, *op. cit.*, pp. 114–115.   The place in 1444 was the highest chamber in the tower next to the Lancaster tower at Windsor. In 1597 the place was under the Banqueting Hall at Whitehall, where all the records were burnt in the fire of 15 January 1618–19. Until 1415 letters of signet were mostly in French, thereafter mostly in English. On the signet, cf. Maxwell-Lyte, *The Great Seal*, pp. 117–131. The emergence of a secretary for the French tongue from 1422 and for the Latin tongue from 1495 did not affect the position of the king's secretary.

The Yorkist kings thus had to hand an efficient means of expressing their personal will, and there is ample evidence of their use of it. As yet, however, the importance of the secretary in general administration was overshadowed by the other household officials, the steward, chamberlains, and controller, who shared most of such work of government as fell to household officers. Under Edward IV, the chancellor was still the chief minister, and the keeper of the privy seal occupied a position in some respects comparable with that of the secretaries of a later generation ; the privy seal was not as yet only a formal stage between the signet and the great seal ; its letters were still used for missive purposes, and indeed the signet or privy seal seems often to have been used indifferently. The sphere of the secretary's activities was still largely that of diplomatic correspondence. But most of the elements of the future great expansions of the secretaryship under the Tudors were already there—the king's confidence, membership of the Council, and an organized secretarial office ; it remained for the force of circumstances and of personalities to bring the office to the very forefront of the executive.

It is clear enough that the Yorkist kings did much to revive the executive authority of the Crown by making an extensive use of the signet seal, and that by this means the administration was made to depend for its initiative upon the king himself to a much greater degree than had been the case since the later years of Richard II. But it seems equally clear that the Yorkists did not learn to combine royal initiative and direction with the vigilance and collective energies and abilities of an effective administrative Council. If they had done so, we might not have heard of the Tudors ; but as it was, the secret of the combination was reserved to Richard III's successors. Edward IV, perhaps, was not willing to profit from the Lancastrian Fortescue's advice in this matter, if indeed, he was ever aware of the nature of this advice.[1] The dearth of materials[2] for the history of the

[1] There is no evidence for the exact date of the composition of the *Governance of England*. Cf. Fortescue, *De Laudibus Legum Anglie*, ed. Chrimes (1942), p. lxxiv, n. 6 ; *Governance*, ed. Plummer, pp. 95–6. Only two fifteenth-century copies of the *Governance* are known to exist, with possibly a third.

[2] *V.* Baldwin, *op. cit.*, ch. xvi.

Council under the Yorkists is not, of course, conclusive evidence
for the absence of conciliar activity, but it is certainly significant
in some degree in itself, and at the same time makes generalizations on the subject both difficult and tentative. It is probably
true to say that the Lancastrian Council foundered during the
Wars of the Roses[1]—if indeed it had not foundered before the Wars
began. In any case it is reasonable enough to suppose that
Edward IV could, and did, largely please himself in the matter of
the composition and functions of his Council; he at any rate
was free from ' Lancastrian ' prejudices and trammels in this
connection. But the difficulty is to determine what it was that he
did do in this respect. Certainly little is heard of Great Councils
in his reign, and these from this time cease to play any important
part in government. It has been alleged that no continual
council at all was appointed.[2] and in the sense of the ' continual
council ' of the Lancastrian period, this may well be true ; but
certainly councillors were appointed, and the names of at least
fifty of them are known.[3] The probabilities are that Edward IV
harked back to conceptions of the Council that had been preva-
lent before the Lancastrians came to the throne, and that he
thought in terms of ' counsel ' rather than of a council as a continuous coherent body. Neither the king himself nor the greater
magnates appointed to be of his council seem to have attended
meetings with any frequency, leaving the work done by the
Council as such to the principal officers and a number of lesser
household officers who were appointed to be of the council,
whilst an increasing number of doctors of laws and clerks of
Chancery and of other departments were included. The vague
character of the functions of some of these ' professional '
members suggests that such councillors were in a position
developing towards that of the later ' king's counsel ' rather than
that of the later ' privy councillors '.[4]

We must, no doubt, assume that the principal administrative
officers conferred together from time to time for deliberative

---

[1] A. F. Pollard, 'Council, Star Chamber, and Privy Council under the Tudors',
in *E.H.R.* XXXVII (1922), p. 342.

[2] Jolliffe, *op. cit.*, p. 490.

[3] Plucknett, *op. cit.*, p. 186.

[4] Jolliffe, *op. cit.*, p. 490.

and administrative purposes, re-inforced on occasions by other selected councillors, and together providing the king with the sanction of conciliar advice and assent as might be required. But the administrative activity of the Council as such seems to have declined greatly. Very few issues under the great seal were now made warranted *per concilium*, though some of the king's acts were couched in the form ' rex de avisamento sui consilii voluit et mandavit '.[1] What happened to the former mass of administrative work done by the old Council is a mystery.[2] As the seat of administrative decision and direction, the Council was in eclipse. But as the place of judicial discretion it was far from being eclipsed ; on the contrary, the restriction of its work largely to hearing ' billes betwix partie and partie ' was transmuting it into a body whose specialization of function gave it fresh significance and emphasis. The Council, now no longer the effective governing body of the realm, was rapidly becoming the Council in Star Chamber, the residuary legatee of the judicial discretion of the king's Council. ' The mediaeval king's council continued its existence under the Elizabethan disguise of the court of star chamber '.[3]

In the forty years that elapsed between the accession of Henry VII in 1485 and the promulgation of the Ordinances of Eltham in 1526, and still more, perhaps, in the further fourteen years to the fall of Thomas Cromwell, the mediaeval administrative system underwent substantial modifications,[4] the full effect of which was felt in the later years of Henry VIII, and which went far to determine the nature of the system until late in the eighteenth century. It would, however, be a grave mistake to imagine that this early-modern system of the Tudors and Stuarts represented a fundamental departure from the mediaeval system. The Tudor sovereigns did not, and could not, start afresh ; they inherited and took over the administrative machinery and institutions built up by the monarchy through many centuries,

---

[1] Baldwin, *op. cit.*, p. 426.
[2] Plucknett, *op. cit.*, p. 187, cf. I. S. Leadam, *Select Cases before the King's Council in the Star Chamber*, 1477–1509 (Selden Soc. vol. XVI (1903)).
[3] Pollard, *loc. cit.*, p. 535.
[4] *V.* F. C. Dietz, *English Government Finance*, 1485–1558 (1921). Cf. V. H. Galbraith, *An Introduction to the Use of the Public Records.* p. 53.

and they could not do more than utilize and adapt their inheritance, and turn it towards objectives, some of them new, some of
them old, which they set before them, or which were set for
them by the force of changing circumstances. In a sense, the
Tudors were able to realize in practice the ideals of the mediaeval
monarchy, and their epoch was the epoch of the triumph of the
monarchy over all rivals or potential rivals for administrative
power within the State. The long-drawn struggle for power
between the kingship and the old nobility ended now in the
victory of the monarchy ; the oppositions which confronted the
Tudors, and indeed in due course the Stuarts also, were not at
all of the same kind as had confronted Edward II, Edward III,
or Richard II, or the Lancastrians. No one sought to put the
Tudor kingship into commission, or to fetter its administrative
discretion or initiative. The Tudor monarchy was essentially a
rejuvenated personal monarchy, able to instil vigour into the
old administrative agencies and to create new ones out of the
old ; and by maintaining its mastery over the whole, it was able
to carry the power of the executive to a level scarcely dreamt
of, certainly never attained, in the past. This high-powered and
efficient executive was in turn passed on to the Stuarts, and could
not be made to yield to new forms of political opposition emanating mostly from the Commons in Parliament without struggles
and civil strife unparallelled in the English middle ages. In a
sense the Civil War of the seventeenth century was the legacy of
Tudor power and success, which in its turn was the result of the
rehabilitation and re-adjustment of the administrative system of
the Plantagenets.

We cannot do more here than to summarize briefly what
appear to have been the principal lines of modification of the old
system during these forty or fifty years. Much of the story
remains obscure, and the subject of Tudor administration still
awaits its historian; the work that has so far been done in this field
is piecemeal and disconnected, but enough has been done to
indicate the probable nature of the changes made. These comprised the rehabilitation of the finances of the Crown ; the
disappearance from important national administration of all the
household officers except one—the king's secretary, whose

administrative importance became so great as to surpass that of the chancellor and all other officers ; and the re-constitution of the administrative council, with the king's secretary as the liaison between it and the sovereign. The accumulative effect of these changes was to bring the Crown to an unprecedented level of executive power.[1]

We have noticed above the financial embarrassments of the Lancastrian period, and the importance of these in contributing to the collapse of the régime. Sir John Fortescue was very conscious of the necessity for improving the royal revenue.[2] Edward IV certainly did a good deal to achieve this end. The difficulties of assessing the financial position of the Yorkists are very great ; the administrative system in the financial sphere at least, had largely collapsed during the years of civil strife ; a number of Receipt Rolls are missing during the last years of Henry VI and early years of Edward IV, and for most of Richard III's short reign ; important sources of income are omitted altogether from the Rolls under the new régime. It is evident, nonetheless, that Edward IV, once he was firmly established, was able to get on with much less borrowing than his predecessors had managed to do, and the amount of fictitious borrowing sank to negligible proportions in the later years of the Yorkist period. The financial prosperity which Edward IV enjoyed in the later years of his reign, buttressed as it was with benevolences, the French pension, trading profits, as well as with considerable parliamentary grants, did not, however, survive the king himself, and there are indications that Richard III was being driven to revive old expedients for raising revenue, when the sudden termination of his reign and the accession of Henry Tudor made possible a fresh start in the work of financial rehabilitation.[3]

It is probable that Edward IV had done much to revive the Chamber as a financial organization.[4] Whether this was so or not, Henry VII achieved his great work of financial reconstruction by turning away from the old machinery of collecting the revenue through the Exchequer of Receipt, and instead reviving and

---

[1] For general information, *v.* K. N. Pickthorn, *Early Tudor Government* (1934).
[2] *Governance*, ed. Plummer, ch. v.
[3] *V.* A. B. Steel, *The Receipt of the Exchequer*, 1377–1485 (forthcoming).
[4] Ramsay, *Lancaster and York.* II, p. 467.

enormously expanding the financial system of the Chamber.[1] It was through the oldest administrative organization of the Household that Henry VII brought the Crown not only to solvency but also to riches. The treasurer of the Chamber became the receiver-general of the king's revenues, and the Chamber in effect took over the functions of the Exchequer of Receipt, leaving the machinery of the Exchequer to decline and the treasurership of England to become honorific. Almost all of the royal revenues, apart from parliamentary grants and subsidies, were in his reign paid direct into the Chamber, and there came under the king's own immediate supervision, and subject to his own daily or weekly scrutiny, and controlled by sign-manual or signet bill. The introduction of the system of the declaration of accounts (Declared Accounts) before the king himself or the king's auditors, enhanced the royal control of finance, and reduced the practical importance of the Exchequer.[2] Arrangements of this kind endured into the reign of Mary, though with less close personal supervision by Henry VIII.[3] In Mary's time the exchequer system was revived, but largely on the methods of the *camera regis*. There were, of course, to be many financial difficulties ahead, but the maladministration of finance which had been the ruin of the Lancastrians was never to be repeated. ' By the new institutions and methods which were developed in the course of his reign, Henry VII completely broke away from the mediaeval financial system, and laid the foundations for the more modern English revenue system, which was to be more completely perfected by his immediate successors, who merely elaborated on his ideas.'[4]

The reign of Henry VIII saw for all practical purposes the disappearance of the household agencies as important parts of the national administration.[5] When Henry VIII began his reign

[1] A. P. Newton, ' The King's Chamber under the early Tudors ' in *E.H.R.* XXXII (1917), pp. 348–372.

[2] Dietz, *op. cit.*, pp. 76–77 ; ' We find a new Treasury System created a change reflected in the splendid series of the Declared Accounts, which rendered superfluous without, however, abolishing the old course of the Exchequer ' (Galbraith, *op. cit.*), p. 53. Cf. A. D. George, ' Notes in the margin of the Declared Account,' in *E.H.R.* XXXI (1916), pp. 41–58.

[3] Newton, *op. cit.*, p. 349.   [4] Dietz, *op. cit.*, p. 77.

[5] A. P. Newton, ' Tudor Reforms in the Royal Household ' in *Tudor Studies*, ed. R. W. Seton-Watson (1924), *passim*.

the Household was still an agency of importance, and the usual source of supply of administrative officials ; when the reign was over, the Household and the Chamber with it had shrunk to domestic proportions and become confined to the Lord Chamberlain's and the Lord Steward's departments. ' In 1509 any and every Household officer might be employed in ordinary business of government ; in 1547 none but the very highest who held what had become sinecure Household appointments played any part in national affairs'—none that is, except the king's secretary, who was still perhaps primarily a household officer, but whose office was certainly no sinecure.

The reforms of the Tudors in the Household, which with a few further changes under James I, lasted almost unchanged until the period of Burke's administrative reforms, were inspired more by financial motives, by the need and demand for economies, and by the desire of the king to ' live of his own ' as far as possible, than by any desire or intention to reduce the ' household element ' in the national administration. Under the Lancastrians, the revenue had sufficed to pay neither the expenses of government nor the actual living expenses of the royal family and Household. No adequate solution to the problem of maintaining the royal estate was found until Edward IV in 1472 formally promised parliament to meet his ordinary charges without recourse to parliament for grants for that purpose. The beginnings of what later came to be called the ' civil list ' date from 1482, when an act of parliament assigned a specific sum per year to be paid by the Treasurer of England into the Household, by tallies charged upon the receivers of revenue. This sum was greatly increased during the Tudor period, but the provision of a definite sum in this way both assured and also limited the amount of the ' national ' revenue that could readily be spent on household purposes. The need for restraint in this sphere, the difficulties arising after the disbursement of the treasure left by Henry VII, and the reluctance of parliament to grant supplies in 1523, and other financial problems at this time, seem to have been the principal motives for the series of household reforms promulgated by Wolsey and the Council in the Ordinances of Eltham in 1525–26, and subsequently incorporated in an Act of 1530–31.

These Ordinances thoroughly overhauled the Household, stabilized and defined the functions of its officers, removed some of them ' out of court ', and by its recognition and definition went far to transform ' courtiers into civil servants '. Lists were made of persons to be employed at court, and their remuneration and the number of servants they might keep were prescribed ; ' hangers on ' were to be dismissed or pensioned off ; the use of deputies to perform duties was prohibited ; restrictions were placed upon the employment of household officers outside the Household. Further reforms of this character were introduced by Ordinances of 1540, under the aegis of Thomas Cromwell, which, as re-enacted by Mary in 1554, remained substantially intact until the end of the eighteenth century. The Board of Greencloth and the Compting House became responsible for the finance of the Household, but played no part in the administration of the realm.

As a result of the process of internal reform, the Household receded into those domestic spheres of activity for which in the very remotest days of the kingship it had been created. This could happen, however, without the king's losing his ultimate control over the administration of the realm, because by now the Household had fostered the growth of an officer whose duties were never defined, and who therefore could act over the whole range of the king's executive powers, and provide the link between the king's person and all the organs and officers of the administration. The king's secretary developed into the principal secretary of state, and in so doing preserved the continuity of mediaeval and modern administrative structures, maintained the household element in the king's government, and prolonged into the nineteenth century the ultimate supremacy of the sovereign's will. But the secretaries themselves were destined to develop from being primarily the king's servants into public ministers of state, and in so doing they eased the long and difficult process of development towards modern principles of Cabinet government.[1]

The emergence of the king's secretary to eminence in the

---

[1] Cf. M. A. Thomson, *The Secretaries of State*, 1681–1782 (1932), p. 158, ' The history of the secretaryship is closely connected with the history of the transition from government by the King to government by a Ministry '.

administration was not at all a rapid development, and was not the result of any deliberate plan, unless it were on the part of some of the secretaries themselves, and even so, hardly before the time of Thomas Cromwell. The secretaries of Henry VII were not in a position markedly different from that of Edward IV's, even though the growing importance of the office is shown by its retention by Thomas Ruthal for six years after he became bishop of Durham (until 1516).[1] It was not until the reign of Henry VIII that the secretaries began to assume a position of prominence in general administration, and even then not until after the fall of Wolsey. The Cardinal proved to be the last of the chancellors to dominate the administration as a whole (apart from Clarendon after the Restoration). Thereafter the importance, both administrative and political, of the chancellorship declined, and its duties tended to become more specifically legal, judicial, and formal, and as the sixteenth century passed, much of the general administrative work that had been associated with the Chancery fell to the secretary. The prestige and dignity of the chancellorship, of the treasurership, and of the keepership of the privy seal remained high, higher indeed than those of the secretaryship, but the practical potentiality of the latter as the key post in the administration constantly increased and soon surpassed that of the older and more dignified officers. Based at first largely upon its close connection with diplomatic affairs and correspondence, the secretaryship in the right hands could expand its range of interest and influence over the whole field of domestic administration as well.

These potentialities, however, were not fully revealed until the appointment of Thomas Cromwell to the secretaryship in 1533. This appointment undoubtedly marks a new epoch in the history of the office,[2] and set the precedent for the great secretaryship of the Elizabethan era. ' Cromwell was the first layman to be secretary, a man apt in intrigue, able and unscrupulous, guided neither by rule nor tradition, but by the ever-varying claims of policy and expediency. An undefined office, not yet in the public

[1] Evans, *op. cit.*, p. 15.
[2] *Ibid.*, p. 31 ff. Cromwell became lord keeper of the privy seal in 1536, but probably retained the secretaryship, to which no new appointment was made until 1540.

notice but full of latent possibilities, suited such a one admirably,
and his letters written when secretary illustrate the almost
bewildering variety of his spheres of influence '. They show . . .
' the secretary as the binding force of the State, holding together
all the various units of administration in a band which held
because of its very elasticity '—all as yet, of course, as the king's
instrument and on the king's authority '.

The full story of Cromwell's place in the history of administration is only now in process of adequate investigation. There
is, however, good reason to suppose that ' he, more than any
one else, provided the bureaucratic foundations of the Tudor
monarchy '.[1] He, it seems, encouraged the decline of the household departments in administration, for he himself did not at
any time control the household offices ; he reduced the importance of the privy seal office as a general clearing-house of government business, and promoted the growth of an organized
Council, of which he himself was virtually the head. When this
story comes to be told more fully, there is little doubt that the
career of Thomas Cromwell will be seen to have been of outstanding importance in English administrative history, and to
represent something like a genuine dividing line between the late
mediaeval and early modern characteristics in this sphere.

At any rate, the secretaryship, by the time of Cromwell's fall,
had been brought to potential predominance in the administration, and the way had been paved for the great Elizabethan
principal secretaries, William Cecil, Francis Walsingham, Robert
Cecil, and the long line of their successors, of varying degrees of
eminence and importance.[2]

The source of the Tudor secretary's power was his influence
over the privy council as the mouthpiece of the king,[3] and it is
to the Council and the secretaries' relations with it that we must
now turn.

We have noticed above that the Council under the Yorkists
was becoming the Council in Star Chamber, and occupied largely
with the more important parts of the Council's judicial business,

[1] G. R. Elton, ' Thomas Cromwell : aspects of his administrative work '
(Summaries of Theses no. cciv) in *Bull. Inst. Hist. Res.* XXII (1949), p. 172.
[2] *V.* Evans, *op. cit.*, and Thomson, *op. cit.*, *passim.*
[3] Evans, ' The Pre-Tudor Secretary ', *loc. cit.*, p. 363.

and was laying the foundations of the future court of star chamber under the presidency of the lord chancellor; other parts of that business (poor men's causes) were falling to the Council of Requests in the time of Richard III if not of Edward IV, under the presidency of the lord keeper of the privy seal, and so laying the foundations of the future Court of Requests. We need not pursue these councils any further, but we need to conclude this survey by reference to the revival of a small administrative council, to which the term ' Privy Council ' was to be applied.[2]

Henry VII's accession to the powers of the monarchy is no more triumphantly signalized than by the fact that he found himself free to choose his councillors as he wished. It seems that he started off with a large number of councillors, some hundred or more. Many of these appointments, however, were honorific in character, but a small group of them were appointed for life, took the oath, and were allotted a fee. These formed the nucleus of Henry VII's administrative council, attendant upon the king, often presided over by him, even after the emergence of a lord president of the council. ' The Council attendant [upon the king] confined itself more and more to matters of State, and became more and more a Privy Council '.[3] Sharp distinctions were not as yet drawn; in Henry VII's time the difference between the ' counsel attendant ' and the ' counsel in star chamber ' was merely the difference between the councillors accompanying the king and those remaining in London. Further differentiation was perhaps delayed by the eminence of Cardinal Wolsey as chancellor, who made the Council in the Star Chamber his own and greatly expanded its business and exalted its prestige. But he himself contributed to the process of differentiation by his share in the promulgation of the Ordinances of Eltham of 1525–26, which sought to define the Council, to limit it to twenty members, ten of whom were to be in continual attendance upon the king, and the other ten, including the chancellor, treasurer, and keeper of the privy seal, were to constitute the council in

---

[1] *V. supra*, p. 261.
[2] For what follows, *v.* Pollard, *op. cit.*, in *E.H.R.* XXXVII (1922), pp. 337–360, 516–539, XXXVIII (1923), pp. 42–60.
[3] *Ib.* p. 355.

star chamber. There is, however, no evidence that these provisions were carried out with any precision. After the fall of Wolsey, the Council in Star Chamber did not maintain the position it had enjoyed during his régime ; it could claim to be the true descendant of the old mediaeval Council, and its clerk was the clerk of the old council. But from now on its primacy of place passed to what was soon to be known as the Privy Council, with a clerk of its own, and which was soon to attain to administrative supremacy in the State under the sovereign. In this development, Thomas Cromwell played the leading part ; it was, it seems, his deliberate policy to organize the ' inner council ' into a privy council, with himself as the virtual head of it and the mainspring of its administrative activity.[1] But it was not until twelve days after his death, on 10 August, 1540, that a definite organization of the Privy Council, differentiated from the Council in Star Chamber, was actually constituted, with a clerk of its own.[2] The labours antecedent to this result, however, were Cromwell's, and in his conception of administration lies the root of Tudor success. Supreme executive authority remained vested in the sovereign himself ; but his secretary, armed with the signet seal and the personal confidence of the king, with all the threads of foreign and domestic affairs passing through his hands, fortified in council and in parliament by his capacity as the king's personal representative and by his own unrivalled knowledge of affairs, could and did, bring the king's government to a concentrated pitch of efficiency and vigour impossible to achieve in any earlier period of English history. The way to combine royal authority with conciliar administration had been found. It remained to reconcile both with parliamentary government.[3]

[1] Elton, *loc. cit.*, p. 176.
[2] Pollard, *op. cit.*, p. 60.
[3] Cf. Pollard, *op. cit.*, p. 535, ' The Crown had before Elizabeth's reign established its claim to be the sole arbiter of the personnel of the privy council, while the peers had established theirs to be hereditary counsellors of the Crown in parliament.'

INDEX

of the Treasury, 27 ff., 53, 56, 59, 192
(*v.* also *Camerarii*)
Chancellor, chancellorship, the, 16,
22 ff., 46, 267; of Hen. III, 109 ff.,
114, 123; of Edw. I; 133, of Edw.
II, 168 ff., 173; of Edw. III, 208 ff.;
of Edw. IV, 259; clerk of, 100; and
the Council, 162, 169, 210; at the
Exchequer, 56, 58 ff.; of the Exchequer, 61, 173; fees of, 112 ff.,
145; judicial sphere of, 24, 168,
210; petitions to, 168, 210; scribe of,
60; (*v.* also *Chancery*; *Seal, the king's
or great*)
Chancery, the, 12, 16, 24 ff., 37, 45; of
Hen. II, 67 ff.; of John, 74 ff., 112;
of Hen. III, 109 ff., 112 ff.; of Edw. I,
146 ff.; of Edw. II, 158, 167 ff.;
of Edw. III, 207 ff.; of Ric. II, 234;
in 15th c., 244, 254; clerks of, 37,
115, 209; enrolments of, 63, 73, 74 ff.;
and the Exchequer, 74, 169; French,
74 n.; *hospicium* of, 116, 145, 209; and
the Household, 111, 113, 138, 159,
167; the justiciars', 37, 71; office of,
116, 146, 210; Ordinances of, 208;
Papal, 74 n.; staff of, 209, and the
Wardrobe, 139, 143, 165 (*v.* also
Chancellor; *Rolls*; *Scriptorium*; *Seal,
the king's, or great*; *Warranties,
Writing-office*)
Chapel, the king's, 12, 26
Charters, 4, 11 ff., 13 n. 3, 26 ff.; con-
firmation of the, 151; the Great,
33, 44, 77 n. 4, 81, 83, 120 (*v.* also
Rolls)
Chevisaunce, 257 n. 1
Chirographs, 13
Civil list, 265
Civil servants, service, 13, 146, 266
Civil war, the, 262
Clarendon, the constitutions of, 39
Clarendon, Edward Hyde, earl of, 267
Cnut, King, 7, 9, 16
Coenwulf, King, 12
Colloquim, of Gloucester, 95
Comitatus, the, 2
Consiliarii regis, 98 ff., 122, 129, 131
Constable, the, 23 ff., 46, 59; clerk of,
61
Constitutio domus regis, 22, 25, 27 ff., 135
Constitutional questions, 71, 120, 121,
270
Contrabrevia, 75
Coram rege, 49, 124
Corfe, 81
Council, the, of Hen. III, 98 ff., 116; of

Edw. I, 130 ff.; of Edw. II, 158,
160 ff., 177; of Edw. III, 193, 216 ff.,
223 ff.; of Ric. II, 205 ff., 219 ff.,
231 ff.; of Hen. IV, 246 ff.; of Hen.
V, 250, 252; of Hen. VI, 251 ff.;
Advice touching, 219; Appellant, 234;
Articles of (1406), 248, 250, 252, 254;
(1423), 248, 252; (1426), 248, 252;
(1440–3), 254; (1444), 259; bills of,
195; the chamber of, 205; clerk of,
206, 219 n. 4, 255, 270; composition
of, 100, 129, 133, 150 ff., 160, 197,
219 ff., 223 ff., 245, 250, 260, 269;
continual, 161, 177 ff., 228, 231 ff.,
239, 244, 248, 253, 260; executive
functions of, 121, 126, 131 ff., 156,
163, 206, 217 ff., 244, 248, 261; *ex-
officio* members of, 231, 236; of
Fifteen, 120 ff., 127; feudal, 45 ff.,
71; governor of, 193, 195; Great,
83, 110, 229, 231, 236, 239, 247 250,
253; as an institution, 101, 244, 248;
journal of, 219, 235; Lancastrian,
244, 251 ff., 255, 260; lords of, 250,
251, 253; meetings of, 101, 133, 162,
206, 236, 245; oath of, 100, 133;
Ordinances of, 219, 235; ordinary,
197, 205, 218; petitions to, 163;
Privy, 246, 253, 269 ff.; and the privy
seal, 163, 205, 217 ff.; records of,
101, 244, 248; seal of, 206; in Star
Chamber, 261, 268 ff.; of Twelve,
126; Yorkist, 268
Counsel, 21, 45, 98, 246, 260; king's,
260
Courts, Byzantine, 15; Carolingian, 5,
6, 15; of Edward the Confessor, 22;
Frankish, 22 ff.,; of the Hundred,
117; Merovingian, 5, 15; of Normandy, 18; Papal, 15; of the Shire,
117; (*v.* also *Bench, Curia regis*)
Court party, the, 229, 232, 254
Coutances, Walter of, abp. of Rouen,
justiciar, 41 ff., 43, 66, 67, 71
Crakehall, John of, treasurer, 125
Crisis, of 1234, 94, 100, 116, 117, 122;
of 1237, 100, 122; of 1244, 100, 122;
of 1258; *v.* Oxford, *Provisions of*;
of 1340–1, 196, 223; of 1376, 252;
of 1377, 252
Cromwell, Thomas, earl of Essex,
king's secretary, 242, 261, 266 ff.
Cubicularii, 6, 8
Curiales, 26, 100, 150
Curia regis, 18, 21, 27, 33, 42, 45 ff.,
64, 72, 74, 87, 116, 121, 125; *ad
scaccarium*, 47, 48, 56, 69, 72